New Perspectives on Bullying

of related interest

Bullying in Schools – and What to Do About it
Ken Rigby
ISBN 1 85302 455 4

Listening to Young People in School, Youth Work and Counselling
Nick Luxmoore
ISBN 1 85302 909 2

Troubles of Children and Adolescents
Edited by Ved Varma
ISBN 1 85302 323 X

Violence in Children and Adolescents
Edited by Ved Varma
ISBN 1 85302 344 2

Challenging Ourselves
Towards Gender Equality and Violence-Free Relationships – A Handbook of Practical Activities
The Metropolitan Toronto School Board
ISBN 1 85302 455 7

How We Feel
An Insight into the Emotional World of Teenagers
Edited by Jacki Gordon and Gillian Grant
ISBN 1 85302 439 2

Mental Health in Your School
A Guide for Teachers and Others Working in Schools
Young Minds
ISBN 1 85302 407 4

Group Work with Children and Adolescents
A Handbook
Edited by Kedar Nath Dwivedi
Foreword by Robin Skynner
ISBN 1 85302 157 1

New Perspectives on Bullying

Ken Rigby

Jessica Kingsley Publishers
London and Philadelphia

First published in the United Kingdom in 2002
by Jessica Kingsley Publishers Ltd
116 Pentonville Road
London N1 9JB, England
and
325 Chestnut Street
Philadelphia, PA 19106, USA

www.jkp.com

Library of Congress Cataloging in Publication Data
Rigby, Ken.
    New perspectives on bullying / Ken Rigby.
        p. cm.
    Includes bibliographical references and index.
    ISBN 1 85302 1-85302-872-X (alk. paper)
    1.Bullying. I.Title.
    BF637.B854 R54 2001
    649`.1-dc21 2001054524

British Library Cataloguing in Publication Data
A CIP catalogue record for this book is available from the British Library

ISBN 1 85302 872 X

Printed and Bound in Great Britain by
Athenaeum Press, Gateshead, Tyne and Wear

Contents

Figures and Tables

Appendices

To my grandchildren:
Christopher, Jessica, Lucy, Lachlan,
Michelle, Austin, Ella and Erin

Acknowledgments

The author wishes to thank the authors and publishers who have given permission to reproduce the following.

Figure 6.1 (p.124): 'The Bullydog', reprinted with permission from Sopris West Educational Services, *Bully Proofing Your School* by Cara Garrity, copyright 1994, *www.SoprisWest.com*

Figure 6.3 (p.128): 'The Eyes Task'. Reprinted with permission from the author, Professor Baron Cohen, taken from an article by Baron-Cohen, S., Wheelwright, S., Spong, A. and Scahill, V. (in press): 'Are intuitive physics and intuitive psychology independent?' A test with children with Asperger Syndrome. *Journal of Developmental and Learning Disorders.*

Figure 11.1 (p. 241). 'Before and after becoming assertive', excerpted from *Bullies are a pain in the brain* by Trevor Romain copyright 1997. Used with permission from Free Spirit Publishing company Inc., Minneapolis, MN; 1-800-735-7322. *www.freespirit.com*. All rights reserved.

Extracts from the works of Tim Field on pages 75–77 and page 124 are from his website (*www.successunlimited.co.uk/*) and with his permission.

The extract on page 122 from *Road Rage* by Ruth Rendell published by Hutchinson/Arrow was reprinted by permission of Random House Group Ltd.

The extract on page 171 *A Miscellany of Men* by G. K. Chesterton is provided with the permission of A.P. Watt Ltd on behalf of the Royal Literary Fund.

Preface

The history of bullying is long and harrowing. If there ever was a paradisal state in which people lived in harmony with each other it was short lived. In the Biblical story not a generation had passed away before brother Cain slew brother Abel. Anthropologists assure us that the Neanderthal were replaced by more advanced and powerful homo sapiens. A major theme of recorded history is the exploitation of the weak by the strong. Not accidentally but purposively. We shrug our shoulders. It was ever thus. Why should we expect things to change?

And yet through the ages people have asked again and again why must it be so. Bold spirits from Jesus Christ to Martin Luther King have told us that the lion can lie down with the lamb; that brother can be at peace with brother, whatever their differences. Meanwhile, the terrorists terrorise and the avengers avenge. Where could we begin?

A new generation of researchers has focussed on children in schools. The systematic study of bullying began in Scandinavia in the 1970s. Professor Dan Olweus conducted his research in schools in Sweden and Norway. He defined, classified and estimated the incidence of bullying behaviour. He sought to explain why some children bullied and others were victimised. He did more that that. He showed that bullying could be significantly reduced in schools. This was a very important achievement. Its implications were potentially colossal. Fellow social researchers were impressed. Before the 20th century had closed, hundreds of similar studies had been conducted in many countries around the world. Books, articles, web-sites, videos, CDs began to appear in profusion explaining what we could do to stop bullying in schools.

This in itself could be seen as the fruits of a new perspective on bullying: a view that at least in one area of human interaction the age-old problem of the strong exploiting the weak could be countered; that people could be educated not to bully or be bullied. School was a natural starting point. No-one doubted that bullying occurred in schools and that some children suffered appallingly as a result of it. For some adults, this is what bullying essentially was: strong, aggressive kids picking on weaker, softer kids. Moreover, here was a "captive" population of young people who could be carefully studied. Here was a gathering of educators who could be persuaded to try out new ways of altering children's behaviour. Here was an opportunity to demonstrate that humans could learn to behave decently with each other.

Easier said than done. Looking back on the two decades in which educators have seriously tried to eradicate bullying in schools we have to confess to only modest success. Most intervention studies, of which there have been about a dozen carefully conducted ones, claim not more that a 15% reduction in the incidence of bullying in a school. But these are "early days." and the enterprise shows no signs of running out of steam.

This book is, in a sense, an attempt to take stock. It is an attempt to describe how the problem of bullying has been, and is being, conceptualised and understood; to explain what researchers and educators (and others) are saying about why there is so much bullying going on; and to examine what solutions are being canvassed. Some of the perspectives on bullying are as old as the hills; some are genuinely new. The systematic study of bullying is constantly throwing up new and challenging ideas.

Moreover, bullying is no longer being viewed exclusively as a problem for schools and for schoolchildren. Over the last few years attention has been directed increasingly to bullying in the workplaces and in prisons. The similarities with schoolyard bullying have been noted; so too have the differences. But why stop there ? Bullying is a phenomenon one can literally find everywhere. It is time that our perspective on bullying extended further afield.

In a way, this book is a testing of the water. It is the first book that has attempted to examine bullying comprehensively. If I am right in thinking that an examination of bullying as "the systematic abuse of power" is an issue that is of vital importance to society at large, then it should indeed be useful to consider bullying in a wide range of contexts: not only in schools, the workplace and prisons, but also and especially in the home, long the preserve of students of domestic violence. We should seek out bullying in the Armed Forces; in Politics; in International Relations, to name but a few. We should seek to understand bullying not only as educational psychologists understand it, but also as the ethologists, the anthropologists, the evolutionary psychologists, the theologians and the sociologists see it. If the issue is as important as I think it is, I will be content to have scratched the surface and stimulated others to dig deeper and find wider applications for the expanding body of knowledge and speculations that I review.

Chapter 1

Introduction

The broader perspective

I believe I have found the missing link between animal and civilised man.
It is us.

— Konrad Lorenz

During the last decade of the 20th century there was an extraordinary rise in interest in the subject of bullying. What had been a largely neglected area of study rapidly became a focus for hundreds of scholars and sundry writers from different parts of the planet. The media fastened on to it. Here was an issue that not only intrigued and challenged empirical researchers, counsellors and theoreticians in psychology, education and sociology, but also offered some kind of hope to thousands of people for whom bullying was a grim, everyday reality.

Twelve years ago, when I first began my own investigations into the nature of bullying in schools in Australia, the reaction of the few who took notice of what I was doing was simply one of surprise, tinged with embarrassment – what a curious thing to be researching. Followed by a look of concern directed at me! There had, of course, been countless investigations of aggression in animals and humans: such studies were well established and respectable. Few, however, had undertaken to study such a 'common' thing as bullying.

There was one outstanding exception. In Scandinavia, Professor Dan Olweus had been busy for more than a decade accumulating data on bullying among children in Sweden and Norway, speculating on why children bully, what effects bullying was having on victims and, most importantly, how bullying could be reduced. In due course this work was to prove immensely significant. But in the 1980s, the time was not ripe for most investigators of social behaviour, even those concerned with children's well-being in schools, to give their attention to what is now acknowledged as a massive and enduring social problem.

In the year 2001, despite the work of thousands of careful investigators of the problems associated with bullying, it remains true that we are still only at the beginning. We have made some headway. There is much more awareness of the problem. People – including academic scholars in their starchy disciplines – are more ready to talk about it with each other. Indeed, academic journals publish papers on bullying; international conferences invite contributions from so-called authorities on bullying; researchers from different nations collaborate in producing authoritative books on bullying. Certainly more is known nowadays about some aspects of bullying. There are now numerous reports on the prevalence of bullying, both in schools and in the workplace. We know far more about how people are harmed by continual victimisation. There have been some demonstrations of how bullying can be reduced in schools, though it is fair to say that not all interventions have been entirely successful.

As in many discoveries of a new area to research, there was a wave of optimism (and credulousness) about what was being found. We read and marvelled at reports from Scandinavia that bullying in schools could be at least halved. I recall this news being relayed by an enthusiastic colleague, a psychiatrist, in more exaggerated terms: 'There is no longer any bullying in Norway.' We had discovered a seriously neglected problem that could now be rigorously investigated with a huge pay-off. More and more aspects of the problem were identified and researched: the relevance to bullying of parenting and family life; the nature of the personalities of bullies and victims; the health consequences of peer victimisation; the impact of the ethos of institutions, such as schools, workplaces and prisons, on bullying; the link between bullying and crime; community and cultural factors relating to bullying; the construction of masculinity and bullying; gender differences in bullying; the role of policy in containing bullying; bystander intervention to stop bullying; counselling approaches to working with bullies and victims; the control of bullying behaviour; bullying and the law; and so on and so on.

As the awareness of the complexity of the problem increased, so too did the potential for disagreement and controversy. It became clear that bullying was being conceptualised by workers in the field in quite different ways, with different implications for what could or might be done. What had seemed clear about the psychological nature of bullies and victims began to appear uncertain. Are bullies, for example, basically insensitive clods who cannot grasp what is going on around them, or are they, in fact, socially perceptive people who have chosen to use their abilities to exploit others? Are bullies generally unpopular with others or are they generally admired? What had to some seemed to be the sensible way of dealing with bullies – applying consequences so that they can learn that bullying does not pay – was being questioned by those who advocated so-called 'no-blame' approaches. Psychologists were increasingly seen as not having a monopoly on the problem of bullying. There were other disciplines such as biology, criminology, history and anthropology that could also provide insights.

I like to think that there are now signs of the maturing of the study of bullying. I think we are becoming less prone to deliver 'truths' and dogmatically proclaim 'solutions'. We are realising that in taking on bullying we are dealing with a problem of great complexity and durability. This is why I think that at this stage we should pause a little in our headlong crusade to root out the monster 'bullying' and try dispassionately and critically to examine the varied perspectives that we have on this problem.

The antiquity of bullying

The first thing we should realise is that although the systematic study of bullying is new the phenomena of bullying are certainly not. Indeed it is salutary that at the beginning of an examination of bullying we should pause to gain, if we can, a sense of how people have from the very earliest times felt about being bullied.

Nowhere is the issue of bullying raised more poignantly than by the Jewish authors of the Psalms, more than 2000 years ago. Many of the Psalms were composed by men who had experienced seemingly unendurable persecution, but still clung desperately to the idea of a personal God who could – and would – help them in their time of need. There is an intense anger, indeed hatred, directed towards those who were oppressing them. At the same time, as believers in God, they appear bewildered and even angry at Him for allowing it all to happen. Their faith is shaken. Although they describe their experiences in ways that seem strange to us, those who have been continually victimised and those who can identify with the victims of persecution, whether in the school, the workplace or the home, can feel their anguish and often enough their rage as well. The following quotations are taken from a modernised version of the bible provided by the American Bible Society (1984).

My oppressors are powerful, numerous and unjust.

- o   My enemies are healthy and strong; there are many who hate me for no reason. (38, 19)
- o   Those who hate me for no reason are more numerous than the hairs on my head. My enemies tell lies against me; they are strong and want to kill me. (69, 4)

- I am surrounded by enemies, who are like man-eating lions. Their teeth are like spears and arrows; their tongues are like sharp swords. (57, 4)
- Deadly enemies surround me; they have no pity and speak proudly. They are around me now; wherever I turn, watching for a chance to pull me down. They are like lions waiting for me, wanting to tear me to pieces. (17, 10–12)

They plan to hurt and destroy me

- My enemies make trouble for me all day long; they are always thinking up some way to hurt me! They gather in hiding places and watch everything I do... (56, 5–6)
- Those who want to kill me lay traps for me and those who want to hurt me threaten to ruin me; they never stop plotting against me. (38, 12)
- I hear many enemies whispering; terror is all around me. They are making plans against me, plotting to kill me. (31, 13)

I am constantly abused and ridiculed

- All day long my enemies insult me; those who mock me use my name in cursing. (102, 8)
- My enemies say cruel things about me. They want me to die and be forgotten. (41, 5)
- They tell lies about me, and they say evil things about me, attacking me for no reason. (109, 2–3)
- Evil men testify against me and accuse me of crimes I know nothing about. (35, 11)
- All who see me make fun of me; they stick out their tongues and shake their heads. (22, 7)
- They talk about me in the streets, and drunkards make up songs about me (69, 12)
- All my enemies, and especially my neighbours, treat me with contempt. (31, 11)
- But when I was in trouble, they were all glad and gathered around to make fun of me; strangers beat me and kept striking me. Like men who would mock a cripple, they glared at me with hate. (35, 15–16)

I feel excluded, without support

- When I look beside me I see that there is no-one to help me, no-one to protect me. No-one cares for me. (142, 4)
- All my enemies and especially my neighbours treat me with contempt; those who know me are afraid of me. When they see me in the street they run away. (31, 11)
- Even my best friend, the one I trusted most, the one who shared my food, has turned against me. (41, 9)
- Everyone has forgotten me, as though I were dead... (31, 12)

I feel shame and distress

- I am always in disgrace. I am covered with shame from hearing the sneers and insults of my enemies and those who hate me. (44, 15–16)
- I am terrified by the threats of my enemies, crushed by the oppression of the wicked. (55, 2–3)
- Insults have broken my heart and I am in despair. I had hoped for sympathy but there was none; for comfort, but I found none. (69, 20)
- My strength is gone, gone like water spilled on the ground... (38, 7)
- I am like a dumb man and cannot speak. (44, 13)

I appeal to God

- Listen to my cry for help, for I am sunk in despair. Save me from my enemies; they are too strong for me. (142, 6)
- Punish them for what they have done, for the evil they have committed. (28, 4)
- My God, my God, why have you abandoned me? (22, 1)

I want revenge

- May those who gloat over my suffering be completely defeated and confused; may those who claim to be better than I am be covered with shame and disgrace. (35, 26)
- May my enemies die before their time; may they go down alive into the world of the dead. (55, 15)
- May they disappear like water draining away; may they be crushed like weeds on a path. May they be like snails that dissolve into

slime; may they be like a baby born dead that never sees the light.
(58, 7–8)

- Choose some corrupt judge to try my enemy and let one of his own enemies accuse him.
- May he be tried and found guilty; may even his prayer be considered a crime.
- May his life soon be ended; may another man take his job.
- May his children become orphans, and his wife a widow.
- May his children be homeless beggars; may they be driven from the ruins they live in.
- May his creditors take away all his property, and may strangers get everything he worked for.
- May no-one ever be kind to him or care for the orphans he leaves behind.
- May all his descendants die, and his name be forgotten in the next generation. (109, 6–13)

This excursion into bullying in early Jewish communities and how these people responded has more than curiosity value. The expressions of pain and grief on the part of people who felt oppressed is as sharp and as moving as one can find anywhere. Time and distance have not lessened the compassion that we can feel for these people. In some ways they are close to us still. Their yearning for a just world with justice for the oppressed is ours. Their values are in many ways ours. Ethically, those who share in the Judaeo-Christian tradition are their heirs.

But there is also this wild and violent demand for revenge: for the divine destruction and damnation of the 'evil' people who had so horribly oppressed them. We may indeed feel pity, but also revulsion towards these 'barbarians' who would have the bullies exterminated, even their prayers considered as crimes; their children reduced to homeless beggars.

But are we different today?
I have a website devoted to bullying: http://www.education.unisa.edu.au/bullying/ In it I pose this question: 'Does bullying really do children any harm?' By email I recently received this anonymous reply:

Hello Ken,

I saw your website. 'Does bullying really do children any harm?' Of course it does. It gets you, slowly but surely, before you turn into someone like me, full of hatred and longing for revenge. Revenge is something that happened with that Trenchcoat Mafia thing. Would I do something like that? Probably not. But I'd like to. It's so tempting.

You know what else? It doesn't end when you're 16. I still get it, all the fucking time. And do you think this is something I enjoy? Fuck, no. And how do we combat bullying? I'll tell you how to combat bullying. You give people like me guns and knives. That'll soon stop bullying.

I should not have been shocked. Revenge as the answer to oppression is both old and new. This is what happens, it seems, to people who have been savagely oppressed. In the USA, people recall with horror the massacres of children at Columbine High School by alienated youths. In Australia we recall how a young man, Martin Bryant, one Sunday afternoon in 1996, took a gun and hunted down and killed 35 holiday makers at the Tasmanian resort at Port Arthur. Who knows why? But we now know that this appalling act was done by a man who as a child was severely bullied by his peers and continually ridiculed as an oddity and a misfit. We have heard that power corrupts, but it looks as if being disempowered through contempt and rejection from others may have a similar effect. As Adlai Stevenson put it: 'Power corrupts but lack of power corrupts absolutely.'

Bullying in nature

It is sometimes said that bullying is a natural and indispensable feature of the way nature works. In Darwinian terms, it serves an evolutionary purpose: it ensures that the fittest survive. This is not just Hitler-talk. The famous (and humane) ethologist Konrad Lorenz is one among other writers who have closely observed animal behaviour and drawn attention to the positive features of intra-species aggression and the formation and maintenance of hierarchical status or *pecking order*.

Lorenz (1969) saw three advantages accruing to species whose members continually acted aggressively towards their 'inferiors', that is, bullying when they could.

(1) Bullies had a much better chance of mating. They could monopolise available sexual partners and deprive others of sexual opportunity. Those fittest in the sense of being able to subdue and exclude others were able to pass on their characteristics to posterity.

(2) The outcome of bullying is a hierarchical social structure that contributes to the stability and viability of the group. One knows whom to follow, and these are (by and large) the strong-willed, the powerful and the wise.

(3)　Intra-species aggression benefits the group in ensuring that each member gives others space. Ecologically this is positive for everyone, as localised resources do not become over-exploited.

This perspective on bullying suggests that no individual organism lives for itself, but should be conceived as a vehicle by means of which a set of genes may be perpetuated. As Samuel Butler long ago argued, it is not the living organism that matters: a chicken is just an egg's way of making another egg. The gene, as Richard Dawkins (1989) maintained, is selfish. Bullying may or may not benefit the individual, but (it is argued) it does benefit the species. It is certainly possible to find evidence of behaviour among birds and animals that we might reasonably call bullying. (If this sounds like anthropomorphising, consider the super-anthropomorphising in the conception of the selfish gene.)

Lorenz (1969) was fond of jackdaws, which he argued 'derive a beneficial firmness of structure from the state of tension arising inside the community from the aggression drive and its results, ranking order' (p.36). Tension, he observed, was greatest between jackdaws who occupy adjoining positions in the ranking order, like football teams similarly positioned in the league table. What is surprising from Lorenz's account is that high-ranking jackdaws, particularly males, interfere in every quarrel between two inferiors. Moreover, the high-ranking birds always intervene in favour of the losing party. One can see why Lorenz, being a nice man, was fond of jackdaws. We learn too that the senior birds enjoy considerable respect: when they express alarm others wisely take notice; the expression of alarm on the part of a younger, less experienced bird is largely ignored. Thus the bullying that establishes a pecking order may confer some benefit to the species. At the same time, the wise old birds see to it that bullying does not get out of hand and prove fatal to members of the group.

Bullying in nature then may seem to be relatively benign. But consider the spotted hyena. Here is Lyall Watson's (1995) account of the birth of baby hyenas:

> Hyenas usually have twins which are well developed at birth, completely furred, eyes open, canine and incisor teeth fully erupted…within minutes of birth, one of the cubs attacks his twin, sometimes savaging a brother or sister that is not yet emerged from its amniotic sac. If both offspring survive this pre-emptive strike the battle begins in earnest as the pair roll in a bitter embrace, each with the skin of the other locked in its jaws. (Watson 1995, p.52)

Rarely does the weaker of the cubs survive. These animals appear to be genetically programmed to attack and kill their siblings immediately on sight.

We may turn with relief (only temporary) to consider the family life of rats, whose members appear to be remarkably kindly disposed to each other. According to Lorenz (1969) 'the tolerance and tenderness towards their children which characterise the mammal mothers extends, in the case of rats, not only to fathers but to all grandparents, uncles, aunts, cousins and so on' (p.136). Further, in the rat pack there is evidently no ranking order. According to Steiniger (cited by Lorenz, p.136) 'the smaller animals are the most forward, the larger ones good humouredly allow the smaller ones to take pieces of food away from them'. Rats are contact animals. They like touching each other. There is a ceremony of 'creeping under' which is performed particularly by young animals while larger animals show their sympathy for smaller ones by creeping over them.

But what happens when a member of a strange rat clan enters the territory? This is Lorenz's description:

> The strange rat may run around for minutes on end without having any idea of the terrible fate awaiting it, and the resident rats may continue for an equally long time with their ordinary affairs, until finally the stranger comes close enough to one of them for them to get wind of the intruder. The information is transmitted like an electrical shock through the resident rat and at once the whole colony is alarmed by the process of mood trans-mission which is communicated by the brown rat by expression move-ments, but in the house rat by a sharp shrill satanic cry which is taken up by all members of the tribe within earshot. (Lorenz 1969, p.138)

Then there is mayhem. 'With their eyes bulging from their sockets, their hair standing on end, the rats set out on their rat hunt' (p.138). The stranger rat is slowly torn to pieces, Lorenz comments that this extreme manifestation of group hate is really a diabolical invention that serves no good evolutionary purpose (p.139).

These examples of animal behaviour illustrate two forms of behaviour that can occur with varying degrees of ferocity among people. There is first the one-to-one bullying – in the hyena's case to the death, purely to establish domi-nance and to reduce the victim to relative or absolute impotence. There appears to be no pay-off for the species. Two hyena cubs could be raised without detriment to either. Indeed, with the death of a sibling the chances of the gene pool's contin-uance may be halved. Evidently the selfish gene is overruled. As far as one can see, it is evil for evil's sake.

Among humans, lethal encounters at birth are not possible, but seemingly motiveless killings by young children have come to light. Among the most chilling was the case of Mary Bell, an 11-year-old who in 1968 in Britain was convicted for her part in the sadistic killing of a 3-year-old, Brian Howe. This little boy was strangled and mutilated in the stomach and genitals. Two girls were involved, each during the investigation continually changing her story to incrim-inate the other. Mary Bell was described in the press as an 'evil child' and a 'freak of nature'. At the time she showed no sense of remorse. A nursing sister who sat in on Mary's statement said that Mary felt nothing: 'I've never seen anything like it. She said all the awful things they had done, but she didn't feel a thing' (Sereny 1998, p.65).

The second kind of bullying, the pack attack of rats on a fellow creature who merely smells different, has its counterpart in human behaviour. Much bullying in fact involves a group against an individual who is seen as different. The attack may or may not promote the interest of the group. We may choose to see echoes of this process in the Nazi pogroms to eliminate the Jews. Or in a mob of schoolchildren who bully a new kid or someone they have chosen to describe as 'not normal'.

Parallels are certainly there between some animal and human behaviours of the kind we can call bullying. But the conclusions we may draw are far from clear. Depending on where we look – at jackdaws, hyenas or rats – we can find support for a variety of views: that bullying is good for us; that bullying is an unspeakable evil; that bullying is the means by which we can, and sometimes do, protect ourselves from 'outsiders' and preserve the purity of our group.

Can human nature change?

It is tempting to paint a picture of overwhelming gloom. I do not think that anybody will ever write a comprehensive history of violence. It would be too exhausting and it would also be profoundly depressing. The nearest thing I know to it is Colin Wilson's *A Criminal History of Mankind* (1984). This tells us more than we would like to know about the agonies inflicted by great tyrants and numerous sadists upon literally millions of innocent victims. We would like to think that these heinous crimes were committed by profoundly sick people or by ancient despots like King Herod or Emperor Caligula. But we should remember that many acts of appalling cruelty were inflicted by people on whom we have bestowed the title of 'great', such people as Alexander the Great, Peter the Great, Catherine the Great and Frederick the Great. One is reminded of Lord Acton's famous dictum, 'Power tends to corrupt, and absolute power corrupts absolutely', to which he added, 'Great men are almost always bad men' (Fears 1985). Sad to say, the exercise of violent means of domination excites both horror and admiration. The bullies in the school playground always have their admirers.

It would be a mistake – an understandable one on the part of that fortunate part of the human race that has enjoyed years of peace and prosperity – to see spectacular acts of oppression as confined to an age of barbarism that we have outlived. Yet on reflection it seems that the twentieth century was perhaps the most violent and cruel of all ages: witness the monstrous persecution of the Jews in Hitler's Germany; the Stalinist purges; the atrocities of Idi Amin; the massed killings of Pol Pot.

Is there evidence that human societies can be radically different from each other in the aggression members show towards each other and the extent to which they bully each other? Is there any evidence that societies or communities change significantly over time in their predilection for violence? Has anybody been able to show that aggression and violence in any society are reducible and sustainably so? Curiously these questions are not often asked. Lyall Watson (1995) has observed that the editor of the *Journal of Peace Research* has complained that prospective contributors overwhelmingly submit articles about aggressive behaviour, rarely about its opposite. Aggression, though hardly news, captures one's attention. When there is a fight in the schoolyard, children flock to watch.

Yet it would be unfair not to point out that historians and anthropologists have been able to identify wide differences between societies in the way their members treat each other. Perhaps the best-known violent society in ancient times was Sparta in the 6th century BC. Theirs was a military society permanently geared for war. Hence toughness, discipline, the capacity to endure pain and contempt for the weak were the highest virtues. Babies who appeared weak and ailing at birth were left to die. Slave children – the vast majority of all children – who showed signs of enterprise (a threat to their masters) were murdered. Husbands unable to produce healthy children were routinely cuckolded. Boys and girls were subjected to equally tough training in the art of fighting. It is notable that for all its inhumanity and ultimate futility – this regime did not survive – the term 'Spartan' still has positive overtones. Literally hundreds of sporting clubs around the world use the name 'Spartan'.

In more recent times anthropologists have identified a number of contemporary societies in which interpersonal hostility is the rule rather than the exception. Chagnon (1977) described Yanomamo who live on the border of Venezuela and Brazil as the 'fierce people'. Yanomamo men assess each other largely on their capacity for violence and treachery and on their willingness to fight. Conflict is commonly about sex. Men constantly battle over the women they seek to possess and once possessed treat with contempt. Men who have killed most have more wives and more children. Such bullying fits like a glove the theories of evolutionary psychologists. The most aggressive men have the greatest reproductive success.

By contrast there are evidently people who have never been seen to kill each other at all. Dentan (1968) has portrayed the Semai people of the Malay peninsula as totally non-violent. These people habitually meet force with flight. Running away from confrontation is not seen as cowardly; no great store is put upon courage. Being called timid is taken as a compliment. The Semai people are said never to punish their children, believing that to bring pressure to bear on a child for his/her behaviour is wrong. Here then is some (limited) vindication of Margaret Mead's claim that human nature is indeed malleable, with a suggestion that style of parenting is a powerful factor in determining how aggressive people will be.

We may also take some comfort from contemporary studies of bullying in schools in different countries. Despite problems in calibrating measurement of bullying across different cultures, the scale of the reported differences between countries does strongly suggest that schoolchildren in some countries are much more likely to be bullied by their peers than in others. For instance, bullying appears to be relatively high in schools in Italy, Greece and Australia compared with Norway and Sweden. Within countries, differences between schools are sometimes large. For example reported peer victimisation in some Australian high schools is more than four times that in others (Rigby 1997a). Finally, there have been some encouraging reports that show that interventions to reduce bullying in schools have been at least partially effective (see Olweus 1993; Petersen and Rigby 1999; Smith and Sharp 1994).

Are we changing?

Are we growing more sensitive to the plight of the oppressed, the bullied? It is hard to answer this question with any assurance. We have little hard evidence either way.

However, consider the word 'bully'. According to the Oxford English Dictionary (Second Edition, 1989), it came into common use in English in the 16th century. It was applied to a particular kind of man. We might be surprised to learn that a bully was a kind of man much admired by men, what people of this time and place would call 'a fine fellow'; what Australians might call 'a beaut bloke'. In Shakespeare's *A Midsummer Night's Dream* the likeable and popular Bottom is referred to as 'Bully Bottom'. The warlike king in Shakespeare's *Henry V,* greatly admired by his men, is eulogised by the soldier Pistol as follows:

'The king's a bawcock, and a heart of gold,
A lad of life, an imp of fame:
Of parents good, of fist most valiant:
I kiss his dirty shoe, and from my heart-string
I love the lovely bully.'

(Act iv, sc.1, 44–48)

However, in the next century the usage changed. No longer is the bully universally admired. He has become a blustering, swashbuckling sort of person, perhaps even something of a coward. In 1780 Duncan described a mob as: 'The most swaggering swearing bullies in fine weather [who] were the most pitiable wretches on earth when death appeared before them.'

In a similar vein, in 1711 Jonathan Swift described someone as 'a bully who will fight for a whore and run away in an army'. By the middle of the 19th century the association between being a bully and being a coward was firmly implanted. In 1850 Dickens, in *Oliver Twist*, wrote: 'Mr. Bumble had a decided propensity for bullying...and consequently was (it is needless to say) a coward.'

What is suggested in this brief analysis from sources cited, I should add, from the Oxford English Dictionary (Second Edition) is a change in the meaning and usage of the term 'bully' from one describing a man who is forceful and widely admired to one describing someone who is derisory, boastful, disreputable and even cowardly.

Still I am unconvinced that we have quite left behind the sentiment contained in the earlier meaning of the word 'bully'. Many of us are still prone (at least in some moods) to admire the practitioner of force for personal ends: the professional wrestling superstar who ruthlessly demolishes his punier opponents; the politician who stuns the opposition with a stream of unanswerable invective; the teacher who subdues the students with a withering stare; the charismatic megalomaniac who smashes all opposition and ends up leading his country into ruin. In the history of the word 'bully' we can see the story of our ambivalence towards those who bully.

But has there been any detectable trend, upwards or downwards, in the prevalence of bullying behaviour itself? Olweus (1993) noted that the evidence from surveys conducted in Scandinavia in the 1970s and 1980s on the bullying of schoolchildren was inconclusive on this point, given the relatively small sample sizes available and the use of unclear and varied definitions of bullying. He goes on to express a personal opinion that 'indirect signs suggest' that 'bullying takes more serious forms and is more prevalent nowadays than 10–15 years ago' (p.17). In fact, the question is difficult to answer, not only because of the paucity of relevant studies but also because people have in recent years become more sensitive to – and more inclusive in their judgements of – what constitutes bullying. If there is a reported rise in bullying, this may reflect greater awareness and sensitivity. The occasional results that suggest a reduction in bullying can usually be taken more seriously as evidence of a real reduction.

One of the areas in which victimisation is commonly reported is in heterosexual dating relationships in which one of the partners, usually the male, seeks to harass or bully the other. In a recent study of dating violence over a ten-year period among students (aged 18–24 years) attending a large American university (Billingham, Bland and Leary 1999), results indicated a reduction in verbal and physical aggression. Increasing numbers of students reported being in non-violent relationships. Whilst this study was restricted to a particular cross-section of people (American university students) and related to one area of interpersonal behaviour (dating), it is nevertheless encouraging, suggesting as it does that changes in community attitudes show signs of affecting people's behaviour.

What then are we to think of the prospects of change in the fearful propensity of the strong to exploit and abuse the weak? To whose voice shall we listen? Must it be to the historians with their endless catalogue of oppressive acts, and emphasis on realpolitik? Or to ethologists such as Konrad Lorenz and the rising band of evolutionary psychologists who see us bound biologically and inexorably to fellow creatures who must dominate or perish? Or to the optimistic (starry-eyed?) anthropologists with their subjective perceptions of societies that they see (or wish to see) giving hope for a more kindly, cooperative world? Or no-one's?

Here in conclusion is a parent's opinion I received a little while ago, anonymously:

> The recent focus on 'bullying' appears to be only the latest 'fad' from the psychologists who seem to need to somehow justify their existence and purpose in life. It is potentially very dangerous and will undoubtedly create a number of innocent victims – both children and parents. When this happens, who will be accountable for the needless and perhaps lasting damage that can be caused? If history is any guide, every so-called professional person involved will either disappear or wash their hands, as did Pontius Pilate.

We have been warned.

Chapter 2

Towards a definition of bullying

'When I use a word,' Humpty Dumpty said, in a rather scornful tone, 'it means just what I choose it to mean – neither more nor less.'

'The question is,' said Alice, 'whether you can make words mean so many different things.'

'The question is,' said Humpty Dumpty, 'which is to be master – that's all.'

– Lewis Carroll, *Through the Looking-Glass*

Nothing frustrates a writer who wants to come to grips with a subject so much as a recognition (alas too late) that his or her readers have all along had a different meaning in their heads for a word – a key word – he thought he had defined with the utmost clarity. Or perhaps hadn't defined at all, assuming a common understanding. In either case, there is much wailing and gnashing of teeth. The key word in this book is of course 'bullying'. This chapter is about how it has been defined.

It seems natural to see bullying as something evil. Not surprisingly in seeking to describe what bullying is, some writers have fastened upon its malign nature, sometimes to the exclusion of almost everything else. Thus in a highly influential definition of bullying, Tattum and Tattum (1992) wrote: 'Bullying is a wilful conscious desire to hurt another and put him/her under stress.' The bully is seen here as wilful, that is, perverse, obstinate, intractable; knowingly wanting to hurt someone. Bullying is conceived as a state of mind, an evil state of mind of someone who really knows better; a person standing condemned before decent people.

We see this view of the bully taken up, with only a slight variation, by the Scottish Council for Research in Education: 'Bullying is a wilful, conscious desire to hurt or threaten or frighten someone else' (Johnson, Munn and Edwards 1991).

To be a bully, then, you don't have to do anything. The fact that you have a desire to hurt and you know that you have a desire to hurt someone is enough to make you a bully. Besag (1989) seems to agree. 'Bullying,' she declared, 'is an attitude rather than an act.'

There is much appeal in this view of bullying. It appeals strongly to the moralist in us. Bullies are people who have bad thoughts. Bullies are bad people. Bullies are demons. Like Lucifer, the fallen angel, they knew what they were doing. They chose to be bad. This offers a solution to the problem of bullying. Stop people having bad thoughts.

There is one glaring difficulty for the researcher in accepting this formulation. The practical difficulty is not that of identifying the bully, but rather identifying the person who is not a bully. In a study of bullying in Australian schools, over 37,000 schoolchildren were asked, 'Have you ever felt like hurting another student?' Across the age range of 8–18 years, some 73 per cent of boys and 60 per cent of girls indicated that they sometimes had the desire to hurt someone (Rigby 1997c). Given that many people provide what they believe are socially desirable responses to questionnaires, these figures certainly underestimate the true percentages. Perhaps it would be fair to say that everyone at times would like to put somebody under pressure. As a definition of bullying, 'the desire to hurt' is so broad as to be practically useless.

In fact, the correlation between expressing the thought that one sometimes has the desire to hurt someone and reporting actually doing so (as derived from the above study) is quite low, being only 0.33 for both boys and girls. This implies that the expressed desire to hurt accounts for less than 10 per cent of the variation between people in their reported bullying behaviour. Feeling that one would like to hurt people and actually doing so are clearly two different things. We often think better of carrying out our malign intentions, being troubled by twinges of conscience, or, less nobly, reasoning that discretion is the better part of valour.

The perspective on bullying espoused by behavioural psychologists could hardly be more different. Their focus is upon what is done rather than on the state of mind of the doer. For example, in his formulation of what bullying is, Olweus draws our attention to 'negative action on the part of one or more other students'. It is not immediately clear what 'negative actions' are. We are left to infer that the victim does not like what is happening. Olweus (1993) adds that bullying is evident when it is 'difficult for the student being bullied to defend himself or herself'.

In fact, Olweus sees bullying from the perspective of the victim. His definition in full reads: 'A student is being bullied or victimised when he or she is exposed repeatedly and over time to negative actions on the part of one or more other students.'

Notice that unlike the Tattums and the Scottish Council for Research in Education, Olweus does not, in his definition, assume any intention on the part of the 'one or more other students'. The victim just happens to be there ('exposed repeatedly') when 'negative actions' are occurring. This formulation neatly avoids one of the traps for which some behaviourists are ever on the look out: that is, unnecessary mentalistic constructs. What goes on in the mind of the bully is neither here nor there. What matters is the behaviour. Olweus calls this behaviour 'negative'.

But despite his careful definition of bullying, which would satisfy the most purist of the empirical behaviourists, Olweus does indicate his belief that bullying is intentional harm-doing.

Olweus (1999) gives examples of negative actions. He explains:

> We say a student is being bullied when another student, or a group of students:
>
> o   say mean and unpleasant things or make fun of him or her or call him or her mean and hurtful names
>
> o   completely ignore or exclude him or her from their group of friends or leave him or her out of things on purpose
>
> o   hit, kick, push and shove around, or threaten him or her
>
> o   tell lies or false rumors about him or her or send mean notes and try to make other students dislike him or her
>
> o   and things like that.
>
> (Olweus 1999, p.31)

This last item rather takes one's breath away. One had rather hoped for further guidance on the nature of 'things like that'.

One fears, at times, that it is open season on what is to be included under the heading of bullying. In France, according to Fabre-Cornali, Emin and Pain (1999), bullying includes 'crime and offences against people or against personal or school property' and 'all the forms of violence of the school itself, as an institution, and also all minor but frequent manifestations of "incivilities" which disturb school life, such as impoliteness, noise, disorder, etc.' (p.130). What is seen as central to bullying in this account appears to depend on the perspective of the potential victim: for example, teachers emphasise 'insolence' from students; students emphasise lack of respect shown towards them by teachers.

The question naturally arises as to whether one should differentiate bullying from aggression, or at least interpersonal aggression. In Randall's (1991) definition of bullying, no distinction is made: 'Bullying is aggressive behaviour arising out of a deliberate intent to cause physical or psychological distress to others.' This definition has affinities with that of the Tattums in explicitly including deliberate intent and recognising that the goal of the bully's negative actions is to hurt someone. But we may ask, further, whether this is anything more than what is generally understood by the term 'aggression', as employed by earlier researchers into aggression, for instance by Berkowitz (1986), who described aggression as simply the intentional injury of another.

To some it may seem like splitting hairs to make a distinction between aggression and bullying, and it is evident that some writers have been reluctant to embrace the term 'bullying', preferring the term 'aggression' – a term more familiar to researchers and less tainted, one may think, by everyday use. But it is sensible to ask whether employing the concept of 'bullying' in research studies does in fact increase one's ability to predict a particular kind of aggression which we can agree to call 'bullying'.

Results from Farrington's (1993) longitudinal study conducted with 411 males over a span of years from 8 to 32 suggests that it does. Farrington claimed that although bullying is clearly related to aggression, by assessing bullying tendencies at an early age as well as general aggressiveness, prediction of who will bully later in life is much improved. Information obtained at an early age about bullying per se can, it is claimed, significantly add to the accuracy of predictions made on the basis of knowledge of a boy's aggressiveness only. This provides an empirical justification for the use of the concept in research.

Not surprisingly, then, a formulation of bullying that equates it with aggressive behaviour has been seen as over-inclusive and attention has been paid to what it is not. One interesting suggestion has been made by Frey and Hoppe-Graff (1994) in their study of aggressive behaviour among Brazilian preschool children. According to them, bullying can be best described as 'dominant aggression which occurs when an unprovoked child taunts, intimidates, coerces, makes fun of or assaults another child – without a clear external goal for this behaviour' (p.250). They see bullying as distinct from 'instrumental aggression' in not having a 'clear goal' as well as being distinct from 'reactive aggression', that is, aggression that has been in some way provoked. Such a conceptualisation of bullying puts severe demands upon the observer who, to identify bullying, must ascertain first whether or not the aggression is a response to a previous provocation. If it is (and this may be difficult to decide upon) it is not bullying. Second, it must be ascertained whether or not there is a clear goal to the action. If there is a clear goal, it is not bullying. Unfortunately, what constitutes a clear goal is not clear. From the observer's point of view, annoying or upsetting or establishing dominance over a targeted person may *not* be seen as a clear goal. It may nevertheless be clear enough to the perpetrator and to the target. Perhaps it is better to say that a distinction can be made between (i) a desired end state achieved by force to hurt another and to demonstrate one's dominance and (ii) an end state in which one has acquired something by force, but in which one's dominance over the target is incidental and irrelevant. Arguably, only the former is bullying.

American researchers have generally been loathe to employ the term 'bullying' – although the American media of late has made use of it quite freely in examining violence in schools. A distinction is sometimes made between 'proactive aggression' and 'reactive aggression', as in the work of Schwartz *et al.* (1998). These authors used 'proactive aggression' to include non-angry goal-oriented aggressive behaviour; 'reactive aggression' was the term used when aggression took the form of angry retaliation. In their observational study of aggression between male primary schoolchildren, proactive aggression was indicated when 'a boy teased, made fun of, physically abused his dyadic partner, or used aversive means to reach an external goal, e.g., acquisition of an object' (Schwartz *et al.* 1998, p.43). Here the authors do not distinguish between different kinds of goals.

Proactive aggression seems similar to what most people would describe as bullying. However, in defining proactive aggression the authors do stipulate that it refers to 'non-angry' behaviour. It is not, however, generally agreed that bullying must be devoid of anger. For the child who has been victimised there may indeed be considerable anger evident if and when he or she turns on others to bully them. This possibility has led some researchers to identify some children as 'bully/victims' (Olweus 1993).

Some have addressed the question of how often an aggressive act must occur before one can call it bullying. Many writers have taken the view that it must be 'repeated'. Olweus (1993) wrote that the victim had to be 'exposed repeatedly and over time' to negative actions; Besag (1989) proposed that there must be 're-peated attacks'; Farrington (1993) stipulated 'repeated oppression'; the Irish Department of Health and Children (1999) indicated 'repeated aggression'; Losel and Bliesener (1999) in Germany described bullying, among other things, as 'relatively frequent and long-lasting aggressiveness' (p.242); the National Police Agency in Japan insisted it was 'pressure continually repeated' (Morita 1996); Roland (1989) used the phrase 'long-standing violence'; Smith and Thompson (1991) opined 'it occurs repeatedly'; Lane (1989) suggested that the behaviour has to be repeated on more than one occasion; Ortega and

Mora-Merchan (1999) state that bullying is 'continuous abusive behaviour' (p.162).

Olweus (1993) offers a pragmatic justification for including in his definition the criterion of repetitiveness. He argues that it enables one to exclude 'non-serious' events. In their joint work in the early 1970s, Olweus and Roland agreed on an operational criterion. For bullying to occur it must happen 'at least once a week for a month or more'.

Despite the imposing list of researchers who have embraced the idea that to constitute bullying aggression must be repeated, there has been some dissent. Randall (1991) maintained that bullying can be a one-off experience. Stephenson and Smith (1991) proposed that bullying is a form of social interaction not necessarily long-standing. Arora (1996) argued that 'one physical attack or threat to an individual who is powerless might make a person frightened, restricted or upset over a considerable length of time, both because of the emotional trauma following such an attack but also due to the fear of renewed attacks' (p.319). It may be added that common usage does allow one to speak of being bullied during a single encounter. No-one would say: 'You weren't bullied. You never met the guy again.' As to the suggestion that one-off bullying cannot be serious, this is plainly wrong. A colleague recently told me how his son (aged four years) had been harassed and threatened by an older boy during an unescorted coach trip in a foreign country. He was severely frightened by this experience, had great difficulties in sleeping and for many nights would wake up crying. We know that a single horrific incident can be traumatising.

Some writers have sought to differentiate interpersonal aggression from bullying by arguing that bullying should only be used to describe aggressive behaviour which (so they claim) occurs in situations in which the aggressor(s) are in some way more powerful than those they attack. This notion of necessary imbalance of power has more recently been incorporated into a number of definitions of bullying: '...the bully is stronger than the victim or is perceived to be stronger...' (Smith and Thompson 1991); '...more dominant individual (the bully) exhibits aggressive behaviour...' (Stephenson and Smith 1991); '...a type of aggressive behaviour in which someone who holds a dominant position...causes mental and/or physical injury to another...' (Morita *et al.* 1999); '...aggressiveness within relationships characterised by an imbalance of power' (Losel and Bliesener 1999); '...a behaviour...by those in a position of power' (Besag 1989); '...repeated oppression...of a less powerful person by a more powerful person' (Farrington 1993).

Although the idea of a power imbalance as being a necessary condition of bullying has been widely accepted, it is not without difficulties. Many of these relate to the trickiness of the concept of power itself and the practical difficulties of identifying the relevant aspects of power in a given encounter.

Power imbalance

Broadly, power may be defined along the lines suggested by Bertrand Russell: that is, as the production of an intended effect. At an interpersonal level, it may be said that Person A's power over Person B is a function of the extent to which A can influence B to act or think in a certain way in spite of the fact that B initially did not favour this action or thought (Berkowitz 1986). The bases of such power may be many.

Still one of the most widely employed analyses of social power is that of French and Raven (1959). Their analysis suggests that the capacity to bully may derive from one or more of six bases. These are: (i) reward power, as when desired resources are allocated unfairly or withheld in order to control or humiliate someone; (ii) coercive power, when people are forced to do something against their will; (iii) expert power, when an expert uses his or her superior knowledge to dominate or mislead; (iv) referent power, when an individual or group with which you identify induces you to do something you really don't want to do – often the same thing as peer-group pressure; (v) legitimate power, when a person in author-ity, such as a policeman or teacher, is able to impose unfairly on someone by virtue of their position; (vi) informational power, when one is deprived of access to what one has a right to know, e.g. information about a grievance procedure.

An individual's power may have several of these bases. For example, a princi-pal of a school may be in a position to reward another staff member by recom-mending promotion; coerce another by giving an uncongenial order; insist upon obedience by referring to his or her legitimate power as a principal; impress and persuade a colleague by demonstrating some expertise; provide information that will help a teacher to solve a problem; and serve as a model for the kind of person someone would like to be, thereby demonstrating referent power. Conceived in this way, power is ethically neutral. It may be used to support or to bully others.

We should bear in mind that an imbalance of power need not involve a person or persons with what would generally be recognised as 'impressive' powers. The weakness of victims also contributes markedly to the imbalance. In any analysis of imbalances that precede bullying one may include a low capacity to reward or coerce others, an absence of legitimate power, little relevant exper-tise, being generally uninformed, and being the kind of person with whom few, if any, wish to identify. Such a person may, of course, not be bullied – in a benign environment – but is likely in many places to be a prime target.

There are difficulties in recognising power imbalances. Whilst some have power which appears obvious, being physically stronger, verbally more skilled, more highly qualified, or positioned higher in a hierarchy of command, others may exercise unsuspected power, having unexpected qualities of assertiveness or support from others. In any case, over time power imbalances may change, as potential victims acquire the means of defending themselves, or potential bullies lose their supporters. Added to this, power imbalances are sometimes situationally bound. The power to physically coerce someone may be useable in some situations but not others. Expertise and informational power can operate only when they are needed. Legitimate power can normally only be used in situations where its legitimacy is acknowledged. Referent power lasts as long as the user has fans or admirers.

In some cases, two people in a bully/victim situation may have different bases of power which enable each of them to bully the other in one situation but not in another. We find this illustrated in Bernard Shaw's (1932) play *Misalliance* when the clever, intellectual but physically undeveloped Bentley torments his cousin through arguments which invariably tie the slower, conventionally minded but physically robust adversary, in painful knots. The tables are momentarily turned when Bentley's cousin, frustrated by the fact that he cannot win an argument, raises his fist to intimidate his 'feeble' tormentor. This is only temporary, because Bentley lets out such fearful screams that family members rush to his assistance and castigate the offender, now doubly frustrated, leaving Bentley comforted and in control of the situation once more.

In research with children, it has become common practice to highlight the relevance of power imbalance by asking respondents to consider only events in which they recognise that one person or persons are more powerful than those they attack. For example, in his questionnaire for children, Olweus (1993) wrote: 'It is not bullying when two students of about the same strength or power argue or fight.'

This helps, but it does not entirely overcome the practical difficulty of getting students to concentrate on only those situations in which there is a power imbalance. As far as physical bullying is concerned (in most contexts the least common form of bullying) it may do so. Children generally know what constitutes a 'fair fight' even when one of the combatants gains the upper hand and wins. But if we include (as we must) other forms of bullying such as exclusion, hurtful sarcasm and rumour spreading, each with less obvious bases of power to make them possible, the difficulties of defining whether an overall power imbalance exists are sometimes great.

Despite these difficulties, it is, in my view, an advance to conceive bullying as involving a power imbalance, as long as it is recognised that the imbalance may be context-bound and fluid. It has the advantage of focusing our attention on a means by which bullying may be avoided, that is, by reducing, where possible, differences in the power of individuals in an organisation, especially where the power imbalances have negative effects on the well-being of individuals and do not contribute to the efficiency of the organisation.

Justified and unjustified aggression

A further issue, one under-examined, is that of distinguishing between aggression by a more powerful person that is justified (and therefore not bullying) from that which is not justified – and therefore *is* bullying.

It should not be assumed that when more powerful persons act forcefully in a given situation that they are necessarily engaged in bullying. They may be bullying, or they may not. Standard definitions of bullying, like those reviewed above, provide little or no recognition that acts intended to put people under pressure can be other than bullying. Yet we encounter many situations in which a more powerful person coerces another without anyone raising the cry of 'bully'. Consider: a mother who drags a child back from running across a dangerous roadway; a teacher who sends a child out of a classroom for constantly disrupting the class; a rugby player who barges over for a try; the policeman who intervenes when someone is being assaulted; a judge who sentences a seemingly incorrigible criminal. We may not entirely exonerate but we are understanding of an older child who unceremoniously puts a junior in his place after repeated warnings to stop provoking him or her. In many situations in everyday life we weigh up the circumstances and invoke the charge of 'bully' when force is being used unfairly or unjustifiably, or when we think that the reaction to provocation is disproportionate. Curiously, this is rarely recognised by those who seek to define bullying.

There are exceptions. Smith and Sharp (1994) define bullying as 'the systematic abuse of power'. This draws our attention to the ways in which power can be abused: what is the justified use of power and what is not. Farrington (1993) has provided us with a useful and more extended definition of bullying: 'Bullying is repeated oppression of a less powerful person, physical or psychological, by a more powerful person.'

The key word here is 'oppression'. The Macquarie Dictionary (1987) defines oppression as 'the exercise of authority or power in a burdensome, cruel or unjust manner'. What is burdensome may be inferred from the reactions of those who carry the burden in the case of bullying – namely, the victims. Yet, we may agree that the fact that you are carrying a heavy burden imposed by another more powerful person is not proof that you are being bullied. You may have chosen to be subject to heavy demands being made upon you. Whether what is being imposed is cruel or unjust is a different matter that cannot be deduced from the victim's feelings. To decide upon this one must raise issues of morality and justice.

It is no good appealing to the self-proclaimed victim as the sole arbiter of what is just and therefore (if we are to incorporate the criterion of justice into bullying) what is bullying. It is clearly possible to feel that one is being treated unjustly when this is not the case. Prisons contain some people vigorously proclaiming they are innocencent when they are not. Hence, if a person feels oppressed we must still reserve our judgement as to whether he or she is really being bullied. In taking the final decision as to whether a person is being bullied out of the hands of the alleged victim, one is not discounting the relevance of that person's experience. It is, indeed, prima facie evidence. One is simply asserting that there are other considerations.

We may also venture to suggest that a person may be being bullied without knowing it. Tim Field, a leading authority on workplace bullying, argues: 'The person being bullied may not realise they are being bullied for weeks or months – until there is a moment of enlightenment.' Indeed, the realisation may not come at all. We see the dumb incapacity to see that one is being bullied in C. S. Lewis's (1956) mythical tale *The Last Battle*, in which Puzzle, the donkey, is being constantly manipulated and exploited by Shift, the crafty ape who poses as his friend. Their relationship is worth examining as an example of bullying unrecognised as such by the victim.

In this story Puzzle does all the difficult and arduous things. He brings home the shopping in back-breaking panniers; then Shift helps himself to the tastiest food. Sadly, Shift explains, apes cannot eat thistles like donkeys can. When they see a curious object floating in the river, Puzzle is asked to dive into the icy water to retrieve it. When Puzzle mildly remonstrates, Shift explains: 'Now Puzzle, I understand what needs to be done better than you. You know you're not clever.' Still, Puzzle cannot immediately see why it should be he who dives into the icy river: after all he has hoofs that make it hard to grab things, while the Ape has hands. That is, not until Shift reminds him that 'apes have weak chests and easily catch colds'. Martyr-like, Shift prepares to meet his end. 'But I'll go in,' he says. 'I shall probably die. Then you'll be sorry.' Puzzle is forced to plead: 'I never meant anything of the sort, Shift, really I didn't. You know how stupid I am and how I can't think of more than one thing at a time. I'd forgotten about your weak chest. Of course I'll go in. You mustn't think of doing it yourself. Promise me you won't, Shift.' And, of course, with much show of reluctance, the crafty ape promises. Bullying may be subtle, manipulative. The target may be deceived. Sometimes even blissfully unaware that his or her companion is a bully. In the British television serial *Blackadder*, the clever insults directed at Baldrick have no impact, so profoundly and blissfully unaware is he of their meaning and malicious intent.

Over time what may be seen as the legitimate exercise of power may come to be regarded as bullying. Slavery is perhaps the most striking example. For much of human history it has been acceptable to have slaves. The limits to what slaves could be expected to do were ill defined. In private schools until recently senior students were expected to have 'fags' whom they could direct to do things for them and punish if they disobeyed. We now acknowledge that in patriarchal societies women have been, and may still be, unreasonably burdened and oppressed by men. In our own society many are still unsure of what are acceptable roles for men and women. What constitutes bullying clearly changes over time with evolving mores.

Sub-types of bullying

You sometimes come across lists of actions that *could* constitute bullying, such as the list proposed by Dan Olweus (1999) cited above. Various attempts have been made to establish separate bundles or sub-types of bullying or (in some cases) aggressiveness in general. This may be done by providing categories according to the manner in which bullying or aggression is delivered:

- physically, e.g. by hitting or kicking
- verbally, e.g. by name-calling
- gesturally, e.g. by staring deliberately at someone.

But somehow this does not catch all we may want to convey. We recognise that people may seek to hurt people in an indirect way, by actions that may not be observed by the victim at the time but which are deliberate and have intentional negative consequences for the victim. We may have in mind excluding people, spreading rumours about a person or turning people against someone. Not surprisingly, 'indirect aggression' has been seen by some – for example, by the influential Finnish researchers Bjorqvist, Lagerspetz, Salmivalli and Kukainen (1992) – to constitute a form of bullying. They saw indirect aggression as 'a noxious behaviour in which the target person is attacked not physically nor directly through verbal intimidation but in a more circuitous way through social manipulation'. Is this really part of bullying?

One way of answering this question is to ask students directly. Stanley and Arora (1998) did this with secondary schoolgirls in England. The focus was on social exclusion. Although a large proportion of the girls (32%) reported that they had been socially excluded at times by their peers, both those excluded and those not excluded generally thought that exclusion did not constitute 'bullying'. But how children choose to interpret a word need not determine how the word should be used. An alternative way of considering whether being excluded is an aspect of bullying is to see how well it correlates with reports of being overtly bullied, physically and verbally. Rigby (1997c) reported moderately high correlations (over .5) with over 20,000 Australian students, between reports of being excluded by peers and being bullied overtly. Victimised children who are frequently hurt in one way (overtly) by their peers tend also to be hurt in other ways (covertly). Many researchers think that they are justified in including both kinds of ill treatment under a single heading of bullying or peer victimisation. We may nevertheless question whether some forms of so-called indirect bullying actually involve an imbalance of power which many see as an essential feature of bullying. One can easily imagine a person who is in every respect less powerful than another spreading untrue rumours about that person.

Rather than categorise bullying or aggression according to the means by which either is carried out, some researchers have drawn attention to the purpose behind non-physical aggression. Thus Crick and Grotpeter (1995) defined 'relational aggression' as 'harming others through the purposeful manipulation and damage of their peer relationships' (p.711). This led them to make a two-fold distinction between physical or overt aggression and relational aggression. This is in some ways problematic. One type of aggression (or bullying), i.e. 'relational', is defined according to its purpose; the other, 'physical', is defined according to overt acts only, as in hitting or kicking. We may ask whether overt actions, such as when a person is physically humiliated, may also have the intended effect of depriving him or her of peer support. I have heard children say: 'I wouldn't be friends with a wimp.' May not social isolation of the target be intended by the physical bully?

A similar problem applies to the formulation of 'social aggression' by Galen and Underwood (1997) as 'aggression directed towards damaging another's self esteem or social status or both'. They add that this 'may take such forms as verbal rejection, negative facial expressions or body movements, or more direct forms such as slanderous rumours or social exclusion' (p.589). Again we may ask whether physical aggression does not sometimes also have precisely these intended effects: to reduce another's 'self esteem and/or social status'. In seeking to get rid of the admittedly imprecise term 'indirect aggression', it appears that other serious problems of categorisation are created.

Racial bullying

Another way of identifying kinds of bullying is to focus on the nature of target groups that are thought to elicit the negative treatment. Thus if the negative treatment is directed towards a person who is of a different racial group from the perpetrator it is often called 'racial bullying' or 'racial harassment'. But to confirm that it is 'racial bullying' it is really necessary to have evidence that it is the racial difference between bully and target that has occasioned the bullying. This is sometimes hard to establish. A child of a different racial group may be the target of bullying for non-racial reasons. A child who bullies one member of a racial group may be good friends with another person of that same racial group. This is a difficult area and misunderstandings and misjudgments are inevitable.

One useful definition of racial harassment is 'all actions and behaviours that intentionally or otherwise either discriminate against someone or make them feel unwelcome or marginalised because of their racial identity' (Connolly and Keenan 2000). They add that racial identity 'in this instance can either be defined in terms of a person's race, colour, nationality and ethnic and/or national origin'.

Bullying due to disability

We know that children who are disabled in some way are more likely than others to be bullied at school (see Chapter 8). As yet, however, few have identified as a special kind of bullying that relating specifically to disability. An exception is in the work of Holzbauer and Berven (1996). They write about 'harassment', practically a synonym for 'bullying'. Disablement harassment is defined as the unwelcome bothering, tormenting, troubling, ridiculing or coercing of another person related to the disability of that person and is composed of verbal behaviour as distinguished from physical violence or force. The harassing behaviour is typically repeated and often takes place in a social context with the harasser attempting to gain power over the individual being harassed (p.479).

It may be that its nature does deserve special treatment. The extraordinary thing about bullying directed at disabled people is that it is so much at variance with the reactions that most people have towards those who have had the misfortune to become crippled or to suffer very serious damage, as, for example, in becoming blind. To maliciously hurt such a person is an evil difficult for most people to comprehend.

Sexual bullying

Recently, the term 'sexual bullying' has been coined (N. Duncan 1999). This appears to be distinct from sexual harassment, a form of behaviour that certainly overlaps with what is generally understood as bullying behaviour. Unfortunately, Duncan does not attempt to define 'sexual bullying' but rather gives copious examples taken from what children have told him. Here is a typical example (p.1):

> Lend me your ruler.
> No.
> You tight bitch, fucking slag.

From the many examples Duncan gives we may infer that: (i) such exchanges are commonplace between boys and girls at secondary school in England; (ii) one or both of the children in the exchange are being offensive; (iii) language with sexual connotations is being used; and (iv) they constitute a kind of behaviour we may call 'sexual bullying'.

Certainly it is not difficult to collect copious examples of such language being used by schoolchildren, just as it has now become easy to collect examples from dialogue in books and films involving adults. However, we may question whether the use of such words generally has any real sexual connotations at all. To people who habitually use words carefully and meaningfully, it may seem strange that 'bad language' can be almost entirely meaningless, but you discover this when you listen to people who use 'obscene' words in every other sentence or simply for emphasis, or, as sometimes happens, to stall for time when searching for a *mot juste*. Expressed in anger, such words happen to be ones that the speaker thinks will make an impact. If the aggressor thinks that other words will do the trick, say 'shit' or 'turd' or more meaningfully – or perhaps more hurtfully – 'loser', then these others may well be used. True, the words that are held to imply sexual bullying do have a sexual referent – if you think about it – but, like much of our talk, the meaning of the metaphor we are using (if any) is at least temporarily lost to us.

A second problem lies in the fact that the use of such language does not enable us to infer that the user is in some sense more powerful than the recipient. Moreover, the words themselves may well have lost their power to offend, and have become mere noise. Both aggressor and target may know this.

Of course it may be argued that the frequent choice of words that have sexual connotations in somebody's lexicon, if not in the mind of the user, implies a world in which adolescent boys and girls are obsessed with sex – which is not exactly a surprising discovery. But it is hard to accept that when a boy or girl uses 'bad language' to describe a peer he or she is essentially engaging in bullying. To demonstrate that this is the case one must go further and show that the person using the language is (a) more powerful than the other person and (b) seeking to hurt that person. This may or may not be so.

One of the consequences of seeing 'bad language' as infallible evidence of bullying is the occasional witch-hunt for those who use it. Recently it was reported in a South Australian newspaper that a school principal on an anti-bullying crusade had ruled that any child found to be using one or other of a prepared list of 'bad words', sexual in connotation, was to be summarily convicted of bullying and dealt with accordingly.

'Real bullying' or bullying on a continuum

In an account of bullying in Spain, Ortega and Mora-Merchan (1999) write of the need to identify 'real bullying' which occurs when the victim feels 'totally defenceless and can't escape'. This they see as different from what can be viewed as a mere joke or game that 'does not produce the same level of anxiety and help-lessness'. Here we see the problem of deciding when bullying is 'real'. From a pragmatic point of view we may ask: should action be taken to discourage behav-iours that presumably cause only 'low levels of anxiety and helplessness'?

Personally, I think it is better to think of bullying actions as occurring along a continuum of severity. Askew (1989) appears to have been the first to conceive bullying along these lines. She wrote: 'Bullying is a continuum that involves an attempt to gain power and dominance over another'.

We may note, in passing, that unlike other writers Askew does not assume that the bully is invariably successful, nor that the hurting of a victim is a neces-sary objective. Or even that there is any hurt. Demonstrating dominance is enough. But quite possibly – depending upon the area in which dominance is demonstrated – the victim may not care. (Perhaps this is 'not real' bullying. Cer-tainly we may reasonably be disinclined to intervene.) For instance I will not be unduly disturbed if a grandmaster demolishes my defences and checkmates me in a trice. After all, it is only chess and I am a pretty hopeless amateur at it.

But the notion of bullying as a continuum suggested by Askew is a useful one. We find it echoed some years later by the Japanese sociologist Morita (1996). He points out that bullying is not a matter of black and white. At one end it may appear exceedingly black, as in violent and repeated assaults. At the other we have a pale shade of grey, as in insensitive but relatively harmless teasing. Gradually along the continuum, a dirty white shades into grey, then into the blackest of black.

I think it should be acknowledged that most bullying is at the relatively mild (or grey) end of the continuum. It is not easy to get agreement on precisely what constitutes mild, intermediate and extreme forms of bullying. In part this is because the consequences of different forms of bullying may vary from one indi-vidual to another. One person may be devastated by being teased on some matter about which he or she is highly sensitive. The same person may be unconcerned about being hit by someone. Nevertheless, if the notion of a continuum of severity is to be of value, we need criteria about what should be taken into account in making judgements about severity. These are my suggestions:

(1)   The nature of the action, e.g. mild teasing versus physical assault.

(2)   The duration of bullying, whether over a short or long time.

(3)   The frequency of bullying acts, e.g. whether daily, weekly or less often.

Low severity would commonly involve thoughtless periodic teasing, name-calling and occasional exclusion. This can be annoying and unpleasant and can escalate and then involve more serious forms of bullying. Most bullying is at this level.

An intermediate level of bullying occurs when a child is subjected for a time to forms of harassment which are both systematic and hurtful. These may include cruel teasing, continual exclusion and some threats or some relatively mild physical abuse, e.g. pushing or tripping.

Severe bullying occurs when the harassment is particularly cruel and intense, especially if it occurs over an extended period and is very distressing to the victim. It frequently involves serious physical assaults but it can still be severe when the bullying is non-physical as in total or almost total exclusion from groups.

One may ask whether, given the difficulty of classifying acts of bullying along such a continuum, there is really any need to do so. I think the justification for doing so is largely pragmatic. First, if we classify as bullying only those acts which in Ortega's view are 'real' we may ignore a great deal of bullying that is clearly undesirable (causing low levels of anxiety and helplessness). Second, if we suggest that 'bullying is all the same' we may create the impression that all bullying should be dealt with in the same way; for example, that we should treat a case of occasional mild teasing in much the same way as we treat repeated physical assault.

What hurts

At the same time, one must admit that it is by no means obvious what forms of bullying will hurt an individual most. Sometimes, from the outside, what the bully does may seem trivial. Victor Frankl (1964) in his account of his experiences in a Nazi concentration camp describes an incident that he found particularly distressing.

> One day I was standing on a railway track in a snowstorm. In spite of the weather our party had to keep on working. I worked quite hard at mending the track with gravel, since that was the only way to keep warm. For only one moment I paused to get my breath and to lean on my shovel. Unfortunately the guard turned around just then and thought I was loafing. The pain he caused me was not from the insults or the blows. That guard did not think it worth his while to say anything, not even a swear word, to the ragged, emaciated figure standing before him, which probably reminded him only vaguely of a human form. Instead, he playfully picked up a stone and threw it at me. That, to me, seemed the way to attract the attention of a beast, to call a domestic animal back to its job, a creature with which you have so little in common that you do not even punish it. (p.34)

To understand his distress one needs to comprehend the total context: the years of intense and accumulating abuse preceding this incident – and what the casual action of the guard meant to him and to his status as a human being.

Individual and group perpetration of bullying

In the early days of research into bullying, there was much talk of so-called 'mobbing' as a bullying phenomenon. The term was popularised by Scandinavian researchers, such as Heinemann (1972) and, in the early years of his work, by Olweus. It suggested to English-speaking readers a group combining to act aggressively towards selected individuals. The term however was apt to be confusing. Lorenz (1969) used the term to describe the 'counter offensive' of the prey against the predator. Crows or other birds, he observed, 'mob' a cat or any other nocturnal predator, if they catch sight of it by day. Yet the term may sometimes be used to describe alleged bullying by an individual, even in places where people speak English. In Norfolk, England, I heard a man remonstrate with his wife whom he thought was nagging him: 'Don't you mob me, gal.' The term is clearly too fraught with ambiguity to help in an analysis of types of bullying and has more or less been dropped.

However, the question of whether bullying is predominantly carried out through group involvement or by individuals acting alone is a live one. One prominent Swedish psychologist, Anatol Pikas (1989), stresses the almost universal involvement of groups even when a given bullying action may be delivered by an individual. Ross (1996) has expressed strong disagreement, seeing bullying as predominantly an individual matter. The question is an important one because one may decide to intervene to stop the bullying differently, according to whether the offending behaviour is seen as determined by an individual's personality or by the functioning of a group. Hence, Pikas has argued that we must take into account the dynamics of the group to which an individual bully belongs and how individual members are influenced. Intervention, he maintains, should at some stage involve the group. By contrast, Ross emphasises treating bullies individually, applying appropriate sanctions and training children to be able to stand up to such bullies.

Typing bullying according to individual / group involvement

Whilst we generally think of the victims of bullying as individuals, sometimes isolated individuals, we might recognise that victims may also constitute groups. The groupings of those who are being victimised may be comprised of individuals who for some reason are put together, as in the case of a class of children or a bunch of army recruits on the parade ground. Alternatively, they may have come together because of some shared interest, as in the case of membership of a computer or chess club. Or again, they may have some features in common besides a common interest; for instance, a racial or ethnic background or a physical disability. The groupings may differ widely in cohesiveness. They may or may not tend to be in the same place at the same time. They may be 'picked off' individually by a bully or group of bullies, or they may be confronted in a group by an individual or group that can hurt them.

We can conceptualise types according to whether perpetrators or targets are groups or individuals, as follows:

Perpetrator	Target or victim
Individual	Individual
Group	Individual
Individual	Group
Group	Group

INDIVIDUAL AS BULLY/INDIVIDUAL AS TARGET

This is the situation with which we are probably most familiar. We should bear in mind, however, that we can rarely discount group influences of one kind or another. The only 'pure' case of one-to-one bullying of which I feel sure is in science fiction. In C. S. Lewis's (1943) *Perelandra*, the hero, Ransome, is pursued by a tormentor in a seemingly uninhabited planet (at least these two know of no others). The bullying consists of the constant repetition of his name: 'Ransome... Ransome... Ransome... ', until Ransome after hours of this torment replies: 'What?' 'Nothing' is the reply. 'Ransome... Ransome... Ransome...' It goes on and on again, interminably. In the real world, there are generally others who know what is going on, bystanders who witness it, encourage it or ignore it. Whilst pure one-to-one bullying may indeed be rare, some bullying is often largely independent of the influences of others.

Bullying may occur within relatively long-standing relationships. These relationships may be quite complex and their quality may vary widely between different dyads. There may be positives (shared interests, good memories) which help to maintain the relationship as well as painful negatives recalled periodically by the person who is the butt of the bullying. The bullying may be an expression of the exploitative style of relating practised successfully by the bully, as in the case of Shift, the ape, in the Lewis story, and endured by the victim, who is aware that despite the negative treatment being experienced there are some positives. The bully may indeed sometimes be nice. The alternative may be having no friends at all.

Sometimes bullying occurs after relatively long-standing relationships have ended with a dispute that has been unresolved. This can provide the 'justification' in the eyes of one or both parties for continuing animosity. The more powerful of the two may seek or make opportunities to bully the other, and even encourage others to join in the vendetta.

Alternatively bullying may occur when there is, or has been, virtually no previous relationship between the perpetrator and the target. Here the bully is fastening upon a victim whom he or she can dominate and upset. There may be a series of people who fulfil the role of victim for this so-called 'serial bully'. A true-life account of such a bully is given in Tony Parker's (1990) description of Big Bully Billy, an aggressive school bully who later on as an adult was jailed for murder.

GROUP PERPETRATORS/INDIVIDUAL TARGET

The group may vary in size and cohesiveness.

The small group. At its smallest this will consist of two people who typically encourage and reinforce each other in their dealings with others. In extreme cases such duos may be dangerous 'outsiders'. Examples have included Mary Bell, aged 11, and Norma Bell, aged 13 (no relation), who mutilated and murdered Brian Howe, aged 3, in Scotswood, England, in 1968; 10-year-olds Robert Thompson and Jon Venables who tortured and murdered the 2-year-old, James Bulger, on a railway line in Merseyside in 1993; teenagers Eric Harris, aged 18, and Dylan Klebold, aged 17, who in 1999 stormed Columbine High School with guns and bombs, killing a dozen classmates and a teacher before committing suicide. Such events are rare and are generally 'explained' as extreme reactions to abuse and trauma in childhood and/or isolation and alienation from others in later life.

More commonly, however, small groups who participate in bullying, though sometimes highly destructive, are less malign. They may swagger around looking for others they can dominate and ridicule without engaging in serious assaults. One of them may act as the leader, as in the portrayal of bullying in the video, *Only Playing, Miss!*, produced by Casdagli, Goki and Griffin (1990). The role of the 'assistant' is largely to stand by and reinforce the more active partner. Occasionally, the bullying is orchestrated by the leader who may 'select' a potential victim and persuade members of his small gang, singly or as a group, to bully that person. In interviewing children who bully others, I have found that such children may not fit the psychopathic stereotype at all, but may sometimes present as happy, extraverted individuals for whom the bullying is an acceptable and enjoyable way of spending one's time at school. Their behaviour is, of course, highly unacceptable to most other children and especially to the victims of such bullying.

Intermediate-sized group. This group may be somewhat larger (approximately four to ten members), fairly cohesive, engaging in a range of social activities besides bullying. For this group, bullying is likely to be seen as a diversion, an entertainment in which members participate to varying degrees. The victim may be selected because he or she is 'bully-able' and perhaps a pleasure to bully because of an 'absurd over-reaction' to being teased. Alternatively, the victim may be someone who has irritated or antagonised the group in some way, and bullying is seen as a way to 'get even'. Sometimes the victim is an ex-group member.

In some cases a group may feel that they have a right to impose upon new people joining an organisation. Because they were treated severely when they joined the organisation, they may come to believe that it is OK for them to treat others likewise. Hence, initiation rites may be devised, sometimes extremely hurtful ones. In Australia cases of such 'hazing', as a form of bullying, have come to light in military training establishments. In schools similar things may happen when senior students feel that they can treat younger students as they wish. In one boarding school with which I became familiar, younger students were reported as having been used as 'tackling bags' for members of the rugby team. Here the practice of bullying is being sustained by a tradition which seems to absolve individuals from a sense of personal responsibility.

It is sometimes found that when you get to know the group members as individuals they do not individually feel all that happy about what is being done to the victim. However, when they are all together, their feelings change. They get a 'charge' from their involvement in the group activity. Individual consciences are clear. It seems like good fun, adds to group cohesiveness (which is in itself pleasurable) and somehow (they tell themselves) the victim deserved it! The group may also contain some members whom we may call 'hangers on'. These are individuals who have found that identifying with the tough guys who bully is insurance against being bullied themselves.

The large group. This includes everybody or practically everybody who comes into contact with the targeted person. The target is a rank outsider. The victimisation once in full swing becomes automatic, a kind of reflex action. Fraser Harrison (1990) describes one such victim in recalling his days and nights at a boys' boarding school in England in the late 1950s and early 1960s. He writes:

> Owing to the unusually bloodless complexion and cadaverous physique, he was known as 'Corpse', and whenever he passed we would pretend to shiver, rolling our eyes in mock horror and making ghoulish noises. He was

also known as 'Bones', which prompted us to rattle invisible skeletons in his face and click our teeth at him like animated skulls. This ritual was performed as casual reflex actions rather than gestures of calculated malice, but they were the invariable greeting he met with wherever he went and whatever he said, which was precious little. He was two years older than I, and by the time I joined the house he had been teased so unremittingly that he had been forced to imprison himself in a cage of silence, a sort of solitary confinement. In an effort to efface himself and to avoid attracting further notice, he had taken his nickname further: he was more ghostly than corpse-like and no longer lived in the house but haunted it, creeping elusively along its edges, never speaking or looking at anyone, his pale eyes in their hollow sockets. I never saw a boy so lonely. (pp.115–116)

Looking back on his days at the boarding school, the author comments: 'I am ashamed to say that although I was horrified by his plight, I still added my voice to his regular torturers. I had a glib and facetious tongue which I did not hesitate to use in the cause of self-promotion.' I am reminded of a focus group meeting which I helped to conduct with 14-year-old boys in South Australia. They spoke of someone whom everyone bullied. 'Why?' I asked. The answer was unanimous: 'He isn't normal'.

It should be added that the target of group bullying is sometimes a teacher. Most people have memories of a teacher who was continually the target of collective bullying both within and outside class periods. This can take the form of disrespectful comment, the sabotaging of lessons (preventing the teacher from getting on with the job), and calling out, invisibly from a distance, whenever the teacher appears. The motivation of the children is commonly to have fun, the teacher appearing (to them) ridiculous, being unable to maintain authority. But the pain experienced by the teacher can be extreme and result in the teacher leaving the profession. Less commonly, it involves physical assaults. During a recent visit to Israel I was met by two distressed female teachers who told me that they had been physically attacked by elementary schoolboys at their school.

INDIVIDUAL PERPETRATOR/GROUP TARGET

A highly dominant person may sometimes bully a group. This is more likely to occur when legitimate power is allied with a dominating personality operating in a situation in which it is difficult or impossible to resist. Perhaps the most striking examples occur in military organisations where groups of recruits are deliberately intimidated by leaders or instructors selected for such a purpose. The stage on which this happens is frequently the parade ground; the bully, in the army the sergeant major; in the navy, the appropriately named petty officer. The aim ostensibly is to instil obedience by establishing conditioned reflexes to commands. Intimidation is the means of achieving this. As shouting abuse and seeking to humiliate in front of others makes most people highly anxious and less capable of executing commands, such as 'about turns' or 'slope arms', the aim is clearly not to achieve precision or coordination in movement. Rather it is to create a feeling that one's commanders are dangerous, perhaps more so than the enemy. The exercise provides considerable entertainment and pleasure those for sergeant majors and petty officers who have a taste for bullying recruits on the parade ground, and also, one may add, for those recruits who identify, as some do, with their 'oppressors', and provide reinforcement for their antics.

In schools, it can sometimes happen that a teacher is able and inclined to bully whole classes of students. In the past such bullying was conducted by teachers through the continued use of physical punishment. In his autobiography Roald Dahl (1984) tells of the savage beatings meted out at his school by his teacher, the future Archbishop of Canterbury, religious affiliation evidently being no guarantee of non-aggression. In my own school, the school tyrant was a teacher of mathematics who instructed students to memorise geometrical theorems which they were subsequently to write down in class and bring up to his desk for checking. If the student made a mistake, he (girls were exempt) was struck violently across the face. It is doubtful whether this process was an aid to learning but it had the effect of producing the quietest classroom in the school.

GROUP PERPETRATOR/GROUP TARGET

The groups may, as before, vary in size and cohesiveness. At one extreme we may have members of a sporting team that seek to harass members of another group, say, a group of computer 'nerds', whom they view with some contempt. Both groups may have a high measure of solidarity. This kind of situation has been amusingly portrayed in the cult classic, *Revenge of the Nerds*, which despite its light-heartedness successfully captures the arrogance of the tormentors and the dismay of the tormented. In some schools children in senior classes may sometimes systematically harass and bully children in a class below them; children in one ethnic group may seek to bully those in another. In the latter case, one would generally expect the majority or mainstream group to dominate. This is not always so. A minority group, with a background or culture where violence is not uncommon, may sometimes terrorise the majority.

Sometimes neither the target group nor the perpetrators have much cohesiveness. This can occur when children who are in some way disabled are subjected to bullying. The victims do not necessarily band together; the perpetrators are unlikely to be acting in a coordinated way. But one can see clearly enough that belonging to one group (the disabled) is likely to evoke disparagement, sometimes ridicule, as in the case of children who stammer, at the hands of those who do not. In an Australian high school I discovered that students were classified by fellow students as footballers, fatties and faggots. It is easy to guess which of the three Fs was likely to be dominant and which more subjected to bullying of one kind or another.

Bullying from the child's perspective

One approach to defining bullying in schools is through discovering what students understand by the term. This is certainly desirable if the term is used in a questionnaire without explanation or illustration. There is evidence that children often use the term in ways different from the researcher. Some children confuse bullying with 'fighting with some one' – as do some adults. Smith and Levan (1995) have pointed out that 87 per cent of the English schoolchildren in their sample of 6- to 7-year-olds said that fighting with somebody was bullying. Age may be important in determining how children view bullying. Madsen (1996) found that older groups were more likely than others to include as bullying indirect forms of aggression. Madsen also pointed out that relatively few respondents in her study saw an 'imbalance of power' as crucial in defining bullying.

Whilst it is important in studying bullying to discover how children of different ages use the term 'bullying', it does not follow that the researcher should be bound by the children's definition, any more than a teacher should accept as 'correct' a definition of a word at variance with a dictionary definition on the grounds that many children use it in a different way. Yet it is not impossible to find serious researchers who believe that by not accepting a child's view of what a word means – for whatever purpose – one is somehow trampling on the inalienable Rights of the Child. They can quote chapter and verse – the United Nations (1989) – in defence of this perspective. We seem to be in Lewis Carroll country.

Non-malign bullying

Thus far we have been concerned with what may be called malign bullying (Rigby 1997a), that is bullying which is deliberate, intended to hurt and gratifying to the successful bully. Whilst such bullying is of major concern, it should be observed that the term 'bullying' is sometimes used to describe bullying that does not have these characteristics. Certainly, pressure may be exercised by a more powerful person or group. The target of such oppression may feel oppressed. An observer may reasonably describe the action as 'oppressive', that is burdensome and unjustified. But to the perpetrator the goal does not lie simply in the hurting of the target, nor is the discomfort of the target once recognised enjoyed.

It is important to identify non-malign bullying for several reasons. First, the target of such oppression feels hurt and is likely to feel resentful. He or she may well think that the bullying is deliberate, intended to hurt and is enjoyed by the oppressor. Under these circumstances the resentment is almost certainly going to increase, and may result in a revengeful act. Further, the oppressor may be bliss-fully unaware of the strength of the resistance that is being created. If there were to be a full appreciation of the pain being experienced, the oppressor might well feel mortified. Such bullying can be seen as a failure on the part of the oppressor, lacking in sensitivity or imagination, to put himself or herself in the place of the person being oppressed.

It is not uncommon for parents to bully their children without recognising what they are doing. They may be bullying their child because they have in mind a 'higher goal' which blinds them to what they are doing to the child. In the past, the higher goal was often religious, and a misguided concern for the child's immortal soul. We find this described in 19th-century novels such as Charlotte Bronte's *Jane Eyre* and Samuel Butler's *The Way of all Flesh*.

Butler describes an interaction between a father and his four-year-old son who was unable to sound a hard 'c' or 'k' in the word 'come'.

> 'Ernest,' said the father, 'don't you think it would be nice if you were able to say "come" like other people instead of "tum"?
>
> 'I do say "tum", replied Ernest, meaning he had said "come".
>
> 'No, Ernest, you don't,' said father, 'you say nothing of the kind, you say "tum" not "come". Now say "come" after me.'
>
> After several unsuccessful attempts by the child to say 'come', his father said that he would give him one more chance to say 'come', failing which he adds: 'I shall know you are self-willed and naughty.'
>
> The child said 'tum' once more.
>
> Father concluded: 'Very well, Ernest, I have done my best to save you, but if you will have it so, you will.'
>
> Whereupon he lugged the boy away, crying in anticipation, to another room where he was beaten. A little while later the father returned, saying, 'I have sent him to bed. Now we will have the servants in for prayers.'

More commonly nowadays the bullying is done by fathers who want their child to be tough and a credit to them. We find fathers who threaten their children with smacking if they cry at night, labelling their evident distress as mere manipula-tion. There are fathers who demand that their child eats food at the proper time, whether hungry or not, to avoid the problem of feeding the child at an inconve-nient time. At best this is to instil self-discipline, a laudable end, but using means which are generally counter-productive and increasingly unacceptable by com-munity standards. Again, it must be stressed that this is not malign bullying; it is not sadism. It is ignorance.

Conclusion

A variety of perspectives has been offered in defining and describing bullying. If I am right, there has been an evolution in the way in which bullying has been conceptualised, leading to continual improvements and refinements which we recognise as we begin to appreciate the shortcomings and weaknesses of earlier formulations. I have suggested that we make a distinction between malign and non-malign bullying, placing, in my discussion, an emphasis upon the former, but by no means neglecting the latter. In conclusion I offer my own tentative definition of malign bullying based upon an analysis of previously published views of what bullying is:

Bullying involves a desire to hurt + hurtful action + a power imbalance + (typically) repetition + an unjust use of power + evident enjoyment by the aggressor and generally a sense of being oppressed on the part of the victim.

Chapter 3

Bullying in childhood

Show me the man who has enjoyed his school days and I will show you a bully and a bore.

– Robert Morley

Not surprisingly, bullying has been studied mostly among children. In fact, for some people 'bullying' carries connotations of immaturity; the sort of thing children do. Adults generally like to think they have outgrown being a bully and can no longer be bullied. Of course, this is a fantasy, but it is fair to conclude that bullying is more commonly observed among children.

Bullying in early childhood

Conflict between children occurs at a very early age, for example over possession of a prized toy or attention from a parent. This can and frequently does involve sporadic acts of aggression, but is not the same thing as bullying. However, when an older and more powerful child persistently seeks to hurt a weaker sibling, this can legitimately be called bullying. There have been few systematic studies of such behaviour in the family context and for an understanding of bullying among very young children we must turn to studies conducted in preschool and kindergarten settings. Here again, compared with studies of older children, there are relatively few. To some extent this may be due to the difficulties of obtaining reliable data from the self-reports of young children, especially through the use of questionnaires which constitute the most widely used method of generating data on bullying and are more appropriately answered by older, more literate children. For younger children alternative and time-consuming methods are needed, such as one-to-one interviews with children and with teachers, and the use of direct observational methods.

One such study was undertaken at four early childhood centres in Canberra, Australia, in 1994 (Main 1999). Some 98 hours of non-participant observation focused on the behaviour of infants (6 weeks to 18 months), toddlers (18 months to 3 years) and preschoolers (3 to 5 years). In addition, 20 hours of semi-structured interviews were conducted with 17 staff members of the selected child care organisations. Main reported that in all the sub-groups (infants, toddlers and pre-schoolers) a relatively few children were responsible for initiating aggressive actions which included pushing, biting and hitting. Altogether 1441 violent incidents were observed. In many cases a clear imbalance of power was apparent. For example:

> Tom is running around poking many children. He has a texta lid on his finger, and smiles as he pokes the children hard with it. He comes over to the observer and pokes her with his finger and says, 'Do you want to see my powerful finger?' (The observer responds that she is not interested because he had poked her with it.) He runs off and continues to poke children with it. A little later, when the children have moved inside, he grabs Rob and pushes his face hard into a pillow and holds him down. Rob is very distressed. A member of staff suggests that Tom does some hammering. Tom replies, 'No! I don't have to!'

Here is another example.

> A preschool boy throws a sandpit spade at a toddler girl as she comes out of the toddler's room. He misses and laughs with the other boys sitting with him. Then he grabs a sandpit spade from her and hits her hard on the body with it.

Often the observed behaviour included a variety of bullying acts: aggressive gestures, physical attack and verbal abuse.

> Jim (a preschool boy) goes over to the corner where Sal is playing with a group of girls on a pile of pillows. He growls at them, putting his face very close to theirs and grimacing. They scream and grab the pillows around them. Jim tells them to share the pillows. He then lies down on the pillows and the girls say, 'We had them first.' Jim does not respond and the girls move away, going back only to retrieve their shoes. Jim then moves from the pillows and gets a piece of string. He grabs Sybi and puts the string around her neck, pulling it around her neck. Sybi cries. A member of staff comes over and tells him to play with Ian. He turns to Sybi and says, 'Cry Baby.' Jim then goes over to Melanie and, smiling, pulls her hair.

Many such examples were given. According to Main, such behaviour, commonplace at kindergarten, cannot be explained as simply due to an 'inability to share'. Nor should it be seen as something that adults should ignore, as some early childhood educators have suggested, on the grounds that it would be interfering with their 'free play'.

Another study by Kochenderfer and Ladd (1996) conducted in the USA provides further evidence of peer victimisation in kindergartens. They interviewed 200 students attending kindergarten (105 males and 95 females) at the beginning of their school year. The mean age of these children was 5.5 years. They were asked to say whether any of the children in their class had done any of the following things to them, and, if so, how often: (i) picked on them; (ii) hit them; (iii) said mean things to them; (iv) said bad things about them to other kids at school. Some 20.5 per cent of the children were identified as being 'repeatedly victimised' by others. This estimate agreed closely with the judgements made by teachers. It was also similar to an estimate of peer victimisation in a slightly older age group of children in Norway by the Swedish researcher Dan Olweus (1993), who reported that some 17 per cent of these children were victims of school bullying in a given year.

A more recent study of bullying has been conducted with 190 boys and 154 girls aged 5 to 8 years in Berne, Switzerland (Alsaker and Valkanover 2001). Based upon data obtained from a combination of peer nominations and teacher ratings, the researchers estimated that 6.1 per cent of the children could be classified as repeated victims; 10.2 per cent as bully/victims (that is, sometimes bullying others and sometimes being bullied themselves); and 10.8 per cent as bullies. This study suggests that about one child in four is involved in bully/victim problems. There was little difference between boys and girls in the proportions of victims. However, boys were notably more likely to be identified as bullies.

Here we may note that attempts to clearly distinguish bullying from other forms of aggression among young children have rarely been attempted. An exception, however, is a study of interpersonal aggressiveness conducted in Brazil with children aged two to four attending so-called nursery schools (Frey and Hoppe-Graff 1994). Observational methods were employed to identify incidents of aggression that could be described as reactive aggression (provoked); instrumental aggression (to achieve a specific goal); and dominant aggression or bullying for which no clear goal beyond dominance was evident. The value of making these distinctions was justified through their findings that although there were no significant differences between boys and girls in total aggressiveness, boys were found to engage in bullying behaviour more often than girls, especially in a sample of children from a middle-class background as opposed to children from a *favella* (slum district). It seems, from this study, that it is not so much aggressiveness in general that distinguishes boy behaviour but rather a tendency for boys to express their aggression through bullying.

Although overt forms of bullying are most common among young children, it should not be assumed that there is an absence of indirect or relational bullying. In a study by Crick, Casas and Mosher (1997) children between three and five years were observed to engage in hurtful non-physical actions, such as isolating those they did not like by telling others not to play or be friends with them. As children get older they often become more adept at manipulating situations so that some students can be hurt through being excluded and isolated. In these early years, however, the targets of bullying appear to be relatively random. With increasing experience of who can be bullied, a few children begin to attract a disproportionate amount of bullying. A child may come to expect to be bullied, and this may result in a self-fulfilling prophecy.

Bullying in later childhood

Numerous surveys have now been conducted in many countries to assess the extent to which peer victimisation occurs in older children. The survey data with which I am most familiar is that gathered using the Peer Relations Questionnaire, the PRQ (Rigby and Slee 1993b), in Australia. Between 1993 and 1998 more than 38,000 schoolchildren between the ages of 8 and 18 years anonymously answered this questionnaire. The results are thus based upon a very large sample, probably the largest employed to study bullying among English-speaking students.

It is made clear to students answering the PRQ that bullying occurs when some person or a group of persons is deliberately and repeatedly hurting or frightening someone who is less powerful. We rule out aggressive acts between people who are equally powerful, for example when two people of about the same strength have the odd fight or quarrel. Examples of bullying are provided which include physical, verbal and indirect bullying.

We may begin with the most general estimate of the prevalence of bullying. One question asks, how often 'this year' have you been bullied by another student or group of students? Answers to this question were obtained from students from some 86 Australian schools. The sample included 22,194 boys and 15,703 girls; their mean age was 13.8 years. About half the students replied that they had not been bullied that year. As expected, however, some children reported that they were continually being bullied. Table 3.1 provides a breakdown according to reported frequency.

Table 3.1 Incidence of victimisation in Australian schools (Percentages reported during the school year)		
	Boys	**Girls**
Every day	2.9	1.2
Most days	5.7	3.8
One or twice a week	14.3	11.0
Less than once a week	27.3	26.2
Never	49.8	57.9

Source: Rigby (1997c)

We can see from Table 3.1 that for most children who are bullied it is not a regular, weekly occurrence. But a substantial number of children do report that they are continually being bullied or harassed. As many as one in five boys report that they are bullied weekly; the figure for girls is one in six. There is no reason to suppose that these children are exaggerating; in fact, many children, especially boys, are predisposed to deny that they are being bullied. Translate these statistics into human terms and one has the picture of one or two children in classrooms throughout the country *expecting* to be bullied by other students every day or most days of the week, and many more thinking that it will happen some time during the week.

Of course, the nature and severity of the bullying that children experience may differ widely. Not surprisingly, what happens often depends on the age and gender of the child. Some of the questions in the PRQ enable us to examine different ways in which the bullying may be delivered (see Appendix 1).

As in all reported studies, the Australian data shows that bullying is carried out mainly by verbal means – by teasing and name-calling. Whether physical bullying is more common than exclusion from groups depends on whether the child is a boy or a girl. Boys are more likely to be hurt by physical means, girls by relational means, as in exclusion. Bullying occurs predominantly within gender groups. Where there is cross-gender bullying it is more likely to be boys bullying girls verbally. For all forms of bullying reported in this study there is a general reduction with age.

These generalisations should not obscure the fact that there are often quite big differences between schools for children in the same age group. For example, we have found that in some schools, reported weekly bullying may be as much as four times that of another (Rigby 1997a). We shall return to the question of why such differences may exist later.

There is an important qualification to the generalisation that bullying decreases with age. Getting older and becoming in some ways more mature can certainly be expected to lead to more and more children abandoning childish bullying tactics and recognising that they can become more dominant in a group by employing non-aggressive ways of relating to others. However, the social context in which children of a given age find themselves is so important that it can override effects of increasing maturity. This has been demonstrated neatly in an Australian study (see Rigby 1996).

It happens that in some states in Australia children normally transfer from primary school in Year 7, that is in the states of Tasmania, Victoria, New South Wales, and Australian Capital Territory. In the other states of South Australia, Queensland, Western Australia and Northern Territory they transfer in Year 8. Results for levels of bullying (percentages reporting being bullied at least once a week) for students who transfer to secondary school in Year 7 could be compared with results for children who transfer in Year 8. Figures 3.1 and 3.2 present data for boys and girls respectively.

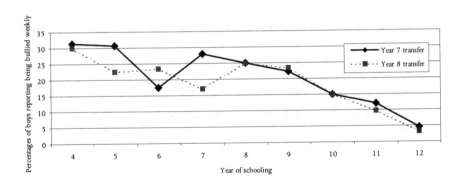

Figure 3.1 Reported victimisation of Australian boys by peers in coeducational schools (Years 4 to 12) for those starting secondary school at Year 7 (early transfer) and at Year 8 (later transfer)

The results in both figures show a general reduction in reported bullying with age. However, there is a temporary rise in reported bullying about midway through a child's school career, that is when they first enter secondary school. The precise timing of this increase depends upon the state where the child attends school. For example, if he or she lives in Victoria the rise in bullying is in Year 7; if the child lives in South Australia, the rise is in Year 8. Thus for Australia the year in which a child enters secondary school is a more important determinant of whether he or she will be bullied than chronological age. Social factors take precedence over developmental ones.

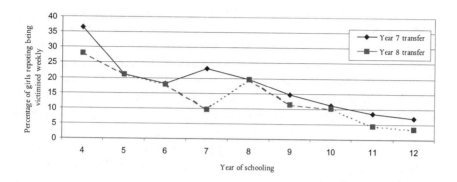

Figure 3.2 Reported victimisation of Australian girls by peers in coeducational schools (Years 4 to 12) for those starting secondary school at Year 7 (early transfer) and at Year 8 (late transfer)

The agents of peer bullying in schools

Earlier (in Chapter 2) we saw that there was some controversy over whether schoolchildren are more likely to be bullied by groups (as in mobbing) or by individuals. Rarely has the question been addressed empirically. However, there are data, obtained from a large sample of Australian schoolchildren, that throw some light on this question (see Appendix 2).

In this sample, the most common experience – reported by 44 per cent of the students during a school year – was not to be bullied at all. The next most common experience was to have been bullied sometimes (but not often) by individuals but never by a group (approximately 22%). Some 16 per cent reported that they had been bullied sometimes by both. For every gender/age group, these results indicate that students were more likely to be bullied (if bullied at all) by an individual rather than by a group of peers.

An alternative way of addressing this question is to ask students to say if they have bullied anyone at school over the school year, and, if so, how – as an individual, as a group member or both. Data from children who say they have bullied others show a somewhat different picture (details in Appendix 3). Apart from boys (8–11 years), who appear from these results to bully as individuals more often than as members of a group, the indications are that students tend to bully more in groups rather than as individuals. This is especially so among older students and among girls.

There are several ways of reconciling the seemingly contradictory results from self-reported victims and self-reported bullies. First, it may be that the comparatively high level of reporting being bullied by individuals is because some individual bullies have multiple victims and groups tend to concentrate on the same targets. Second, it may be that many victims of bullying are unaware that the person doing the bullying is part of a group or sees himself or herself as part of a group. Third, it may be that those who bully do not want to report – even in an anonymous questionnaire – that they have bullied as individuals, but prefer to diffuse responsibility for the bullying acts in which they have engaged.

The finding that girls are more likely than boys to bully in a group is not surprising, since indirect forms of bullying, e.g. exclusion, have often been reported as more commonly experienced by girls. Because girls experience indirect bullying more often than boys, one might expect them to sympathise more with victims of group bullying, and boys to sympathise more with victims of individual bullies. This is indeed what has been reported to be the case in a recent study of bullying behaviour among Italian schoolchildren (Baldry 2001).

Bullying within and between genders

We have seen that, generally speaking, boys are bullied rather more often than girls – although it must be admitted that comparisons are difficult because boys and girls tend to be bullied in somewhat different ways. It appears that in coeducational schools, within-gender bullying is more common than between-gender bullying. But there is one notable asymmetry. A boy rarely reports that he has been bullied just by girls. Girls, however, not uncommonly indicate that it is boys not girls who have bullied them. (For details from a large Australian sample, see Appendix 4.)

Another asymmetry is that whilst most boys (over 70%) indicated that the person who bullied them was always a boy, less than 25 per cent of girls report that the bully is always a girl. The conclusion we can draw is that girls are much more likely to be bullied by boys *and* girls (some 50% or so of girls indicate this) whilst boys are predominantly bullied by their own sex.

We might therefore expect that girls in single-sex schools would be bullied less than girls in coeducational schools. This appears to be the case. Estimates based on results of reported bullying in Australian coeducational and single-sex schools indicate that in coeducational schools, approximately one child in five is bullied weekly compared with one in seven in girls-only schools (Rigby 1997c). The differences are not large and in no way suggest that girls' schools are bully-free. There are wide variations between schools of each type in the extent of reported bullying. In the recurrent debate about whether girls are better off in single-sex schools, safety from being bullied is not a major factor.

We need also to consider the kind of bullying that boys and girls direct at each other. Relevant results are available from a study conducted by Rigby and Bagshaw (2001), which involved 190 boys and 202 girls attending second-year high school with a mean age of 14 years. They were all asked in an anonymous questionnaire to say how they had been treated by boys and by girls at their school during the current year. Three kinds of treatment were described: verbal abuse, e.g. name-calling; physical abuse, e.g. being kicked or hit; and indirect abuse, as in having unpleasant rumours spread about you. (Details in Appendix 5.)

For both sexes of this age (around 14 years) verbal abuse is the most common form of ill treatment from peers at school. Girls are slightly more likely to be abused verbally by boys than by girls (74% against 68.2%) whereas boys are much more likely to be verbally abused by members of their own sex than by girls (75.8% against 46.9%).

As we might expect, physical abuse is something that happens mainly between boys: 62.7 per cent of boys report being physically abused by another boy or group of boys as against 24.7 per cent of girls being physically abused by another girl or group of girls. Cross-gender physical bullying is experienced relatively rarely, but is nevertheless not insignificant. Among girls 17 per cent reported having experienced physically abusive treatment from boys. Unexpectedly, boys claimed to be physically bullied by girls rather more often (27.2%). As in studies of domestic violence we need to examine the impact of the physically aggressive acts in some detail before drawing further conclusions.

Girls are clearly the recipients of more indirect bullying than boys, especially from other girls (51.6%). Some boys (25.8%) are also targeted by members of their own sex practicing indirect bullying, though somewhat more frequently by girls (31.1%). Among young Australian adolescents we can say that girls are more often bullied by boys than boys are bullied by girls, but it is worth noting that the imbalance is specifically in the area of verbal abuse. As far as indirect bullying is concerned, boys might expect to be bullied indirectly more often by girls than by their own sex.

Sexual identity and bullying

In Australia it has been reported that some 90 per cent of students believe that sex-based harassment occurs at their school, with approximately 40 per cent reporting that it happens 'often' (Collins *et al.* 1996). A prime target for bullying in most, if not all, schools are students who are gay or who appear to be gay. So called 'gay put-downs' in Australian schools are exceedingly common. Collins *et al.* cite an example from a Year 10 Australian student: 'If a boy did sewing I reckon he'd be tagged as a fag for about a week' (p.26).

The use of derogatory names to describe children who are perceived to be gay begins well before puberty. In a study of name-calling and nicknames among 60 primary school students (aged 8–11 years) in Wales, Crozier and Dimmock (1999) reported that the use of terms 'poofta' or 'queer' was commonplace. As students grow older and become more sexually active, the bullying of students thought to be gay intensifies and can become extremely distressing, especially, as is sometimes the case, if parents of the victimised child are unsympathetic.

The severity of bullying

We have thus far assumed that acts of bullying are equally severe. This of course is not so. In some cases the bullying experienced by a person can be extremely stressful; in other cases the bullying may be mild. It is not easy to say with any certainty what will be experienced as severe. Some people are extremely sensitive to negative actions from others and are easily hurt, whilst others are surprisingly resilient. Again, some children are hurt by one kind of negative treatment; some by another. Nevertheless there are some criteria that can be suggested.

One obvious criterion has already been suggested, namely the frequency with which the bullying happens. There is abundant evidence that those who are bullied most are most bothered by it, are more likely to suffer a loss of self-esteem and to experience feelings of sadness and/or anger (Rigby 1997a, 1997c). If we look at the distribution of reported bullying in schools according to reported incidence (as in Figure 3.3), we see that it is highly skewed. A small proportion of children are bullied every day; a much larger proportion are bullied occasionally (less than weekly); an even larger proportion appear not to be bullied at all. Some children appear to attract a disproportionate amount of negative attention and to suffer accordingly.

We should also recognise that it is not just the current intensity of the bullying that counts when we try to assess severity. It is also the duration over which bullying behaviour has been endured. Some children have had to put up with being bullied throughout their school careers, sometimes from the same persons. For others it has been a passing phase, a period that was nasty at the time but happily came to a conclusion or at least a considerable abatement. Again there is empirical evidence to show that very long-term bullying is much less common than short-term bullying. Figure 3.3 shows some results from older (16–18-year-old) students who answered a PRQ question about what was the longest period over which they had been bullied at school.

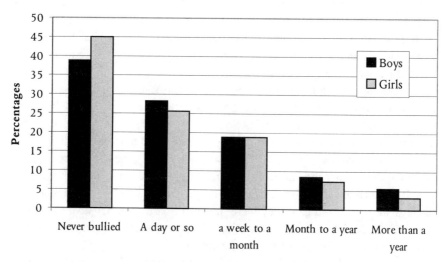

Figure 3.3 Australian students aged 16–18 reporting being bullied over periods of time

As we can see, most commonly bullying goes on for a day or so. But it is disturb-ing to see that some 14 per cent of boys and 10.4 per cent of girls reported having suffered long-term or relatively long-term bullying from peers, that is for more than a month.

But still we have not taken into account the quality or nature of the bullying. Our first guess is that physical assault or the threat of assault is the most severe form of bullying. (This is what teachers tend to think.) Whether verbal or indirect bullying have greater impact has rarely been considered.

Recently the matter was put to an empirical test by asking secondary school students in Australia how hurt or upset they had been by different sorts of negative treatment by peers at school. The population sampled was of Year 9 students (mean age of 14 years). Questionnaires were prepared containing a list of 50 negative treatments of widely different kinds, physical, verbal and relational, encountered by students from their peers at school. (This list had been generated previously through group discussions with students of their own age.) Some 652 students in 7 schools were asked to report anonymously on which of the negative treatments they had experienced at school that year, how often, and how hurt or upset they had felt afterwards. Statistical tests (Principal Components Analyses) conducted on the responses were applied to selected sets of ten items which best assessed physical, verbal and relational forms of aggression.

My fellow researcher (Dale Bagshaw) and I expected to find that boys would rate physical aggression as most hurtful and that they would tend to dismiss verbal and relational abuse as 'girls' stuff'. Indeed, in the discussion groups preceding this study, boys had repeatedly spoken up denying that they had feelings that could be hurt. We noticed some girls were highly sceptical – and amused – when the boys made such a claim.

Details of the results are given in Appendix 6. What is most striking about these results is that the most hurtful aggressive acts were those that we had categorised as relational, such as 'somebody trying to break up my friendships', 'people ganging up on me' and 'being excluded'. 'Being deliberately hit or kicked' was way down the list. By and large, boys and girls gave us results that indicated that in fact they ranked the hurtfulness of the items in much the same way. It did turn out to be the case (as one might expect) that boys were much less likely than girls to indicate they were hurt or upset by the negative treatments they had received. But this was true of practically every item, whether it reflected relational or other forms of negative treatment.

From this study we were left to conclude that we could have greatly underestimated the effects of relational aggression, especially on boys. The stereotypical picture that boys don't have feelings to be hurt when people quit speaking to them or tell their secrets to others or spread rumours about them and so on turned out to be nonsense. (The girls knew this all along.)

We should recognise that different kinds of negative treatments are not experienced equally often. Being teased was experienced by most students; being touched sexually by relatively few (about one in ten). Interestingly, equal proportions of boys and girls reported being touched sexually against their will, in the case of boys usually by other boys. Both boys and girls rated it as highly distressing.

The study I have described examines the hurtfulness of things that children had actually experienced. However, one can be hurt or upset by the threat of things that have not happened but may well happen. Hence it is relevant to consider how safe children feel at school from being bullied. The data on this question generally come as a great surprise to teachers. From the PRQ results we find that only a minority of students believe that their school is a safe place for children who find it hard to defend themselves. Seventeen per cent of children in secondary schools (similar proportions of boys and girls) have reported that it is *never* safe or *hardly ever* safe.

Thinking back on the things that hurt – and what hurts more, what hurts less – have I been unduly analytic? In a sense, yes. When a child is bullied he or she may be hit by a combination of things – by jeers and sneers, insults and slurs, punches and shoves, rejection and rumours – by all manner of negative things.

These treatments often go together, rarely are they encountered singly. Estimating severity becomes very complex, even without factoring in individual vulnerability. What we are learning from these studies is that if we are to understand the stress that is felt by the victimised child we must recognise the diversity of events that contribute to it, not least of which is the kind of bullying we may well ignore, that is the most covert, the destructive manipulation of a child's social relations at school. There are, as we shall see, good practical reasons for seeking to assess the severity of peer victimisation. Because it is complex does not mean that we should not try to understand it.

The process of bullying

Now we can turn away from our analysis of what happens and what hurts and seek to understand how bullying comes about in a school. As we have said, it can occur when there is an imbalance of power between individuals and/or between groups in a school. All that is needed is a more powerful person or group relishing the opportunity to put somebody down. This is not inevitably the case. Some more powerful children are simply not motivated to take advantage of their less powerful peers. Many children tell us – and I believe them – that they would be ashamed if they bullied someone. But unfortunately there are generally some who are not so inhibited who are on the lookout for someone they can bully. And the opportunity presents itself.

The process according to which bullying begins and develops can be illustrated in a series of diagrams.

The cycle of bullying begins when a child is seen as relatively weak and vulnerable to attack from others. We know from research that such children tend to be introverted, physically weaker than most, anxious, isolated and/or the objects of group prejudice. A more powerful child or group of children decides to target potential victims and to subject them to various forms of abuse. It may start with teasing and mild ridicule and go no further, but often it advances. Other children may join in. The victim's belongings may be moved or stolen; he or she may be verbally abused, pushed around or, in extreme cases, physically attacked. Periods of unwelcome attention may alternate with periods in which he or she is isolated. If the victim is passive, unresisting, the cycle may continue in the way suggested by Figure 3.4.

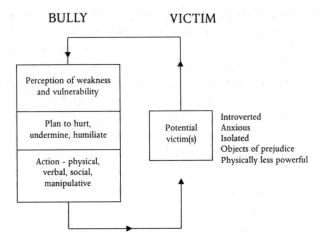

Figure 3.4 Bullying cycle begins

Such a victim typically feels threatened and fearful. If the victim shows signs of being disturbed or upset, this is evidence that the bullying is succeeding. The bully is then able to enjoy a pleasurable sense of dominance. If there is approval from others – friends and bystanders – any concern or empathy the bully may have for the plight of the victim quickly dissipates. It all seems like fun, and the cycle is likely to continue and the harassment to become more intense and the means more elaborate (see Figure 3.5). As we have seen, for many children the nightmare can go on for months and even years.

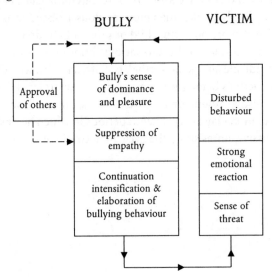

Figure 3.5 Bully and passive victim

Sometimes, of course, the victim may resist or take action to stop the bullying, as suggested in Figure 3.6.

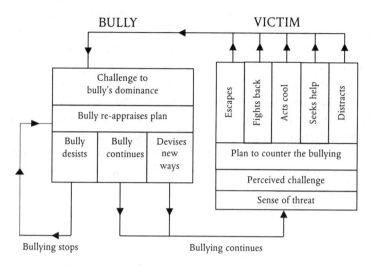

Figure 3.6 Bully and resistant victim

The victim may seek (and sometimes find) ways of escaping or avoiding the tormentors – for instance by keeping close to teachers or spending time in the school library. Alternatively, he or she may fight back, act assertively or perhaps even nonchalantly. But if the imbalance of power is too great and the bullying persistent, which it often is, such 'resistance' is likely to fail. Some children try to find others to help them, or, failing that, think up ways in which they can distract or amuse children who might otherwise bully them.

How successful are the strategies that victimised children adopt? It is hard to generalise because situations in which victims of school bullying find themselves vary so widely. Some bullies may indeed be put off when they find that their taunts have little or no effect. Sometimes it is not difficult to avoid the attentions of potential bullies; sometimes impossible. Escape may be at little cost (one goes home a different way); sometimes at great cost – for example, staying home from school for extended periods. We know that in Australia some 6 per cent of boys and 9 per cent of girls report staying home to avoid being bullied. An assertive response may induce a bully to look for an easier target – or redouble his or her efforts to get under the target's skin. Occasionally, bullying may turn out to be less fun for the bully than enjoying a game with a person initially targeted. But we must remember that for many children bullying itself is 'a lot of fun'. Getting help may be easy – for instance if you have a big brother; all but impossible if you are the target of group prejudice.

Informing

Because many schools emphasise the importance of 'telling' – 'Make ours a telling school' is a familiar slogan – it is worth examining in some detail what outcomes one might expect when a child informs on someone who is bullying him or her. Data from the large-scale Australian study show that both boys and girls do generally tell someone – a friend, a parent, a teacher or a counsellor. This is despite the stigma that may be attached to 'dobbing' on someone. Girls are more likely to tell. Among those who have been bullied, over the age range from 8 to 17 years, approximately 86 per cent of girls and 70 per cent of boys reported that they had told somebody about it. The outcome appears to depend very much on the age of the student. In Figures 3.7 and 3.8 we have a summary of results for 8135 girls and 9606 boys who told someone that they had been bullied and also recorded the outcome anonymously.

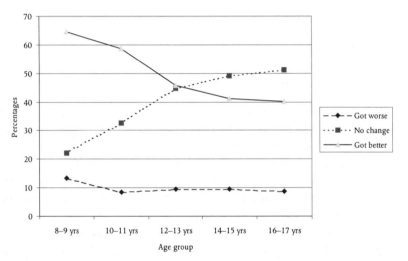

Figure 3.7 What happens when boys tell about being bullied: Percentages reporting outcomes

The outcomes follow a similar pattern for both boys and girls. Although overall there is a reasonable chance that telling will lead to an improvement in the victim's situation – about 50 per cent of students report an improvement – the chances of an improvement become progressively lower with age. For example, among boys aged 8–9 years there is a 65 per cent chance of improvement; among older boys aged 16–17 years, the chances of an improvement after telling drop to about 40 per cent. Among girls the corresponding drop is a little less steep: from 62 per cent to 45 per cent. As the chances of an improvement drop with age, the likelihood of there being no change in the objective situation increases, again for both boys and girls. (One should not ignore the possibility that telling might help an individual psychologically, especially if he or she receives emotional or moral support.) What appears to be relatively constant over the age range is the percentage of students who claim that telling made matters worse. This is generally around 10 per cent, the risk of telling being only slightly higher for boys.

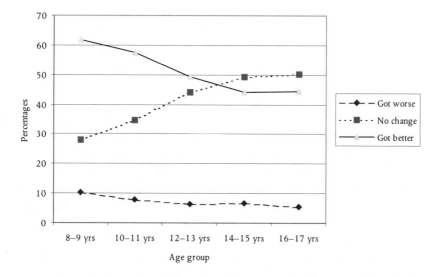

Figure 3.8 What happens when girls tell about being bullied: Percentages reporting outcomes

Of course, the outcome may depend on who is told and what they do. Curiously enough there has been hardly any research on this vital question. A beginning has been made in a recent study undertaken in Victoria, Australia, where children were asked to indicate what were the outcomes of telling someone they had been bullied in relation to the different people they told: friends, parents, teachers and the school counsellor. Friends were the most likely people to be told; the school counsellor the least likely. The results of this pilot study conducted in one school indicated that improvement in a victim's situation was greatest when the counsellor was informed, and least when a fellow student was told about it (Rigby and Barnes 2001).

School factors

It may be objected that the cycle of bullying that has been described above places undue emphasis upon the personalities of individual children; in particular, encounters between strong, aggressive children motivated to hurt and enjoy hurting others and weak, vulnerable children who are unable to resist. This is only part of the story. It is doubtful whether schools differ much in the imbalances of power that exist between individual children or in the proportions of children who enjoy hurting others. But schools most certainly do differ widely in the amount of bullying that goes on between the children who attend. School factors are important.

The school ethos

Emphasis is often placed upon the school ethos. This is a difficult matter to define to everybody's satisfaction. A dictionary definition is 'the fundamental and distinctive character or spirit of a social group, culture or community' (Heinemann 1992).

The school ethos is most evident in the way members of the school community – students, staff, parents – treat each other, whether with respect or disrespect. In some schools there is a sense of caring for others. This is felt not only as a moral obligation but also as something people want to experience and promote. It is generally (but not always) evident more in primary schools than secondary schools. Sometimes it is informed and promoted by a religious or spiritual culture, or by a school philosophy that is effectively communicated and practised. There is evidence that this is the case in at least some Steiner schools, where it appears that bullying, especially physical bullying, is very rare (Rivers and Soutter 1996).

Schools differ in the extent to which members care about children who are victimised by their peers. In Chapter 10 we examine the attitudes and beliefs of people towards victims and bullying in some detail. Here we may note that there are in fact wide differences both within and between schools in the extent to which children and teachers care about the issue and seek to counter bullying when they see it. There is now evidence that differences in the levels of bullying in schools can be predicted on the basis of what is known about the attitudes of children in those schools towards bullying (Rigby 1997d).

Are attitudes and beliefs conducive to bullying imported, as Randall (1996) has suggested, from the community, from which come a stream of schoolchildren already predisposed to bully or be bullied? Or are they generated somehow by the schools themselves, in some schools more than others? It would be foolish to discount either of these possibilities, but again it should be noted that the vast scale of differences between schools in the prevalence of bullying argues for a substantial influence from the school itself. Next we will note some of the factors that can be located in the school.

Classroom climate

One factor often neglected in studies of bullying is what may be called the classroom climate. This involves both the formal learning environment and the emotional reactions of students to this environment. Currently we know little about how students are affected in their relations with each other as a result of spending a major part of their lives in classrooms. A study is now being undertaken by Shoko Yoneyama and Ken Rigby in Japan and Australia to assess the possible impact of the 'classroom climate' as a determinant of level of bullying in a school. These are four aspects of the classroom environment we think are most relevant, as conceptualised and operationalised by Marjoribanks (1994). We have hypothesised that peer victimisation will be low among children who are educated in classrooms where lessons are well planned and capture their imagination and where teachers are genuinely concerned about the children's feelings and do not oppress them by unnecessary rules and regulations. In such ideal classrooms children are unlikely to feel bored, angry and frustrated – and less inclined to take it out on children less powerful than themselves.

Bystander behaviour

An area of considerable importance in accounting for the prevalence of bullying in a school is bystander behaviour. We know from studies conducted in Canada, Finland and England that bystanders are usually present when bullying takes place. The model describing the process of bullying (Figure 3.5) indicates that reinforcement by bystanders of bullying behaviour, either positively through encouragement given to bullies or through the withholding of any adverse comment, practically guarantees that the bullying will go on and on. What is currently not known is what differences exist between bystander behaviour in different cultures and in different schools and (more importantly) what can be done to increase the level of active discouragement by bystanders of bullying behaviour at school. (See Chapter 9 for a further discussion of this important situational factor.)

Action to stop bullying

More and more schools are beginning to see that bullying can be reduced by systematic, planned action on the part of schools specifically directed towards preventing and reducing bullying.

My own experience, supported by data from teacher questionnaires, is that staff in schools differ greatly in what they know about the bullying going on around them, and that teachers within particular schools also differ widely in their attitude towards bullying. Some schools are acquiring detailed knowledge about what is actually going on between students in the area of bullying and the effects it is having on more vulnerable children, and then discussing what they have found. Others remain ignorant or in denial. When staff in schools move towards a realistic consensus on what is happening, they are taking an essential step towards effectively countering school bullying.

Given such a basis of understanding, some schools are developing and implementing a systematic, whole-school approach to school bullying. The specific elements in the approach may differ, but generally they include the development of a well supported anti-bullying policy; talking with and enlisting the support of students through group discussion and (sometimes) the provision of training for students in such skills as conflict resolution and mediation; systematic ways of dealing with cases of bullying; and close and constructive working with parents on bully/victim problems.

These actions and others (examined in detail in Chapter 11) are changing the dynamics of peer interaction in an increasing number of schools. Although the situation in schools remains one in which bullying occurs with sickening regularity, inroads are at last being made.

Chapter 4

The school and beyond

It may be proved, with much certainty, that God intends no man to live in the world without working, but it seems to me no less evident that he intends every man to be happy in his work. It is written 'in the sweat of thy brow' but it was never written 'in the breaking of thy heart'.

– Attributed to John Ruskin
by Lord Lea in the House of Lords
debate on workplace bullying, 4 December 1996

Most attention to bullying has focused on the school, and there are good reasons for that. Of all communities schools contain the greatest imbalances of power and they are attended at a time when people are at their most vulnerable to abuse from their peers. Practically everybody goes to school and feels they have to do so. Unless you belong to a very small (but growing) minority of children for whom home schooling is an option, or unless you are too sick to attend, there is no escape. One may be in the predicament that Les Murray describes (see Rigby 1997a, p.7):

Where children can't leave and mustn't complain
There some will emerge who enjoy giving pain
A dreary intense groove leads them to each one
They pick to torment, and the rest will then shun.

In school there is this extreme diversity of human types with whom one is destined to spend one's days – and in boarding schools one's nights as well, like it or not. And, of course, many do like it. But for those who do not, and continually fail the test of standing up to the bullies – and receive little or no sympathy for failing – school is not the place to be. By contrast, the outside world is generally a kinder place. People can choose, within limits, their occupation, where they live, with whom they live, the games they play or do not play.

Nevertheless, this increased freedom does not insure people against being bullied. With new found freedom the risk of harassment diminishes. Maturity will often have brought with it new ways of protecting oneself: new skills, new strategies, new friends, new escape exits. With deeper interests and commitments the barbs of others matter less. But as we know there are new challenges to be faced. Bullying does not always end.

In this chapter we will examine perspectives on bullying in a variety of non-school contexts. I will argue that the idea of bullying as 'the systematic abuse of power' is applicable in each case. We will see differences in the predominant ways in which bullying occurs and that some factors that contribute to bullying are more important in some contexts than others. It may also be that different solutions or ameliorations will apply. Let us see how 'bullying' as an overarching concept can apply.

Contexts

In situations where people interact continually for a period of time a potential for bullying is always present. The choice of contexts for this chapter is to some extent arbitrary. In some of the areas we will consider, a substantial amount of research has already been done, though more is needed. These areas include the workplace and prisons.

Conspicuously lacking are studies of bullying in the home. Nobody doubts that it happens there, but we are disposed to use other terms to describe the phenomena, such as spouse abuse, child abuse and domestic violence. We need to ask: would it be helpful to call some of this 'bullying' and seek to broaden our understanding by viewing it in this way?

Other areas in which bullying behaviour can be usefully examined include sport, politics and international relations. These have in common an intense concern with power – to beat one's rival or the opposing team; to acquire, maintain and utilise the capacity to govern; to promote one's version of the national and/or international interest. Again we may ask whether it is useful to examine behaviour within each of these areas to shed light on the nature and ramifications of bullying.

The workplace

Workplaces are exceedingly diverse. These range from the rudimentary workshop with as few as two people working together continually or intermittently, to the complex, large enterprises that may include thousands of employees in many different roles. Striking differences may also be found in the structure of work organisations, some having tier after tier of management levels; others being essentially non-hierarchical. In addition, the nature of the work done in a workplace will help to determine the nature and composition of staff. For example, some work is done predominantly by women, e.g. nursing; some by men, e.g. truck driving. Some work is seen as requiring considerable supervision, under conditions in which monitoring of performance is intense; other work may require little if any monitoring by supervisors.

The possibilities for power to be abused by management or others is much greater in some work areas than others. With tasks requiring a great deal of coordination, the scope for criticism of individuals who are seen (rightly or wrongly) as not performing adequately is relatively great. Given the range of alternative workplace situations, generalisations about 'workplace bullying' are difficult to make.

It is not surprising then that estimates of the extent of bullying in the workplace vary greatly from study to study (see Table 4.1).

Table 4.1 Estimates of the prevalence of bullying in the workplace		
Source of report	**% age bullied**	**Period**
Staffordshire University: UNISON (Rayner 1997)	53%	working life
* Institute of Personnel and Development (1996)	12%	5 years
UNISON (Rayner 1998)	14%	6 months
University of Glamorgan School (Lewis 1999)	18%	working life
National Health Service (Quine 1999)	38%	1 year
Manchester School of Management (Hoel and Cooper 2000)	10%	6 months

* For survey results from the Institute of Personnel and Development, see http://www.successunlimited.co.uk/press.htm#PR2, 13 April 2001.)

What strikes one immediately is the wide variation in the estimates, from 10 per cent to 53 per cent. To some extent this may be explained by the estimates being based upon different time periods over which bullying may be reported as taking place. But notice that one estimate gives 38 per cent over 1 year, another 12 per cent over 5 years.

A cynic might suggest that figures have been bullied into a shape to suit the researcher. But I do not think that is the case. The reports were provided by conscientious researchers from prestigious centres. What maybe suggested is that 'bullying' itself may be conceived and/or operationally defined differently in different studies. In addition, there may indeed be large differences in the prevalence of bullying in different places of work, as we have found to be the case in schools.

Defining bullying in the workplace

As in the literature in which bullying in schools is defined, so too with workplace bullying, we get a variety of definitions, some emphasising one supposed aspect or characteristic of bullying, some another. Generally, however, we see four features present in a definition: (i) the malicious intent of the aggressor; (ii) the pained reaction of the target; (iii) the aggression being repeated; and (iv) its unfairness. For example: 'Bullying involves a deliberate, hurtful and repeated mistreatment of a target' (Neuman 2000).

Sometimes the definition is fuller:

> Bullying is…'persistent, offensive, abusive, intimidating, malicious or insulting behaviour, abuse of power or unfair penal sanctions, which makes the recipient feel upset, threatened, humiliated or vulnerable, which undermines their self-confidence and which makes them suffer stress'. (Lyons, Tivey and Ball 1995)

Again we can identify each of the four elements, the bullying being malicious, painful to the target, repeated and unfair. But it adds further detail, especially in explaining how the 'recipient' must feel. It also suggests that if one's confidence remains high, bullying has not occurred.

Leymann (1996) adds details which from a definitional viewpoint seem unnecessary and open to question. Bullying is seen as a particular kind of social interaction

> through which one person (seldom more) is attacked by one or more (seldom more than four) individuals almost (sic) on a daily basis and for periods of many months, bringing the person into an almost helpless position with potentially high risk of expulsion.

Leymann is not explicit, as are Neuman and Lyons, in stating that the actions of bullies are intended to harm someone, although we may suppose that 'an attack' is essentially an act directed towards hurting someone. He does not suggest that the actions of bullies necessarily constitute an abuse of power. His attempts at quantification leave one puzzled. (How many months is 'many months'?) One may reasonably wonder whether being bullied necessarily increases one's risk of expulsion, even 'potentially'. (Is it not possible that having somebody around to bully may be an asset that an employer may not want to lose?) Leymann seems to have in mind the 'mobbing' phenomenon whereby there is a concerted attempt to drive somebody away.

Unlike bullying in schools, a definition of workplace bullying may specify one means of bullying, as in: 'Workplace bullying is deliberate, repeated, hurtful verbal harassment of a person (the target) by a cruel perpetrator (the bully)' (Namie and Namie 1998).

Here the authors do not mince words – the bully is a 'cruel' person, but the mode of bullying is simply verbal, which is certainly usually the case, as it is for children. But the narrowness of this definition must raise the eyebrows of those that have been punched or even beaten up at work.

Sometimes the definition appears to be non-judgemental as far as the 'perpetrator' is concerned.

> We define bullying as a situation where one or several individuals persistently over time perceive themselves to be on the receiving end of negative actions from one or several persons, in a situation where the target of bullying has difficulty in defending him or herself against these actions. (Hoel and Cooper 2000)

Here the identifying characteristics of bullying are to be inferred from the perceptions of a possible target. If people think that negative actions are being directed towards them and find it hard to cope, they are, *ipso facto*, being bullied. This has some things going for it. It avoids the problem of intentionality, a constant bugbear to behaviourally inclined researchers. One doesn't have to make assumptions about what a perpetrator is intending. It allows one to say, reasonably, that a person may be being bullied even when the bully does not intend that anybody be hurt. Being harmed may be an unintended consequence of a bully trying to get something he or she wants. The person who gets hurt, it might be said, just happened to be in the way. The hurt may be regarded by the perpetrator (and even by the observer) as collateral damage. The person hurt is more likely to see it in a different way. But whose perception is right? We might feel inclined to go for the old legal standby, the reasonable man – or woman – and ask: is it reasonable to suppose that a reasonable person would have realised the hurtfulness – and (one might like to add) the wrongness – of what was likely to result, and call that bullying?

A further advantage of defining bullying in this way is that it greatly simplifies the work of the researcher. Following the Italian dramatist Luigi Pirandello (1922), we can say to the complainant: 'Cosie, se vipare' ('Right you are, if you think so'). No need to get tangled up in motives and moral dilemmas.

The definition chosen may, in part, reflect the values and experiences of people in particular professions. Nurses for example have emphasised the prevalence of horizontal bullying, that is bullying by colleagues. One interesting definition proposed by Queensland Nurses' Union defines bullying as: 'Less favourable treatment of a person by another in the workplace, beyond that which may be considered reasonable and appropriate workplace practice' (www.qnu.org.av/bullying.htm).

But what is appropriate? Spring and Stern (1998) state that bullying is 'behaviour that is designed to humiliate, degrade and injure the dignity and worth of an individual'. One yardstick, they suggest, may be derived from reflecting on how nurses treat patients. They feel that the sensitive way in which patients are treated should extend to relations between peers. They suggest that bullying include 'abuse that we direct towards each other that would be inappropriate if we directed that same behaviour, action, word, tone, attitude towards a patient'.

If we follow this line we will be inclined to include a large amount of everyday behaviour under the heading of bullying, such as minimising another's concerns, making sarcastic remarks, raising one's voice in anger, ignoring another's needs, and so on.

It is evident from this brief review of definitions that we have in the area of workplace bullying a large range of different kinds of definitions, which could easily explain why estimates of the prevalence of bullying vary so widely. Is it possible to provide a parsimonious and comprehensive definition that can reasonably cover the field? For me the best candidate at the present time is the one proposed by Smith and Sharp (1994): 'the systematic abuse of power'. Many people are happy with this definition, but some are not. I think the main objections come from those who do not want to view the bully as a more powerful person because being 'powerful' seems to be a positive characteristic, not something to be applied to a bad character such as a bully.

This is how a leading figure in the world of anti-bullying experts, Tim Field, defines or, more accurately, describes bullying in his website:

> Bullying is a compulsive need to displace aggression and is achieved by the expression of inadequacy (social, personal, interpersonal, behavioural, professional) by projection of that inadequacy onto others through control and subjugation (criticism, exclusion, isolation etc). Bullying is sustained by abdication of responsibility (denial, counter-accusation, pretence of victimhood) and perpetuated by a climate of fear, ignorance, indifference, silence, denial, disbelief, deception, evasion of accountability, tolerance and reward (e.g. promotion) for the bully. (www.successunlimited.co.uk/)

Field follows up his definition by itemising the kinds of things that bullies in the workplace do:

They constantly criticise – explanations and proof of achievement are ridiculed, overruled, dismissed or ignored.

They are forever subject to nit-picking and trivial fault-finding (the triviality is the give away).

They undermine, especially in front of others; they express doubts about a person's performance or standard of work – in the absence of substantive and quantifiable evidence, for they are only the bully's unreliable opinion.

They overrule, ignore, sideline, marginalise, ostracise, isolate and exclude others from what's happening, thus making people more vulnerable and easier to control and subjugate. They single out and treat individuals differently (for example everyone else can have long lunch breaks but if they are one minute late it's a disciplinary offence). They belittle, degrade, demean, ridicule, patronise, threaten, shout at and humiliate, especially in front of others, taunt and tease with the intention of embarrassing and humiliating.

Bullies set unrealistic goals and deadlines which are unachievable or which are changed without notice or reason or whenever they get near achieving them.

Victims are denied information or knowledge necessary for undertaking work and achieving objectives; they are denied support by their manager and thus find themselves working in a management vacuum. They are either overloaded with work (this keeps people busy [with no time to tackle bullying] and makes it harder to achieve targets) or have all their work taken away (which is sometimes replaced with menial jobs, e.g. photocopying, filing, making coffee). Their responsibility may be increased but their authority removed. Their work may be plagiarised, stolen and copied – the bully then presents their target's work (e.g. to senior management) as their own. They are given the silent treatment: the bully refuses to communicate and avoids eye contact; often instructions are received only via email, memos, or a succession of yellow stickies.

They are subject to excessive monitoring, supervision, micro-management, recording, snooping etc. They become the subject of written complaints by other members of staff (most of whom have been coerced into fabricating allegations – the complaints are trivial, often bizarre ['He looked at me in a funny way'] and often bear striking similarity to each other, suggesting a common origin).

They find requests for leave have unacceptable and unnecessary conditions attached, sometimes overturning previous approval, especially if the person has taken action to address bullying in the meantime. They are denied annual leave, sickness leave, or – especially – compassionate leave. When on leave, they are harassed by calls at home or on holiday, often at unsocial hours and receive unpleasant or threatening calls or are harassed with intimidating memos, notes or emails immediately prior to weekends and holidays (e.g. 4pm Friday or Christmas Eve – often these are hand-delivered). There is an absence of clear job description, or [they] have one that is exceedingly long or vague. The bully often deliberately makes the person's role unclear. Victims are invited to 'informal' meetings which turn out to be disciplinary hearings. They are denied representation at meetings, often under threat of further disciplinary action; sometimes the bully abuses their position of power by excluding any representative who is competent to deal with bullying. They are encouraged to feel guilty, and to believe they're always the one at fault; they are subjected to unwarranted and unjustified verbal or written warnings. They face unjusti-fied disciplinary action on trivial or specious or false charges or face dis-missal on fabricated charges or flimsy excuses, often using a trivial incident from months or years previously. They may be coerced into reluctant res-ignation, enforced redundancy, early or ill-health retirement.

It is evident from this list that bullying is conceived primarily as oppression by management – especially (one might add) by managers who are personally inade-quate.

It is fair to say that Field does recognise that bullying is not explicable entirely in terms of wilful oppressive acts by inadequate individuals in managerial roles. For example, he identifies 'organisational bullying' which occurs 'when an organisation struggles to adapt to changing markets, reduced income, cuts in budgets, imposed expectations, and other external pressures', and also 'corporate bullying…where the employer abuses employees with impunity knowing that the law is weak and jobs are scarce'. But generally he sees bullying as traceable to the dysfunctional individual 'who picks on one employee after another and destroys them'. This he sees as the most common type of bullying, and is perpe-trated by a so-called 'serial bully who exhibits the symptoms of Antisocial Per-sonality Disorder (APD)'. He claims that 1 person in 30 fits this category.

One suspects that there are strong motives at work in seeing bullying in this way. Being badly hurt by being bullied may be one of them. By calling the bully inadequate one is getting one's own back. One may feel vindicated because some bullies no doubt are 'inadequate'; some victims are too. (In Chapter 6 we will discuss what is known about the personalities of bullies and victims.) Another motive, I think, is to give hearty encouragement to victims of bullying, to validate their feelings, to get them to feel they are right to be angry and to insist that things be changed. Hence the emotive language. The danger exists, however, that it can make sober research in this field – and its reception – harder to achieve.

What does the research tell us?

Research, albeit of variable quality, is growing rapidly in the field of workplace bullying. Perhaps the most well-researched report (currently in the year 2001 the most recent) is that provided by Helge Hoel and Cary Cooper (2000) at the Manchester School of Management. Based on responses to questionnaires from 5288 employees theirs is the largest and most comprehensive study of workplace bullying ever undertaken in Britain. They sampled a wide range of work organisations, in total employing nearly a million people. The response rate of 42.8 per cent was high for this kind of investigation. Data were available from 18 areas of work, with numbers of respondents ranging from 68 (Brewery) to 535 (NHS Trusts). Unlike previous studies it became possible to compare responses from a substantial range of workplaces.

As a generalisation across occupations the authors report that approximately one in ten workers indicated that they had been bullied over the last six months. Some 1.4 per cent reported that they were exposed to bullying on a daily or weekly basis. Comparisons of bullying prevalence between schools and workplaces is difficult to make, but if we may risk a generalisation here, it appears that reported bullying is considerably less common in the workplace than at school, where weekly bullying has been reliably reported as being as high as one in six (Rigby 1997a). But this is small comfort to those being bullied. As Hoel and Cooper (2000) state:

> With a workplace of approximately 24 million employees, this figure [1 in 10] suggests that more than 2 million British employees may currently be bullied at work making bullying one of the most significant hazards affecting people at work today. (p.11)

It appears that the estimates provided by Hoel and Cooper are conservative, at least compared with the results of a survey reported by Charlotte Rayner (1998). Her report was based upon responses from 761 members of a union representing members employed in local government, health care, higher education, electricity, gas, water, public transport, police and the voluntary sector. In this study it was estimated that 14 per cent of union members were being bullied in any six-month period.

As one might expect, the extent of bullying appears to vary between areas of work. Hoel and Cooper report large differences, ranging from 16.2 per cent bullied weekly in post and telegraph to 4.1 per cent in manufacturing. Bullying reported by employees in prisons, teaching and police service were well above the mean percentage whilst bullying in higher education was relatively low. Explanations for such variations have at this stage been notably absent and one is left to wonder whether the variations are due to working conditions, the kind of people who are employed in given areas, the sensitivity workers may have to being bullied, or what. It would be useful to know what variation in the prevalence of bullying there is between workplaces where people are engaged in the *same* kind of work. We know from studies of school bullying that children in the same year-group in different schools of the same type can experience wide variations in prevalence of bullying (Rigby 1997a). If this turns out to be the case also for workplace bullying we may come to conclude that the nature of the work people do is perhaps unrelated or weakly related with bullying behaviour, and we may need to look more at 'on the spot' explanations.

What sort of bullying?

The lumping together of different kinds of bullying is worrying. There is a big difference between being niggled by a colleague with a tedious and misplaced sense of humour and being mugged in the car park; between being annoyingly teased by one's colleagues and being threatened with the sack by one's employer. Such obvious qualitative differences are lost in summary statistics. Fortunately, however, some researchers in workplace bullying, as in school bullying, have attempted to categorise forms of bullying.

In the summary review of literature relating to workplace bullying, Rayner and Hoel (1997) provide five categories of bullying behaviour. These are:

- Threat to professional status, for example, public professional humiliation, accusation of lack of effort and belittling opinion.

- Threat to personal standing, for example, teasing, insults and name calling.

- Isolation, for example, withholding information and preventing access to opportunities, such as attendance at training workshops.

- Overwork, for example, setting impossible deadlines and making unnecessary disruptions.

- Destabilisation, for example, 'shifting the goal posts', setting meaningless tasks, not giving credit where credit is due, removal from positions of responsibility.

There is clearly an overlap between bullying actions that are evident among schoolchildren and bullying actions perpetrated in the workshop. Perhaps the most obvious overlap is in the area of threat to personal standing. For example, in listing items on a Work Harassment scale relevant to workplace harassment, Bjorqvist and Osterman (1998) included the following:

Being shouted at loudly.

Lies being told about you to others.

Insulting comments about your personal life.

Being sneered at.

Words aimed at hurting you.

In her study of workplace bullying in a NHS community trust, Quine (1999) adds several more kinds of bullying that may be found also in the schoolyard. These include destructive innuendo and sarcasm, verbal and non-verbal threats, making inappropriate and hurtful jokes and, in extreme cases, the use of physical violence. She notes that isolating individuals is a bullying tactic used in workplaces – as it is in schools. The main differences is that workplace isolation is sometimes practised by management in ways that are not applicable to schoolchildren, as in deliberately not considering an employee's applications for leave, training or promotion. In the workplace, particularly heavy burdens may be placed upon targeted individuals without justification, as in putting extreme and unreasonable pressure on them to work harder. This is a form of bullying that may sometimes be inflicted on schoolchildren by an unreasonable taskmaster, but is more likely to occur in the workplace as management has a strong vested interest in maximising productivity, though the undue pressure may have a contrary effect.

Quine draws our attention to yet another form of bullying, where the power of management may be used to destabilise individuals or groups of workers. One tactic has been described as 'shifting the goalposts', which implies that workers committed to achieving a given goal may suddenly find that what they have been doing was not what they were supposed to be doing. This is more likely to occur when there is a high degree of role ambiguity, which may be fostered on occasions by managers who are either unclear themselves as to what they want people to do, or (more maliciously) seeking to provide specious grounds for dismissal or non-promotion of an individual they seek to harm.

It is acknowledged that as individuals move towards and into adulthood, techniques of social manipulation become more and more sophisticated. In the workplace, what others think about your professional skills and your contribution to the business become increasingly important. Hence, creating the impression that certain people whom one doesn't like or favour are inadequate workers may become a consistent aim of some managers and/or some fellow workers. Often how they do it, according to Bjorqvist and Osterman, is by providing what they call 'rational sounding criticism'. Superficially – if one doesn't check the evidence (which is either lacking or equivocal) – the complaints may appear reasonable.

In their study of bullying in the workplace, Hoel and Cooper (2000, p.10) provide a list of the frequency with which particular negative acts were reported by respondents who indicated being bullied over the last six months – that is, currently.

Table 4.2 Frequency of negative acts experienced in the workplace by those currently reporting being bullied compared with other workers		
Negative act	% reporting currently bullied	% not currently bullied
Opinions ignored	53.6	9.9
Information withheld	49.9	17.2
Unmanageable workload	45.9	18.4
Unreasonable deadlines	38.4	14.4
Ordered to work below competence	36.4	11.8
Fault finding	34.9	2.4
Humiliated or ridiculed	33.8	3.2
Facing hostility	32.6	3.4
Excessive monitoring	31.5	7.0
Spreading gossip	31.1	4.6
Insults or offensive remarks	30.6	4.3
Removal of responsibility	29.2	7.3

These data suggest that among those who are bullied many of the negative behaviours they experience are of an indirect kind: having opinions ignored; information withheld; unreasonable deadlines; spreading gossip; and (possibly) excessive monitoring and removal of responsibility. Some appear to involve direct confrontations: being ordered to work below competence; fault finding; being humiliated or ridiculed. What is interesting is that among those who report being bullied relatively rarely, if at all, many believe that they are treated negatively at work, more especially in having information withheld from them, having unmanageable workloads, and unreasonable deadlines. This suggests two things: not all negative experiences are construed as bullying, and that some negative acts are more likely to be seen as bullying than others. For example, receiving an unmanageable workload and having an unreasonable deadline are not always taken as evidence of being bullied personally.

Who bullies whom and how in the workplace?

The general consensus among those who have inquired is that bullying is perpetrated at least as often in the workplace by managers and supervisors as by others.
For example Hoel and Cooper (2000) have reported in their study that some 74.7
per cent of respondents reported that they had been bullied by managers and
supervisors as against 36.7 per cent by colleagues; 6.7 per cent by 'subordinates';
and 7.8 per cent by clients, customers or students. To those who care to add up
these figures, it is evident that some were bullied by more than one of the above.
Not all researchers have reported such a high preponderance of bullying by management. Quine (1999) has reported in her study that bullying by management
and colleagues was about equally prevalent. It could be useful to distinguish
clearly between workplaces in which bullying is predominantly carried out or
seen to be carried out by management and workplaces in which bullying is done
at least equally by colleagues or other workers.

The means of bullying by management and co-workers are often similar. A
study conducted by the Working Women's Centre of South Australia (1998) of
148 male and female employees who claimed to have been bullied at work indicated that the following were the most frequently encountered forms of bullying:
being regularly humiliated with put-downs/insults/sarcasm; having one's views
and opinions continually trivialised; and being constantly criticised over one's
work. Over 65 per cent of respondents reported that they received such treatment
from employers and from co-workers. Of particular concern was the proportion
of respondents who reported that they had been further victimised for lodging a
complaint about a work-related matter: some 49 per cent by employers and 39
per cent by co-workers. Many respondents reported that other workers had been
encouraged to 'gang up' on them. Some 46 per cent indicated that this had been
done by management, and 70 per cent by co-workers. These results suggest that
often management and workers carry out similar acts of bullying – sometimes, it
would seem, in collusion.

The most common forms of bullying identified in the South Australian study
were personal, for example approximately 60 per cent of respondents reported
that managers and co-workers had attributed work problems to the personality
flaws of workers. By contrast, relatively little bullying was seen as attributable to
being a member of a social group. Only 10 per cent cited prejudice against
disabled people as a reason for being bullied; only 7 per cent mentioned racial
discrimination. Sexual harassment was reported by 14 per cent of the respondents. It is worth noting that bullying directed against people because of disability, race and gender has over the last ten years or so monopolised the attention of
sociologists and the framers of anti-harassment policies. Bullying on personal
grounds has until recently been virtually ignored in both workplaces and schools.

Detailed comparisons between who bullies whom in schools and other workplaces are difficult to make. If, however, we equate school staff with managers or supervisors, there are some grounds for a somewhat casual comparison. We know that teachers do sometimes bully children (their subordinates?) although defining where appropriate discipline ends and bullying begins is fraught with difficulties (see Terry 1998). But it would be fair to say that there is this important difference between the bullying generally experienced by children at school and that experienced by adults in the workplace: children are on the whole bullied by their peers, adults by people in a management role.

The contrast between children and adults should not blind us to some notable similarities. Adults at work can and do behave like some children do in identifying someone they dislike or want to hurt and tormenting him or her. In some workplaces this appears to be more common than others. There may in fact be a tradition of selecting individuals for 'special treatment' which may include physical as well as mental torture, as we periodically discover and rediscover happening in military or paramilitary organisations where violent initiating rites are sometimes carried out. This is no different from what we sometimes find going on in boys' boarding schools even today. We also find that being victimised by someone or some group of people at work can continue, as it does at school, for many months or years. Hoel and Cooper (2000) report that among their respondents who reported being bullied, a large proportion (39.3%) reported having been bullied for more than two years.

The involvement of males and females in bullying appears to follow a similar pattern in schools and workplaces. In both areas where the sexes work together the male is more likely to be the perpetrator. At school, boys are generally bullied by boys; girls by both boys and girls. The situation is much the same in the workplace. However, one difference has been suggested in recent research. In the workplace, it appears from Hoel and Cooper that women are somewhat more likely to report being bullied (12% of women against 10% of men); whilst at school – more especially at secondary school level – boys appear to report being bullied significantly more (Rigby 1997a).

A further sex difference in bullying in the workplace relates to the proportions of men and women who are bullied by employers and colleagues. Hoel and Cooper (2000) provide data indicating that although both men and women are more likely to be bullied by management than by their colleagues, for men being bullied by management is a more common experience, and being bullied by colleagues a less common experience. As yet, there has been little or no speculation as to why this may be so. We may ask: is it because men are still, as traditionally has been the case, more concerned about status at work and professional advancement and that this leads them into conflict more often with management – which responds by bullying them? Or is it because women are, as numerous psychologists have claimed, more concerned than are men with achieving and maintaining close personal relations – and more frequently seek to ensure such closeness through social manipulations that amount to indirect bullying? Perhaps both these reasons apply.

Finally, it is natural enough to think of bullying as being a problem primarily for those low in the official pecking order: that is, those at the bottom of the organisational hierarchy. Given the emotional climate that surrounds us when we research and invariably empathise, if not identify, with those who are appallingly treated by management or colleagues, it is hard to maintain objectivity. The standing temptation is to exaggerate the malice of managers. They normally have a preponderance of power and under some circumstances they are prone to abuse it, in some cases systematically to achieve goals that they think (often misguidedly) could not be achieved by any other means. It is therefore as well to reflect that in the study on which we have mainly drawn, self-reported targets of bullying are well represented across all levels of workplace hierarchy (Hoel and Cooper 2000). These are the percentages of those reporting being bullied weekly: workers (9.6%); foreman/woman (9.1%); middle management (10.6%); senior management (8.5%); and other (11.5%). Bullying is no great respecter of position.

Other places

Bullying in schools became an issue for researchers in the 1970s when Dan Olweus began his studies in Scandinavian schools. Slow off the mark, bullying in the workplace began to get serious attention following the publication of Andrea Adams' book *Bullying in the Workplace and How to Confront It* in 1992. Curiously, it has generally stopped there. Yet it is plain to see that bullying goes on in many, if not all, walks of life. We await the 'discovery' and the 'exploration' of bullying in the home, in the church, in sport, in politics, in the theatre, in the club; and involving motorists, entrepreneurs, publishers, bank managers, journalists, politicians, waiters, policemen, car salesmen, cooks, *Encyclopedia Britannica* salesmen, accountants, lawyers, doctors, dentists. It is of course hard to find any human activity that does not produce situations in which the more powerful do not exploit their greater strength or power to impose on others.

The home

The 'other place' which you would most expect to become a target for the study of bullying is of course the home. Mountains of books have been written about domestic violence and child abuse, often I fear producing more heat than light. Nowhere have I been able to find any book or article that deals with bullying per se in the home, although everybody knows it exists; indeed hardly a day goes by without a husband or a wife or a son or a daughter or a grandparent complaining that they are being bullied by another family member. The rule appears to be: conflict in the home when it turns nasty is to be called domestic violence. Because a lot of behaviours in the home are decidedly nasty but not in the everyday meaning of the term 'violent', we are obliged to stretch the meaning of the word 'violent' to include such things as raising one's voice, sarcasm, not recognising another's good points, and generally making another feel upset or fed up. Doing violence to the word 'violence' has become something of an epidemic. We must refuse to be bullied into allowing it to be used in that way.

I think a distinction should be made, if only on pragmatic grounds, between child abuse and abusive acts involving adults. In the former, an imbalance of power between the violator and the violated can normally be assumed; in the latter it can't. In the case of what might be called child abuse, the plea that 'it was justified' has become unacceptable. Regarding acts between adults in the home, community judgements differ widely on the circumstances that may or may not justify one adult person acting in an aggressive manner towards another. We say: it depends on what he or she did and what sort of aggressive action followed. We generally want to know what led up to it and whether the aggressive act was 'understandable'. We can then consider whether to call it bullying or not.

Child abuse

Examples of child abuse may be found not only in the home. Recently I was having lunch at an outdoor café next to a table at which were seated two women in their thirties and two young children around three years of age. It was an exceptionally hot day, even for Australia. The mother of one of the children was hot and bothered, her condition not made any better by her having reached a stage of pregnancy at which movement was becoming noticeably difficult. The children were drinking milkshakes, or were, until one of them accidentally upset his drink over the table, splashing milk everywhere. The consequence was electrifying. The child was yanked by one skinny arm clean out of his seat with terrific force, dragged away, petrified, and severely – and publicly – beaten. He returned to his seat, trembling and sobbing and stifling sobs for a good five minutes whilst his mother sat impassively. I mention this incident not because it is exceptional. It isn't. Nor because the violence was perpetrated by a woman. (I suspect the only reason why we see public displays of child abuse by women more than men is because men commonly absent themselves from such situations.) Nor because there are not more extreme examples I could choose. Rather because such incidents are taken for granted, do not bring in the police, and in fact, often do not evoke even a ripple of public condemnation.

Child abuse is often categorised according to subtypes of sexual, physical, psychological, neglect and exposure to family violence. Precise facts are hard to establish. In the area of childhood sexual assault, probably the best estimate of incidence was provided by a national random survey in the USA by Finkelhor *et al.* (1990) which estimated that 27 per cent of females and 16 per cent of males had been sexually assaulted at some point in childhood. There is always some uncertainty as to what counts as 'abuse' in other areas and it is obvious that some acts can be multiply classified, for example an abusive incident may have both physical and psychological dimensions. In a recent study of maltreatment by parents and peers based upon retrospective reports of adult students in Canada it was estimated that 11 per cent had been abused by parents physically and 18 per cent psychologically (R.D. Duncan 1999).

In the same study some 61 per cent of males and 50 per cent of females reported that they had been bullied at school. Of particular interest was that those who reported being abused at home, physically, sexually or emotionally, were more likely to be bullied at school. For instance suffering sexual abuse at home was reported more than three times as often by those who were bullied by peers at school. When asked about their mothers, bully victims reported a higher level of emotional maltreatment than non-victims in all areas covered in the questionnaire: yelling, insulting, criticising, making feel guilty, ridiculing or humiliating, embarrassing, and made to feel like a bad person.

R.D. Duncan (1999) goes on to describe the psychological well-being of the adults in the study who had provided information on their childhood experiences. On the basis of a wide variety of tests it was found that although victims and non-victims of abuse in the home or at school did not differ in psychological well-being, those who were *dual* victims, that is, had been abused or bullied in the home and at school, fared significantly worse than each of the other groups (non-victims, bully-only victims and abuse-only victims). They were significantly more likely than others to show a range of symptoms of psychological distress. This I think was an important finding. It suggests that long-term psychological damage to individuals is more likely to occur if as children they were abused both at home and at school. Duncan explains why this may be:

> For a child who is experiencing abuse within the home and who is being bullied by peers at school, there may be no safe haven. In addition, because children turn to parents, and to peers in middle and late childhood for validation, when a child is told by both parents and peers that he or she is not valued, it is not surprising that symptoms of distress would surface and even continue into young adulthood. (R.D. Duncan 1999, p.51)

Domestic violence between adults

What, if any, is the relationship between domestic violence and bullying? Let us begin by establishing, if we can, what domestic violence is and what its prevalence might be.

How much domestic violence or abuse actually occurs is difficult to establish for a variety of reasons. Part of the difficulty is definitional. Straus and Gelles (1986) defined domestic violence as occurring when an act is carried out with the intention, or perceived intention, of causing physical pain or injury to another person. They reported that in 1975 in the USA 28 per cent of couples had experienced domestic violence at some point in their lives, and that 3.8 per cent of women in a relationship were subjected to violence in the year of the study. On the basis of a similar survey conducted ten years later they reported somewhat lower figures. Sometimes the term 'violence' is used more inclusively. In a recent study Mieko (1999) assessed the incidence of domestic violence among women of Japanese descent in the USA by including, as well as indicators of physical abuse, 'emotional violence' such as withholding affection, financial neglect and sexual abuse. Not surprisingly, the estimates of prevalence were much higher than those reported by Straus and Gelles, being no less than 80 per cent!

A further issue is whether we can reasonably infer 'abuse' from answers to questions about acts of aggression, without learning about the context in which they occurred or the significance they may have for the participants. When Mieko (1999) asked her respondents whether they considered what had happened to them as abusive, many did not. This led to a downscaling of the estimate of lifetime abuse experienced by the women to 61 per cent – still remarkably high by comparison with other estimates of other populations. We must grant that large differences may well exist for different cultural groups and at different times. Mieko points out that data collection occurred during the hearing of the O. J. Simpson case, when there was heightened interest in the issue.

Making inferences purely from statistics on acts of violence or aggression as to the nature of domestic violence can lead to misleading conclusions. In a recent meta-analytical review of gender differences between heterosexual partners it was concluded that 'women were slightly more likely than men to use more acts of physical aggression and to use such acts more frequently' (Archer 2000, p.651). Whilst this may be factually accurate, it is apt to convey the impression that women are more culpable and tells us nothing about the significance of the acts. Women are far more likely to be physically injured by men than vice versa. Also from these facts we gain no insight into the motivation or reasons behind the acts, and this is what we generally want to know, especially if we wish to link domestic violence with bullying.

Interpretations of acts of domestic violence between couples that are made simply to promote ideological positions may impede our understanding of aggression between family members. It is sometimes taken for granted that if a man abuses a woman it is because society sanctions the abuse and control of women by men, but as Gordon (2000) has put it, 'societal level explanations cannot explain why particular individuals or couples engage in violent behaviour and others do not' (p.759). We should bear in mind that violence between lesbian couples is by no means uncommon (Lockhart *et al.* 1994). These researchers noted that 31 per cent of those surveyed in an American sample reported one or more incidents of physical abuse. They add that such abuse was triggered or erupted around issues of power imbalance and/or a struggle for varying levels of interdependency and autonomy in their relationship. Societal explanations have their place, for example, in helping us to understand how some individuals can come to have rigid sex-role expectations of their partner and feel justified in acting aggressively in order to see them fulfilled. But they provide only a partial explanation for acts of violence and acts of bullying.

Some acts which fall under the heading of domestic violence, whether defined narrowly as aggressive physical acts or more broadly so as to include behaviour intended to hurt emotionally, are what we might usefully think of as bullying, conceived as the systematic abuse of power. These are acts which are intended to be hurtful and typically repeated, are made possible by an imbalance of power between the perpetrator and the victim and are not justified by the usual societal and moral standards. It is the last two considerations that define an act as 'bullying'.

Before we can construe domestic violence as bullying, we must first identify the power bases that enable spouses and partners sharing a home to hurt each other. Some of these are similar to those evident when bullying takes place in schools and in the workplace. We can immediately identify two of them: physical strength and control of access to resources. Although there is evidently a growing overlap in the capacity for men and women to dominate the other physically, it is clear that in most cases of physical conflict women are disadvantaged. As Archer (2000) reports, 'men are more likely to inflict an injury, and overall 62% of those injured by a partner were women' (p.651). Again, although the situation is evidently changing, men in the home, like men in the workplace, generally have greater control over resources than women, especially financial or economic resources.

However, comparisons between factors relating to bullying in the home and elsewhere break down when we think about the quality and emotional intensity of relationships that normally exist in the home. Hostilities between men and women are usually emotionally charged and a great deal may be at stake in how conflicts are resolved. The weapons used are many and varied. Although physical conflicts have caught the attention of most researchers in this area, verbal and indirect means of bullying are more common and sometimes of equal or greater harmfulness.

Some imbalances of power are to the woman's advantage. A tongue-lashing by a woman is frequently more hurtful than that expressed incoherently or inarticulately by a man. As we have seen, girls in schools are far more practised and through practice (or natural talent) more proficient in the art of indirect and manipulative forms of aggression. Although the threat of separation following aggressive or violent encounters may be dreaded by both parties as they skate recklessly on ever thinning ice, men are typically more at risk. Typically they become more devastated at the loss of a partner and women, recognising the greater dependency of their spouse, often realise it.

We cannot discuss bullying without bringing in the judgements people make about whether aggression is justified under this or that circumstance and, if so, what sort of aggression is justified. Particularly relevant are the role expectations that men and women have of each other, especially the expectations men have come to have of women. Traditionally men have felt justified in refusing to help with child care, housework and cooking. The pressure to 'act like a man' may differ from culture to culture and from sub-culture to sub-culture. The precise source of the pressure is sometimes not obvious. During a visit to Korea I was told that increasingly young women were avoiding or indefinitely postponing getting married, because they did not want to lose their 'freedom'. It was not, I understood, uncommon for men to promise sincerely to be model new-age husbands, sharing and caring and living together as equals. Young Korean women, however, know that when they are married they will have a mother-in-law insisting that they become 'proper' wives to their sons.

Physical and sexual assault of women

Where we have clear evidence of physical and/or sexual assault against women it can often be construed as bullying. Physical assault on women is mostly carried out by men. In a survey of over 6000 Australian women carried out by the Office of the Status of Women (reported by the Australian Bureau of Statistics in 1996) approximately 7 per cent reported that they had experienced violence during the previous 12 months. Some 80 per cent of these assaults were by men. These ranged from being pushed, grabbed or shoved – the most common category – to being beaten, the least common. The physical assaults were carried out mostly by the women's partners. It is reasonable to view most, if not all, of these assaults as constituting bullying, that is an abuse of power, though to what extent the abuse was 'systematic' and 'repeated' is unclear. Sexual assaults were found to be less common and more often perpetrated by a man other than the current partner. Some 1.6 per cent of the sample of women reported that they had been sexually assaulted, that is, they had experienced acts of a sexual nature against their will (excluding unwanted sexual touching) through the use of physical force. Many of these acts would have constituted rape. Such behaviour is perhaps the most atrocious form of bullying that people, most commonly women, experience.

We should note that the incidence of physical and sexual assault varies widely between social or cultural groups. In Australia the rate of physical and sexual assault in Aboriginal communities is much higher than in the non-Aboriginal society. According to the Australian Federal Attorney General's Department, in some Aboriginal communities such violence affects up to 90 per cent of families. Police figures in Western Australia show that Aboriginal women are 45 times more likely than non-Aboriginal women to be victims of domestic violence (*The Australian*, 30 June 2001, p.21). Figures provided by National Victim Center in the USA in 1992 indicated that the rate of rape in the USA was greater than in other parts of the world, being 13 times higher than in Britain and 20 times greater than in Japan (www.nvc.org/stats/sa.htm). The reasons for such variation are currently unclear. But the sheer size of the differences would appear to rule out an explanation of rape that attributes such behaviour to variations in biological attributes. According to Anderson and Swainson (2001) both sex and power motives are generally seen by American students as being involved in rape cases. Essentially, however, rape is an abuse of power. For some men it is evidently a premeditated act, a recurring behaviour, that is bullying.

As in the more familiar kind of bullying experienced in the schoolyard, there is the familiar protestation that somehow the bullying was justified. In the schoolyard the victim was 'asking for it' by being a particular kind of person. At the rape scene, the victim was also 'asking for it' – asking for it by being deliberately sexually arousing. And, as in schoolyard bullying, the victim of rape may come to feel that there would be more trouble in store if he or she were to inform.

Prisons

Bullying in prisons takes place under extreme institutional pressure, in degree quite unlike that normally found elsewhere. Not only are prisons peopled by inmates who are, by and large, more aggressive in temperament and often accustomed to imposing their will on others, but importantly prisons provide a climate in which bullying seems virtually inevitable. As a British Home Office Prison Service report put it: 'The strong can exploit the weak to create their own hierarchies. Bullies can get away with it and victims are afraid to report what has happened.'

Not surprisingly, the problem of bullying in prisons is particularly serious. In their study of types of bullying behaviours in prison, Ireland and Archer (1996) list physical assaults, taking belongings, verbal abuse, threats, intimidating, gossiping and/or spreading rumours and ostracising. Brookes (1993) provided a more extensive and detailed description of bullying behaviours in prisons, including kicks and slaps, sexual abuse, practical jokes such as placing excrement in bedding, threatening a victim's family, and forcing inmates to bring drugs to prison.

Comparative figures for bullying in prisons and other contexts are unavailable. This is partly because the contexts themselves place demands upon what may count as bullying. If we ask the inmates themselves about bullying, the term itself may be seen as suggesting immature childish behaviour. They may therefore deny that they engage in it or indeed are ever the target of it. For this reason it is sometimes thought to be preferable to ask questions about *behaviours* that we might – from the outside – describe as bullying. Yet differences between evaluations of such behaviours inside and outside a context may differ widely. From the outside the behaviours may look like an abuse of power, that is, bullying. From the inside the same behaviours may appear as normal: an accepted or even acceptable use of power. The question is: on whose judgements should we rely?

It is sometimes maintained that bullying in prisons has some special features and may require extending the definition of bullying. Ireland (2000) takes issue with the definition of bullying that insists upon describing bullying as 'repeated' negative behaviour. She points out that many incidents of bullying occur when inmates are moved to new locations, either to or from prisons or to different sectors of a prison. Ireland also discusses types of bullying that are seemingly unique to prisons. One of these is 'baroning', whereby certain resources, such as money, drugs, tobacco and alcohol, are lent to inmates and repayment is demanded at a high rate of interest. Physical assaults and threats may then be carried out against those who fail to pay back the loans. Shakespeare's Shylock was familiar with this device, as were generations of unscrupulous money-lenders once pilloried as usurers.

'Taxing' is another mode of bullying singled out as unique to prison life. This is defined by Ireland as 'a behaviour in which new inmates have goods taken away from them under the pretext of a tax'. This raises the more general question: when does a tax become bullying? When the American colonies in the 18th century rebelled and demanded exemption from taxation with the slogan 'No taxation without representation', were they, in essence, objecting to bullying by the British government? In my own state of South Australia some time ago fines were imposed upon parking motorists who displayed their parking permits on the right-hand side of their dashboards rather than on the prescribed left-hand side, thereby punishing those who had failed to read the small print. Cases of trickery and extortion by the state, it seems, can parallel those that occur more often in prisons.

What happens in prisons is not so much unique as extreme. When Bernard Shaw in the preface to *Misalliance* likened schools to prisons he struck not a few responsive chords. They are indeed alike in being places 'where humans can't leave', though the confinement is less unremitting. What has been described in prisons as bullying can be seen, in attenuated forms, in many schools. We find in both prisons and schools the fear of disclosing to the authorities the identity of the bully; the tendency for those who were bullied as newcomers to become bullies later on; and the prevalence of harsh initiating practices.

We need not subscribe to the view that bullying is entirely a response to a specific form of environment – enclosed, authoritarian, frightening and boring by turns, engendering fear, frustration and futility – to conclude that to the degree that people live under such conditions they will be inclined to bully or become the victims of bullying. That is why the study of bullying in such institutions as prisons is so important.

Sport

An examination of bullying in sport raises some difficult questions. Take cricket. In the 1930s England launched the now infamous 'bodyline barrage' against the Australians in general and their star batsman, Bradman, in particular. This unhappily sparked off what was seen as a serious international situation between the two countries. For the uninitiated, 'bodyline' (or as the English called it, elegantly enough, 'leg theory') was a new tactic used to get batsmen out, by bowling at their bodies and placing many fielders in short-fielding positions where they could be caught out as they fended off the ball in a desperate effort to protect themselves. In effect, it was a means of intimidating batsmen so they would more readily give up their wickets; not illegal, not against the rules, but, as some would say, 'against the spirit of the game' or 'not cricket'. But was this what we might call 'bullying'? Many believed it really did amount to 'a systematic abuse of power'. The power that could be exerted by a fast bowler of the kind England had in its armoury in the person of Harold Larwood was supported by an English captain who did everything he could to enable that power to be applied in a systematic and intimidating manner. Eventually the rules were changed to outlaw bodyline, but the problem did not disappear.

In more recent times, controversy arose over the use of the so-called 'bouncer' – a ball delivered at speed and made to rear up at the batsman's head and shoulders; as before, intended to intimidate. Again the bowler could be branded as a bully. As a means of redressing the power imbalance, it was proposed that batsmen might wear protective helmets. Gradually – after first being denounced as 'wimpish' – the idea of wearing helmets caught on. At least for the more expert batsman this was a problem he could live with. He could weave and duck and even, if sufficiently expert, take on the bowler by hooking furiously – and effectively – and smashing the ball for a leg-side boundary. But for the less skilled batsman (the 'tailender') this was not such a viable option. Could there be a rule for the 'weak' batsman and a rule for the 'strong'? Amazingly, this is what the umpires had to decide upon. A less expert batsman was to be protected from the onslaught of bouncers by the umpire calling 'no ball', which counted against the bowler who could, if he persisted, be asked to discontinue. How could one tell who was less expert? First, it could be said, he batted lower in the order; second, he did not bat very well. But what if he did rise to the occasion and show unexpected talent in the course of an innings? Then, it was decreed, the bouncer was justified – in moderation!

This digression into the peculiar technicalities of cricket really does have an important point. At least in the culture of cricket the notion of what constitutes 'a systematic abuse of power' (what I am calling 'bullying') is far from being cut and dried. It operates in a culture that recognises the legitimacy of aggression – up to a point. It is not readily encompassed or perhaps even clearly encompassable by rules. It is sensitive to pressures from other arenas, for example public opinion or even international affairs. It involves continual shifts in judgements as perceptions of power change. It will continue to baffle; these difficulties will not go away.

In the arena of sport, 'bullying' is seen by some as quite acceptable. Here is a statement today (28 June 2001) attributed to the powerfully built tennis player Venus Williams: 'I think if you have the opportunity to bully your opponent, then you have to take that chance. If you have the power, it's perfect to use it.'

There is another issue that a consideration of sport brings to mind. We need to keep in mind that sport is something that people normally choose to be in or out of – I am not forgetting the misery of children forced into compulsory games. If one chooses to be in the ring with Mike Tyson, then (it may be said) it is your lookout, and you must abide by the rules of a sport in which the 'abuse of power' in many respects appears normal and acceptable – though there are, of course, some limitations, even in boxing, as to how we may hurt our adversary. In sport we may be permitted to behave in ways that in another context would constitute bullying. Our concern is limited to whether the rules are being interpreted reasonably – or (more rarely) whether the rules should be changed, failing which one has the option to leave the sport.

A serious situation may arise when the sportsman or sportswoman decides that the rules of the game shall apply to the game of life or, more simply, carries on as if the schoolyard, the workplace or the home is indeed part of the game. We see this happening when schoolboy rugby fanatics in boarding schools line up younger children to serve as tackling bags. And when arguments are decided by the loudness or vehemence of the disputants. Of course, there are those for whom this sporting life is a domain outside the everyday world. There may even be some who behave as Konrad Lorenz said they might: that is, they 'let off steam' on the sports field and become peaceful afterwards. But the danger remains that aggression in one context overflows into aggression in another; that the bully on the football oval becomes a bully at school or in the workplace. As yet, we have no definite proof either way.

Bullying in politics

The arena of political activity is one that can draw out the best and the worst in people. Generally speaking, politics attracts those who are most concerned with the acquisition and exercise of power. Where there has been no effective democratic constitution the abuse of political power has proved awesome. The twentieth century saw the rise to power of Hitler, Mussolini and Stalin, political megalomaniacs who systematically bullied others to achieve ever greater power with devastating effect. But even in countries with democratic institutions, with well considered checks and balances, opposition parties, regular elections, parliamentary conventions and so on, there can be, and sometimes is, a systematic abuse of power by individuals or by groups of the kind that can fairly be called bullying.

Bullying in politics is most public, and therefore most evident, in parliament. In Australia we are continually reminded of the schoolyard. Question time is often bullying time. Questions are couched in the most misleadingly respectful terms – Will the 'honourable member' please explain… ? The intent is to embarrass, humiliate and expose one's political enemies as fools and incompetents. The targeted member rises to his feet, ignores the question, and launches into a spirited attack on the members opposite. The game's afoot. Bystanders now act according to cue. Cries of derision for supporters of the putative bully; expressions of solidarity from the friends of the struggling speaker; a few bystanders – independent members – become spectators watching to see how things develop. Whether the scene unfolds as a bully/victim scenario will depend upon the virulence and pointedness of the attack , the defensive skills of the speaker and the degree of support provided by the party. Often enough it is stalemate: no real harm done - but equally no good done either. Occasionally it is not unfair to characterise the situation as one to which the schoolyard analogy applies.

In the Australian parliament few, if any, political performers have played the role of the bully with greater effect than Paul Keating, Treasurer, then Prime Minister of Australia, in the late 1980s and early 1990s. He was equipped with a breathtaking capacity for personal ridicule and a flair for telling insults. Here is a list of abusive phrases for which he became notorious:

About the then Leader of the Opposition, John Howard:

> What we have got is a dead carcass, swinging in the breeze, but nobody will cut it down and replace him.

> He is the greatest job and investment destroyer since the bubonic plague

> I am not like the Leader of the Opposition. I did not slither out of the Cabinet room like a mangy maggot.

And of the next leader of the Opposition, John Hewson:

> I have a psychological hold over Hewson… He's like a stone statue in the cemetery

Not surprisingly, he earned a reputation as the Head Bully. He was much feared by his political enemies; greatly admired by his friends. In full flight in Parliament he seemed unstoppable. One tactic, however, did have some success. An Opposition Minister, "Ironbark" Wilson Tuckey, notable for his aggressive no-hold-barred political behaviour, made a surprising move. Each time Paul Keating held forth in his inimitable manner, the Honourable Member for O'Connor reminded him by interjection of his Achilles heel, which happened to be (or was thought to be) a possible breach of promise with a young woman some years before he became a happily married man. All that was necessary during a Keating tirade was to call out the name of the young woman in question. According to Alan Ramsey (2001) a parliamentary observer on the historic day (February 18th, 1986), Tuckey warned Keating that if he continued his personal attack on a colleague he would mention Christine, whereupon Keating directed his fire at Tuckey himself, describing him as "the loopy crim from O'Connor." The threat was carried out. Tuckey: "Christine had a little girl called Paul…". Keating, wounded, complained to the press, and threatened Howard for not repudiating his minister with the words: "From this day onwards, Mr Howard will wear his leadership like a crown of thorns, and in Parliament I will do everything I can to destroy him." His status now was that of the hell-bent bully/victim.

There is one more angle to the schoolyard analogy. Mr Speaker (or Madam Speaker) in Parliament is the counterpart of the teacher on yard duty, continually calling upon members to refrain from abusive name-calling or "unparliamentary language" – or words not to be used at our school. Offending members are duly suspended and like naughty children, sent to the 'Reflection Room' to cool off.

Parliament is where the politicians perform for the edification of the public. What happens there should perhaps be seen as the froth on the surface. Politicians sometimes refer to it as "robust debate." But the sad consequence is that it does provide a model for how men and women in authority seek to settle their differences. And for some it increases contempt for the political process.

Stalking

We normally think of bullying as being localised. It is something that happens at school, in the workplace, in the home, in the sporting arena. Yet a kind of bullying can and does occur which has no close association with place. This is stalking. We may add that more than any other kind of bullying it becomes detached from time as well: the stalker may be always with you mentally, no matter where you are.

Stalking has exceedingly sinister connotations. Kohn, Flood and Chase (1998) define it as 'wilful, malicious and repeated following or harassing of another person with the intent to place that person in fear of death or serious bodily injury'. This is how we often think of it. Yet, as with the broader notion of bullying, we tend to focus on the worst of it. Just as bullying conjures up a physical beating so stalking makes us think of violence and even tragedy – of Jodie Foster and John Lennon, for instance.

A less sensational definition has been proposed by Wright *et al.* (1996): 'The act of following, viewing, communicating with, or moving threateningly or menacingly toward another person' (p.487).

As in bullying we may distinguish between malign and non-malign forms. From the viewpoint of the stalker the act of 'following and viewing and communicating with' may lack malevolent intent; indeed, the stalker may wish to 'do good' to their focus of attention. This appears to have been the case for an Australian man who was recently convicted of having stalked the international tennis star Martina Hingis. The argument that he was seriously deluded cut no ice with the jury. It was enough, understandably, that Ms Hingis felt threatened by the stalker's amorous and persistent attentions.

The line between the dogged persistence on the part of a suitor, cheerfully determined to overcome knock-backs, and crass or even criminal insensitivity to the expressed wishes of the *objet d'amour* is not always easy to draw. After all, Beauty eventually said yes to the Beast. Where mental illness is involved, the judgement of the stalker is especially likely to be at fault. According to Zona, Sharma and Lane (1993) a major mental illness was present in 63 per cent of the cases they investigated. Some mental conditions are more likely than others to result in stalking behaviour. People with Asperger syndrome, for instance, have profound difficulties in interpreting the cues that most people readily understand. They do not read a rejection as others do.

As in the case of bullying, so too in stalking, it is sensible to distinguish between sub-types of behaviour. Wright *et al.* (1996) identify first the 'delusional stalker' who lives in a fantasy world, believing that a close intimate relationship has developed with the target of his or her amorous attention. This may or may not pose a serious threat. The target is often a person who because of his or her position or celebrity attracts a good deal of interest. Typically such a person is completely unaware of the identity of the stalker. Sometimes the stalker may find this difficult or impossible to believe. Stalking of this kind takes on features of malign bullying and may become extremely threatening if (as is commonly the case) the stalker feels rebuffed, frustrated and angry.

A second sub-type is the stalker who is not deluded, but who desires to hurt another person by such actions as repeated threatening anonymous phone calls, emails or letters, without revealing his or her identity. Wright *et al.* (1996) describe such a person as an 'organised stalker'. This type conforms closely to that of the classical bully who derives pleasure from feeling in control of the person he or she continues to hurt. Finally, there is the 'domestic stalker' whom the target knows, e.g. a former spouse, boyfriend or girlfriend, and who persists in seeking to resume a close relationship that has become unwelcome. This is perhaps the hardest to deal with, as reconciliations are always a possibility. One may be caught between recommending restraining orders to deter the stalker and mediation to make restraining orders unnecessary.

Estimates of the incidence of stalking have varied widely. As in studies of other forms of bullying, much may depend upon how stalking is defined and the choice of population sampled. For example, in a study reported by Fremouw, Westrup and Pennypacker (1997) of stalking experienced by students (N = 593) at the West Virginia University in the USA, stalking was defined as 'having someone knowingly and repeatedly fooling, harassing and threatening you'. Approximately 30 per cent of female students and 16 per cent of male students reported that they had been stalked on campus. In a much larger US national sample of 16,000 people aged 18 years and over, 'stalking' was defined conservatively as 'a course of conduct directed at a specific person that involves repeated physical or visual proximity, non-consensual communication, or verbal, written or implied threats sufficient to cause fear in a reasonable person' (Tjaden 1997). It was estimated that 8 per cent of women and 2 per cent of men had been stalked at some point in their lives. Between these two published studies, we have a four-fold difference in females and an eight-fold difference in males!

In summary, stalking has much in common with other forms of bullying, both non-malign and malign. Its manifestation is consistent with a view of bullying as a 'systematic abuse of power'. Like other forms of bullying, stalking is practised mainly by males; unlike bullying as it is experienced in schools by schoolchildren, females are more likely than males to be the targets and are much more likely to be stalked by men than by women. (We should nevertheless acknowledge that women are sometimes stalked by members of their own sex.) In some respects stalking may differ from other forms of bullying. Stalking is more likely to have strong sexual connotations, the targeted person often having for the stalker erotic qualities that stimulate fantasy. The obsession typically grows and may lead to physical assault. Finally, it is seen as a more deviant behaviour than most bullying and frequently stemming from a mental disorder.

Chapter 5

Bullying and health

A research perspective

If pleasures are greatest in anticipation, just remember that this is true of trouble.

— Elbert Hubbard

The main reason why most people are concerned about bullying is because they think it is harmful to the health of many vulnerable persons. If they are right, the anti-bullying movement is most clearly vindicated. The trouble is that claims that bullying is the cause of a great deal of avoidable personal suffering and ill health are often highly subjective and based loosely on selected anecdotal evidence. Hence, as far as possible, we need studies of the relationship between health status and involvement in bully/victim problems that are based upon credible, replicated, empirical investigations. This chapter aims to produce such a basis. The perspective in this chapter is that of the researcher.

In fact, very different views are held on the relationship between involvement in bully/victim problems and health. These may be listed as follows:

1. Essentially there is no relationship. Whilst being bullied may not be pleasant at the time, the effects on a victim's health are generally trivial and not enduring. Further, bullying others is typically the expression of 'normal' aggressiveness and has no significant health implications.

2. Being bullied may have a *positive* effect on one's health and well-being in so far as it evokes a positive response to a temporary

stressor and commonly has the effect of making a targeted person more resilient. Successfully bullying others adds to one's self-esteem.

3.   Being continually bullied is stressful and typically undermines one's sense of well-being and can impair one's physical health and the effects can be enduring. Bullying others is generally undertaken by people whose mental health is deficient.

Before examining the evidence that has a bearing upon the validity of these points of view, we should consider what we meant by 'health'. Although it is a familiar enough word, it can and does mean different things to different people.

Defining 'health'

In the highly influential definition of health proposed by the World Health Organisation (WHO) in 1948, 'health' was conceived as 'a state of complete physical, mental and social well being and not merely the absence of disease or infirmity' (World Health Organisation 1986). Such a positive and holistic view of health is nowadays widely accepted, although it has its critics. For example, Saracci (1997) has suggested that the mission statement of the WHO comes closer to the concept of happiness than health. He argues for a clear distinction between feelings of well-being and conditions of physical health. At the same time, there is evidence of a close association (though not a necessary connection) between states of low psychological well-being and symptoms of poor physical health.

We can identify four aspects of health that may be affected by bullying:

(1)   Psychological well-being, as indicated by self-esteem and happiness.

(2)   Social adjustment, as indicated by involvement with others as opposed to being isolated and alienated from one's environment.

(3)   Psychological comfort, as opposed to feeling distressed as in suffering from attacks of anxiety and depression.

(4)   Physical wellness, as indicated by an absence of physical health complaints.

What research can tell us

Generally researchers in this field have sought to examine whether involvement in bully/victim problems – as a bully or a victim or both – is associated with one or more of the aspects of health indicated above. This research has been conducted for the most part with children in schools. However, in recent years increasingly reports have appeared describing the health of people who have been bullied in the workplace.

It is important to see what such studies can and can't tell us. If there is no cor-relation between being bullied and having relatively poor health, then the first of the viewpoints listed above will have been supported, that is, the effects of being bullied on health are negligible, at least for the population being sampled. If there is a correlation, such that those who had been repeatedly bullied by their peers have poorer than average health of one kind or another, then there would be a prima facie case for believing that being victimised a good deal *may* cause a dete-rioration in health. But only a prima facie case. It may be that the health of the people who are victimised a good deal was generally poorer before the bullying began. It may be that if your health is poor, people are more likely to pick on you.

In addition to evidence of a reliable association between being victimised and poor health we need evidence that victims' health has changed for the worse following the experience of being bullied. But let us first satisfy ourselves that there is an association; then (if there is) we can look for evidence that there is a causal link.

The association between poor health and peer victimisation among children

We will begin with a review of studies that have examined the health of school children who have been identified, either through self-reports or through obser-vations by others, as bullies or victims at school or as both bullies and victims.

Psychological well-being

Happiness is perhaps the simplest and most widely used concept suggested by 'psychological well-being'. We may ask, are victims less happy in themselves than others? One of the most commonly used measures of happiness with children is the so-called 'Terrible–Delighted Faces' test developed by Andrews and Withey (1976). This consists of pictorial representations of seven faces depicting expres-sions ranging from a broad smile (A) to a heavy frown (G). It is illustrated in Figure 5.1.

A   B   C   D   E   F   G

Figure 5.1 The happiness measure: The 'Terrible – Delighted Faces' test

In the course of administering the Peer Relations Questionnaire to Australian school children (aged 8 to 18 years) over the past 7 years (Rigby and Slee 1993c), some 31,980 children have responded to the pictorial measure of happiness. They have been asked to indicate 'which face is most like you when you are at school'. The overwhelming majority of children (85% of girls and 77% of boys) have pointed to happy faces, that is faces A, B or C. However, a small minority (4% of girls and 7% of boys) have pointed to unhappy faces, that is faces E, F or G. Among children categorised as 'victims' (those who reported being victimised at least once a week) the proportions of children who saw themselves as unhappy at school were much higher (see Figure 5.2).

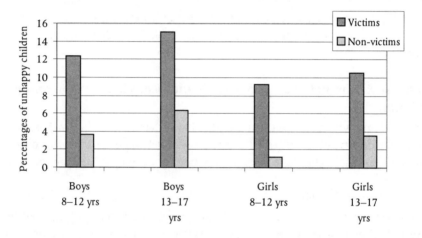

Figure 5.2 Reported unhappiness of Australian schoolchildren according to victim and non-victim status

For each of the age/gender sub-groups indicated in Figure 5.2, the frequently victimised children were more likely to represent themselves as unhappy. The differences are all significant by chi square at the .001 level. The contrasts are most striking for younger children (under 13 years); among girls, frequently victimised children were more than 7 times more likely to see themselves as unhappy; among boys, the ratio was more than 3 to 1.

Other cross-sectional surveys using verbal measures of happiness provide support for a connection between peer victimisation and happiness with students in both primary and secondary schools: in Ireland (O'Moore and Hillery 1991); in England (Boulton and Underwood 1992); and in Australia (Forero *et al.* 1999).

But what of bullies? One study by Rigby and Slee (1993a) does suggest that they too tend to be relatively unhappy children. When asked to indicate the face that best described them at school, they were, like the victims, significantly more likely than others to choose the less happy-looking faces.

So far we have no evidence that children become less happy as a consequence of becoming involved either as a victim or as a bully in bully/victim encounters. Although it seems likely that being bullied does reduce the happiness of those targeted, we have to consider the possibility that simply going around looking miserable can actually result in a person being picked on by others, especially by peers who are lacking in empathy. Similarly, as yet, we do not know whether bullying others makes one more unhappy or whether being unhappy makes one more likely to bully others. It seems more likely that the second possibility is true. It may be that the pleasure that comes from dominating others helps to lift the gloom experienced by some bullies – and transfer it to their victims.

Relatively low levels of self-esteem or self-worth have been reported in a substantial number of studies involving frequently victimised children in different age groups. These have included cross-sectional survey studies conducted with primary school children in England by Boulton and Smith (1994); Callaghan and Joseph (1995) and Mynard and Joseph (1997); in Ireland by O'Moore and Hillery (1991); and in Australia by Rigby and Slee (1993a) and Rigby and Cox (1996).

The link between self-esteem and peer victimisation among older students has been examined in a number of school-based studies. In Australia Rigby and Slee (1993a) assessed secondary students (N = 877) aged 12 to 18 years using a reliable self-report measure of peer victimisation and the Rosenberg (1986) measure of self-esteem. After controlling statistically for the effects of behaving anti-socially and as a bully, being victimised by peers was found to be significantly and independently associated with low self-esteem. This means that we can say that the low self-esteem experienced by children who are often victimised was not due to some of them being anti-social characters. The statistical link between being a victim and having low self-esteem was supported in subsequent studies in England with adolescent schoolgirls by Neary and Joseph (1994) and Stanley and Arora (1998). In this latter study, the authors focused upon one particular aspect of peer victimisation generally considered to be more prevalent among girls, namely that of excluding others.

In a further study of the relationship between peer victimisation and self-esteem, Rigby and Slee (1999b) conducted another study with secondary school students in Australia, this time controlling for the possible effects of social support, psychological introversion and the tendency to disclose one's feelings to others, a factor believed to promote mental health (Larson and Chastain 1990). Low self-esteem remained a significant predictor of peer victimisation, and (it could be claimed) was not due to the kinds of children who are often victimised being introverted, with little social support or being inclined to keep things to themselves – although these qualities may have made them more vulnerable to attack and also contributed to them feeling bad about themselves.

There is some persuasive research evidence that a drop in self-esteem is actually induced by peer victimisation. A longitudinal study conducted in the USA by Egan and Perry (1998) included 189 children of approximately 11 years of age who were assessed on a number of variables relating to peer victimisation (as derived from the results of peer ratings), as well as various measures of self-regard, and then retested using the same measures five months later. The researchers evidence that low self-regard (a concept akin to low self-esteem) may predispose a child to be victimised. They also found that it was the case that being victimised at school actually *induced* a loss of self-regard. The authors claim that their study 'may be the first to show convincingly (i.e. with proper statistical controls) that actual maltreatment by significant others leads to impairment in self-regard over time' (1998, p.307). This is an important finding. But it should be noted that the particular measure of self-regard for which significant results were claimed in predicting effects of peer victimisation was one that reflected 'self-perceived social competence' as inferred, for example, from a child claiming that it is 'pretty easy to make friends'. (Global self-worth was not statistically significant.) These results suggest that being victimised by others may strengthen a child in the belief that he or she is not very successful in interacting with others. This may lead to the child being bullied more frequently.

We may also draw on the reports of children describing how they have felt after being bullied at school. In a large-scale study of Australian schoolchildren (N = 25,273) using an anonymous questionnaire, children who had been bullied were asked to indicate how they felt about themselves afterwards (see Rigby 1997c). About half indicated that they 'felt much the same' and a small proportion (less than 7%), surprisingly, said they 'felt better' – perhaps feeling that they had successfully resisted or even 'turned the tables' on the bully. However, over 40 per cent of the students indicated that they 'felt worse about themselves'. This suggests that some children are more vulnerable than others – or possibly more ready to disclose their feelings. Among children who reported that they were bullied frequently (at least once a week), the percentage of those who felt worse about themselves increased to over 50 per cent among boys and over 60 per cent for girls. Far from adapting to the state of being continually victimised, it appears that those who endured most bullying were more likely to experience a fall in self-esteem.

There are also some indications from longitudinal studies that severe peer victimisation can have long-term effects on self-esteem. A study conducted in Scandinavia by Olweus (1992) focused on 15 men aged approximately 23 years who had been identified previously, through teacher ratings, peer nominations and peer reports, as being severely victimised at school during their adolescence. After applying appropriate statistical controls, Olweus found that compared with other subjects in the study the men who had been victimised at school had significantly lower scores on Rosenberg's (1986) scale of global self-esteem. This suggests that peer victimisation can have serious enduring effects.

We should also ask whether children who bully also experience low self-esteem. Some writers have thought so. It is sometimes argued that children bully because they have low self-esteem, and that one way of treating bullies is to encourage them to feel better about themselves. There is little empirical support for this view. O'Moore and Hillery(1991) have provided some evidence that suggests that bullies at school are more 'troublesome' (an aspect of low self-esteem) than others but failed to provide significant support for the view that overall they have lower self-esteem than non-bullies. The bulk of the evidence suggests that the self-esteem of bullies does not differ significantly from that of others (see Olweus 1993; Rigby 1997a).

Social adjustment of victims of bullying

A number of studies have shown that children who are repeatedly victimised at school, not surprisingly, have an aversion to the school environment. This is evidenced in various ways. Repeatedly victimised children report that they do not like school. At the age of 5 years, according to Kochenderfer and Ladd (1996), children nominated by their peers as being victimised by others are more likely to say that they dislike school. This association has also been reported in relation to older primary and secondary students in Australia (Rigby and Slee 1993a).

Some studies indicate that victimised students tend to avoid going to school. In their large-scale study of children's health in Western Australia, Zubrick *et al.* (1997) reported that victimised children were more likely to be absent from school. The figures for absences from school in Australia are higher for children who are frequently victimised. For example, some 19 per cent of boys and 25 per cent of girls who are bullied frequently (at least weekly) report having stayed at home because of bullying; for those who are bullied less frequently, the corresponding figures are 4 per cent and 12 per cent, that is considerably less (Rigby 1997c). This suggests that absenteeism increases as a function of the severity of being victimised by peers.

Some longitudinal studies throw further light on cause–effect relationships between social adjustment and peer victimisation. Kochenderfer and Ladd (1996) examined the relationship between peer victimisation and school maladjustment among 200 kindergarten children. For the most part these children were meeting and interacting with children they had not met before. On the basis of interviews with the children, they concluded that 20.5 per cent of them were being consistently targeted. Their measure of peer victimisation, repeated on two occasions separated by several months, was significantly correlated with: (i) being lonely at school; (ii) not liking school; and (iii) avoiding school. School avoidance was indicated by children's answers to a series of questions about them attending school such as: 'Do you ask your mom or dad to let you stay home from school?' Subsequent analyses led to the conclusion that 'victimised children tend to become more lonely and school avoidant after they are victimised by peers'. They add that 'whereas children's feelings of loneliness were more pronounced whilst victimisation was occurring, delayed effects were found for school avoidance' (1996, p.1305). There was 'no support for the counter-argument that school adjustment difficulties precede exposure to victimisation' (1996, p.1314).

A further report based upon results for the same sample of children as that described above (Ladd, Kochenderfer and Coleman 1997) examined the question of whether peer victimisation contributed uniquely to school maladjustment, that is, after taking into account effects attributable to other peer relation factors, namely numbers of friends, whether they had a reciprocal best friend and general peer acceptance. On the basis of multiple regression analysis in which all the peer relation variables were entered, it was concluded that peer victimisation among children attending kindergarten was uniquely and significantly associated with school avoidance both currently and predictively.

Longer-term effects on social adjustment have been suggested in several retrospective studies with adults. In a study of 206 American undergraduates aged 18 to 22 years, those reporting having been victimised at school (18 women and 8 men) were as adults significantly more lonely than others (Tritt and Duncan 1997). In a study of 276 adults (aged 15 to 66) in England who had stammering problems at school, nearly one half reported long-term effects, predominantly affecting personal relationships (Hugh-Jones and Smith 1999). This is an example of how a disability (stammering) can attract victimisation through ridicule and increase the likelihood of subsequent 'maladjustment'. In his retrospective study of American adults, Gilmartin (1987) suggested that interpersonal difficulties of males who are subjected to victimisation at school may take the form of disabling shyness in making relationships with the opposite sex.

There is some retrospective evidence that bullying can seriously affect the capacity of victims to form intimate and sexual relationships. In the USA Gilmartin (1987) asked adults to recall their relationships with their peers at school. He found that men who were severely victimised by their peers were more 'love shy', as he put it, than others, that is, they were much less successful in achieving satisfactory intimate relationships with members of the opposite sex. In Australia Dietz (1994) assessed the psychological well-being of both men and women who were victimised at school and likewise found that they had marked difficulties in forming close intimate relationships.

The view that bullying can have destructive consequences for the sexual life of people is strongly supported by the Australian poet and essayist Les Murray (1994). He describes this group as 'almost certainly bigger than the gay population and all the sad victims of literal rape and sexual abuse put together'. They are, he writes, 'folk for whom the sexual revolution remains a chimera, the ones whose sexual morale was destroyed early by scorn, by childhood trauma, by fashion, by lack or defection of allies, by image'. Not all of them are unattractive, but all of them, he says, live and act in the belief that they are. They are described variously as 'wallflowers, ugly, wimps, unstylish, drips, nerds, pathetic, fat, frigid, creepy...'.

According to Murray, this continual denigration should be seen as a crime because it often results in the sexual destruction of a person. It begins at school and is usually called bullying or harassment. The psychological scarring, he observes, may persist for a lifetime. But it is not only the taunting and the jeering that are devastating. It is also, he argues, the 'abandonment that goes with them, the moral cowardice of fellow kids who don't jeer themselves but don't speak out either, or afford the tormented one support for fear of becoming victims themselves'. He adds that 'if the jeering or the avoidance come from the opposite sex, the results are apt to be severe and lasting'.

The social adjustment of bullies

Do bullies also suffer from being poorly adjusted? When bullies are conceptualised as 'deviants' this seems to be so. But adjustment may be adequate within the group with whom they habitually associate. And bullies often have a supportive peer group of those who admire them. The question is further complicated by the fact that some bullies operate in groups or with the support of groups whilst others engage in bullying as isolated individuals. So far, studies have not distinguished, as they should, between different kinds of bullies. Perhaps it is the bully who is a 'loner', who is socially maladjusted.

There are results from research indicating that children who bully appear not to like school as much as others do (Rigby and Slee 1993a) and are absent from school more often than most children. Should we accept such results as signs of maladjustment? Probably not. What may be a reasonable index of maladjustment for one group may not be so for another. It may be, for instance, that their more extraverted and adventurous lifestyle associated with being a bully leads many school bullies to feel bored with school and to seek distractions outside the school. A further question is whether engaging in bullying has consequences for the future adjustment of children. It has been claimed that confirmed and serious bullies at school have a much greater chance than others to come before the courts as young adults on charges of delinquency (Olweus 1993). In the long term, at least, it would appear that maladjustment – according to community standards – may result from habituation to bullying that some children do not grow out of.

Psychological distress

One of the more commonly reported emotional reactions to peer victimisation is chronic anxiety. In an early study in Sweden of so-called 'whipping boys', that is boys who were frequently targeted by aggressive peers, Olweus (1978) reported that such children were significantly more anxious and insecure than others. Subsequently O'Moore and Hillery (1991) and Salmon, Jones and Smith (1998) reported that feelings of anxiety characterised peer-victimised children in Ireland and England respectively. In a large scale study (N = 2692) of English primary school children (aged 7 to 10 years), Williams et al. (1996) noted that 'victimised children were significantly more likely to report "not sleeping well" and also "bed wetting"'. Fear of bullying was reported by 25 per cent of students in a study of 11,535 students aged 13 to 15 attending schools in England and Wales (Francis and Jones 1994). Among English secondary students (N = 703), Sharp (1995) found that victimised children tended to report feeling irritable, nervous and panicky after episodes of bullying. Many of them (32%) said that they had had recurring memories of bullying incidents; some 29 per cent said that they had subsequently found it hard to concentrate.

Depressive reactions on the part of victimised children have been reported in several studies. In Australia, Slee (1995) reported that primary school students (mean age ten years) identified by peers as frequent victims were more likely than others to manifest symptoms of clinical depression. Similar conclusions were drawn in studies of peer victimisation among primary schoolchildren in England (Callaghan and Joseph 1995; Neary and Joseph 1994; and Williams et al. 1996, and in Finland by Kumpulainen et al. (1998). Research with older students has also yielded similar results. In an early study of 110 Finnish schoolchildren aged 14 to 16, Bjorqvist et al. (1982) reported that a sample of 18 students identified by peers as frequently victimised were significantly more depressed than others. More recently, Kaltialo-Heino et al. (1999) have reported results from a large study (N = 16,410) of Finnish adolescent schoolchildren which confirmed this finding.

Students who are frequently victimised may have mixed emotions and show a variety of symptoms of distress. For example, in a nationwide survey in England involving 6282 primary and secondary school students, Borg (1998) reported

that self-declared victims commonly experienced emotions of anger, vengeful-
ness and self-pity, with the latter appearing as more common among girls.

In Australia a programme of research undertaken and reported in detail by
Rigby (1998c) into the possible effects of peer victimisation has made use of a
multi-dimensional measure of mental unwellness, the General Health Questionnaire or GHQ, devised by Goldberg and Williams (1991). This measure contains
sub-scales assessing the prevalence of (i) somatic symptoms, e.g. 'felt run down
and out of sorts'; (ii) anxiety, e.g. 'felt constantly under strain'; (iii) social dysfunction, e.g. 'felt (un)able to enjoy your normal day-to-day activities'; and (iv) depression, e.g. 'felt that life was entirely hopeless'. Results from an analysis of 713
students aged 13 to 16 years who completed the GHQ indicated that children
who are repeatedly victimised at school (at least once a week) were significantly
more likely than others to have high scores on each of the four aspects of mental
ill health as well as on the total GHQ scale. Mean scores on the GHQ and
sub-scales are given for boys and for girls in Figures 5.3 and 5.4, according to
victim status and gender.

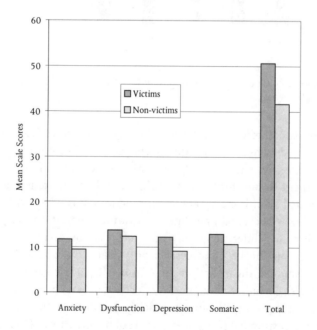

*Figure 5.3 Mean scores on the General Health Questionnaire and sub-scales for Australian
adolescent boys*

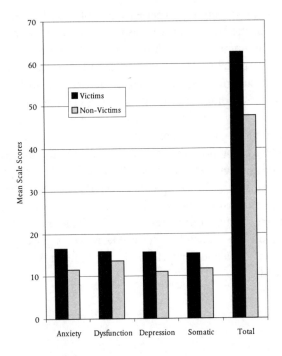

Figure 5.4 Mean scores on the General Health Questionnaire and sub-scales for Australian adolescent girls

For every comparison indicated for boys and for girls in Figures 5.3 and 5.4 the students categorised as victims (reporting having been bullied during the year of testing at least weekly) showed a significantly higher level of psychological distress than others. Results for two-way ANOVA with victim status and gender as factors indicated significant differences for victim status with girls generally having higher levels of mental unwellness. Of further interest was a significant interaction effect for gender suggesting that peer victimisation is related more strongly to the mental health of adolescent girls than is the case with boys.

In a further study of the mental health of Australian adolescents Rigby, Slee and Martin (1999), examined whether the 'effects' of peer victimisation could be explained as being due to inadequate parenting. Schoolchildren completed the Parental Bonding Instrument (PBI) of Parker, Tupling and Brown (1979) assessing perceived parental care and perceived parental over-control, as well as measures of peer victimisation and the GHQ. It was found that parenting factors and peer victimisation each independently accounted for a significant amount of variance in adolescent mental health. A further study addressed the question of whether the apparent effects of peer victimisation could be due to low levels of social support. Results indicated that low social support does indeed contribute significantly to poor mental health, but, again, does so independently of peer victimisation (Rigby 2000).

Whether psychological distress is a consequence or cause (or both) of peer victimisation has received relatively little attention. But a few studies have suggested that being bullied is a precursor to psychological distress. Rigby (1998c) reported that a relatively high proportion of students who had been frequently victimised indicated that they had felt either angry (32%) or sad (37%) as a result of being bullied at school. A substantial proportion (33% of boys and 55% of girls) of those frequently victimised expressed the view that their general health had deteriorated as a result of how they had been treated by other students. Gender differences in reactions to bullying were particularly marked, with girls more likely to report feeling sad rather than angry and to have been affected more by peer victimisation. Student judgements certainly suggest that negative health effects of being bullied are not uncommon.

Evidence from longitudinal studies provides supportive evidence that being bullied tends to increase the likelihood of psychological distress. A longitudinal study discussed earlier (see Olweus 1993) focused upon the mental health of adults who had been victimised at school. Olweus' questionnaire included a reliable measure of depression (the Beck Inventory). Through multiple regression analyses, he was able to show a significant relationship between victim/non-victim status of his subjects as adolescents and elevated scores on the depression measure some six years later. He concluded that an intervening variable, feelings of maladjustment and inadequacy, mediated the effect of peer victimisation on level of depression.

A further longitudinal study on the relationship between peer victimisation and psychological distress among 78 Australian adolescents examined changes in peer victimisation and health indices over a three-year period among Australian students attending a secondary school (Rigby 1998a, 1999). A shortened version of the GHQ was used in pre- and post-test administrations of the questionnaire. This included GHQ sub-scale measures of somatic symptoms, anxiety and poor coping. Being victimised frequently as a student during the first two years of attending secondary school was predictive of experiencing relatively high levels of psychological distress as a student three years later at the same school. Again, a stronger effect on the health of girls was evident.

Are bullies also more likely to be psychologically distressed than others? Results from a study of the psychiatric health of self-reported bullies suggests that they too are more troubled than others. This is particularly true of male bullies aged between 13 and 16 years. On each of the four indices of psychiatric ill health on the GHQ – somatic disorder, anxiety, poor coping and depression – the degree to which Australian male students (n = 338) engaged in bullying others corre-lated significantly with mental ill health scores. For female students (n = 361) attending the same schools and in the same age group the correlations were notably lower, yet still statistically significant on each of the indices except coping. Hence there is reason to believe that adolescents who frequently engage in bullying others tend to be somewhat distressed.

Suicidal tendencies

One extreme consequence of peer victimisation that has been suggested is suicide. Several cases of suicide by schoolchildren have been attributed to the experience of repeated victimisation (see Morita *et al.* 1999; Olweus 1993). However, because suicidal behaviour is commonly determined by multiple factors it is difficult to validate particular claims, even when suicide notes point to peer victimisation as the cause (Morita *et al.* 1999). Research into suicidal tenden-cies is commonly carried out by assessing the frequency with which people think of killing themselves. This varies widely, with some people rarely or never having suicidal thoughts, and others continually dwelling on taking their own lives. Whilst evidence of such thinking, often called suicidal ideation, cannot be regarded as being equivalent to actually attempting suicide, thinking about suicide is a common precursor to such action.

The relationship between peer victimisation and suicidal ideation was examined with two samples of adolescent schoolchildren (n = 1103 and n = 849) attending South Australian secondary schools (Rigby 1998d; Rigby and Slee 1999a). Assessment of peer victimisation employed both self-reports and peer ratings. As a measure of suicidal ideation, four items from the GHQ were used. For example: 'Over the last few weeks the idea of taking my own life kept continually coming to my mind.' Results indicated that frequently victimised students of either gender, whether identified by self-reports or by peer ratings, were significantly more likely than others to think of taking their own lives.

In a Finnish study Kaltialo-Heino *et al.* (1999) also examined the relationship between peer victimisation and suicidal ideation. Suicidal ideation was indicated if a student endorsed either of two items: 'I have definite plans of committing suicide' and 'I would kill myself if I had the chance'. This study showed that suicidal ideation was significantly related to peer victimisation after controlling for level of depression and perceived social support. We do not, as yet, have answers to the important question of whether suicidal ideation precedes or follows being bullied at schools. The existence of suicide notes and cases of suicide that followed being repeatedly bullied certainly strongly suggests that being bullied can induce thinking about suicide.

Bullies too have higher than average tendencies to think of killing them-selves. In conducting the study of bullying and suicidal thinking (described above) Rigby and Slee (1999a) also identified children who, according to their peers and according to self-reports, repeatedly engaged in bullying others. Levels of suicidal ideation were significantly higher than average for these students.

Physical ill-health symptoms

Relatively few studies have been concerned with physical aspects of health, yet there are suggestions from some studies that symptoms of poor physical health may be reliably associated with severe peer victimisation. In their study of peer victimisation among primary school children, Williams et al. (1996) included several questions designed to discover whether the children had frequently (more than once a week) experienced headaches and 'tummy aches'. They reported that peer-victimised children (those who reported having been bullied at school) were more than twice as likely to say they had, compared with non-victimised children. In a study of secondary students in Australia, Forero et al. (1999) included questions as to whether respondents had experienced the following health symptoms: headache, stomach ache, backache, feeling low, irritable or bad tempered, feeling nervous, difficulties in getting to sleep and feeling dizzy, and if so, how frequently. In terms of the four aspects of health outlined in this chapter, some of the items might be categorised as relating to psychological well-being; others to psychological distress; others more clearly to physical symptoms. Somewhat surprisingly in view of results from previous studies, 'bullied students', defined as those who reported that they had been bullied but had not bullied others, did not differ in so-called psychosomatic symptoms from a comparison group of students who were uninvolved in bullying. On the other hand, students who were bullied and bullied others did show significantly high levels of physical complaints, suggesting that bully/victims were particularly at risk of poor health.

In another Australian study with a similar sample of students, Rigby (2000) made use of a measure of physical complaints which overlapped in content with that of Forero et al. (1999). Students were also presented with a list of 21 common ill-health symptoms or physical complaints and asked to indicate how often during the year they had experienced them. The list was devised with the assistance of nurse educators from the School of Nursing at the University of South Australia who had conducted routine health assessments with adolescent students in South Australian schools. The items were as follows: colds, ear infections, hay fever, injury from accidents, headaches, rashes, sore throats, anorexia or bulimia, dizziness, sinus problems, asthma, a bad cough, stomach ache, mouth sores, diarrhoea, difficulty in seeing, fainting, 'thumping' in the chest, vomiting, wheezing. Students were asked to respond to each one by saying how often they had experienced it during the school year: 'not at all', 'a bit' or 'a lot'. The resultant Physical Complaints Scale (PCS) was found to be internally consistent for both boys and girls as reflected by alpha coefficients of .84 and .74 respectively. Children who reported having been frequently victimised (at least once a week over the school year) were significantly more likely to report a high frequency of physical complaints. The largest differences between victims and others were in relation to headaches, mouth sores and 'thumping' in the chest: for each of these, differences were significant at the .001 level. Figure 5.5 shows overall differences on the measures of physical health for victims and non-victims (see Rigby 1998c for further details).

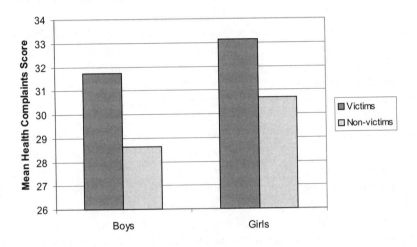

Figure 5.5 Mean scores on the Physical Complaints Scale for Australian adolescent schoolchildren

Two Australian studies have provided results that suggest that bullying can lead to a deterioration in the physical health of children. One was a simple study (Rigby 1997a) in which children were asked to say how they had felt after being bullied. Here are some statements children made:

- Not feeling well, not wanting to eat or do anything.
- Nervousness, worrying, loss of sleep, sick and scared feeling in the stomach.
- I've felt dizzy like I was going to faint or something.
- Getting very depressed, staying home, vomiting, attempting suicide.
- I just hated school and everything in it so bad that the thought of coming here made me sick and vomit.
- Headaches, hay fever, vomiting.

- Can't sleep, tiredness.

- Stomach aches, feeling sick every morning about going to school because of bullying.

- Stressed out and upset.

- Tense, headaches, nausea, all that crap. Bullying sucks, that's all there is to it.

We may notice that a lot of the symptoms described above involve physical ill-health conditions. However, qualitative studies of this kind need to be supplemented by quantitative, longitudinal studies. One such study made use of the Physical Complaints Scale (PCS) described above, administered on two occasions (1994 and 1997) to secondary school children in a study reported in Rigby (1998b, 1999). The results for correlations between peer victimisation in 1994 and the Physical Complaints Scale in 1997 were significant for both boys and girls. Analyses controlling for differences between levels of health in 1994 among the students in the study enabled one to conclude that having been victimised by peers was the likely cause of the relatively poor physical health of the victimised students three years later.

Finally, again we should ask whether bullies are generally physically less well than others. What evidence exists – and it is currently sparse – suggests that they do generally report having more symptoms of poor health than most students. For example, boy bullies were more likely to report frequent vomiting and girl bullies more frequent mouth sores (Rigby 1998c).

Health and victimisation in the workplace

The link between victimisation and health is in some respects harder to establish in the workplace than in schools. Children in schools often constitute a captive audience. Typically they dutifully complete questionnaires and ensure a representative sample. Longitudinal studies to establish cause and effect are usually easier to conduct as respondents can usually be kept track of during their years of compulsory education. Not surprisingly, detailed empirical studies of the relationship between victimisation and health are more readily available for school populations. However, there has been of late an increase in studies of the connection between bullying in the workplace and the health of workers.

A good example is a study of workplace bullying in a National Health Service community trust in the United Kingdom (Quine 1999). The 1100 respondents who answered a questionnaire consisted of a wide cross-section of employees, comprising nurses, therapists, administrative staff, doctors, psychologists, other professionals, residential care workers and ancilliary staff. The response rate of 70 per cent was unusually high for workplace studies. A substantial proportion of respondents (38%) reported that they had experienced bullying more than once over the last five years. As in school studies reported earlier, there was strong evidence that those identified as 'victims' were less psychologically well than others. They showed significantly higher levels of anxiety and depression. Many more of those victimised appeared to be alienated from their environment and showed a greater propensity to leave. Also, as in school studies (see Rigby 2000), having good social support significantly lessened the stressfulness of the victimisation.

One area that appears to have gained more attention in workplace bullying studies than in school studies focuses on the occurrence among victimised individuals of post-traumatic stress disorder or PTSD. This severe and sometimes incapacitating condition is characterised by the experience of frequent and disturbing flashbacks of traumatising events, a tendency to avoid stimuli associated with the traumata and a persistent feeling of irritability sustained for long periods of time. According to Leymann and Gustafsson (1996) victims of workplace bullying being treated in a Swedish rehabilitation clinic were often given the diagnosis of PTSD. It has been claimed that their characters had undergone drastic changes as a result of severe victimisation.

Although the social environments of children at school and employees at work have much in common, especially in being places where people have to spend time with others who may be inclined to dominate or bully them, workplaces are typically organised in an hierarchical manner that has little or no counterpart among children in school. True, there are status differences among schoolchildren, for example some may have positions of leadership conferred upon them by school authorities; others may be looked up to for their sporting or (more rarely) scholastic achievements. By contrast, workplaces are typically structured so that there is a line of command, with those in the upper echelons having the power to direct those lower down, power that can be and inevitably is sometimes abused, even systematically. In short, top-down bullying among people at work is much more likely than among students at school. This being so, it is not unreasonable to look at the health status of people at different levels in the work hierarchy – after making appropriate controls.

Examination of differences that might be attributed to status in organisations may be most readily carried out in the British Civil Service, where employees are divided into 13 grades in descending order of status from permanent secretary to clerical assistants, messengers and porters. In a study of 12,000 civil servants, Marmot et al. (1991, 1997) reported a steady rise in mortality and sickness absence the lower the status. Statistical controls were, however, necessary in order to draw conclusions. Marmot chose to control for the following known health-risk factors: high cholesterol, smoking, little or no exercise and inadequate diet – and found that together they accounted for only one third of the mortality, the rest being attributed at least in part to work experience. A further finding suggested that high workload was not associated with higher sickness absence. The crucial factor was perceived control over one's work tasks. Where one feels over-directed, over-controlled – as occurs when an employee is pressured from above – one's health may be undermined. To what extent such 'pressure' constitutes bullying, however, requires further analysis.

The question of whether poor health is a cause or consequence of bullying in the workplace has not, as yet, been addressed as in school studies, using longitudinal research designs. However, a useful distinction has been made between different kinds of victims for whom different health outcomes appear likely. Zapf (1999) has distinguished between the kind of victims who appear to be highly vulnerable to victimisation at work and those who do not. The former, he claims, have a pre-existing condition of anxiety and depression. They are also non-assertive, seek to avoid conflict, are shy and make little effort to integrate in the work group. By contrast, there are others who may be victimised who are stable, assertive and socially skilled. These people do not show elevated levels of anxiety and depression after being bullied. They would thus appear to be resilient – or alternatively inclined to deny that they have emotional problems. However, like the other kind of victim they are more likely than non-victims to experience psychosomatic problems. Perhaps the existence of psychosomatic problems provides a more reliable indicator of stress induced by repeated victimisation.

Zapf (1999) also suggests that the effects of victimisation on a person's health may in part be due to the kinds of attributions he or she makes regarding the cause of being bullied. Most workers blame hostile persons; a minority blame the 'social system'. It is this latter group who do not personalise the victimisation process that suffer the least anxiety, depression and negative affect, but they do experience relatively high levels of psychosomatic conditions. This work by Zapf is particularly interesting because it warns us against considering victims as a homogeneous group reacting in the same way to being bullied. Thus far the distinctions suggested by Zapf have not been made in studying victimisation among schoolchildren.

Assessing the research on peer victimisation and health

We are now in a position to give some answers to the questions raised at the beginning of this chapter.

(1)   The view that there is no relationship between being victimised and health status is simply untenable. Both in schools and among adults in the workplace relatively poor health is characteristic of people who

tend to be victimised by others. In schools at least the health of children who are identified as bullies also tends to be below average.

(2)   There is no evidence that being bullied has any positive health consequences. Whether successfully bullying others has positive effects on one's self-esteem seems unlikely in view of the fact that bullies do not generally have higher self-esteem than average. (The question of whether their self-esteem would be lower than average if they did not bully has never been investigated.)

(3)   Whether being continually bullied is stressful, undermines one's sense of well-being and impairs one's physical health with potentially enduring effects is the most difficult question to answer. However, the growing number of studies providing retrospective reports and (more importantly) using longitudinal research designs strongly support the view that, among children at least, victimisation at school contributes to ill health.

We still need further research. For example, it would be useful to know to what extent family background and parenting are responsible for changes in both the health of children and their proneness to be victimised or their readiness to bully others. We still have the thorny problem of taking into account genetic predispositions that affect both health and interpersonal behaviour. Definitive answers to the questions we are raising may well have to involve the behavioural geneticists before everybody is convinced that bullying can make you ill.

Especially we need good longitudinal studies in the workplace to establish that victimisation at work makes a significant contribution to poor health. There are good theoretical reasons for expecting such a causal relationship, as we shall see in the next section, but for those who are sceptical, as many are, about the claims that bullying can make you ill, such studies are needed.

To increase our understanding, we need to know more about the kinds of bullying that are more likely to be associated with bad health outcomes. It may turn out to be the case that relational or social bullying is not only the most hurtful (as we have seen among children) but also the most devastating to one's health. We need to know in more detail the conditions under which bullying may have the most effect on health; for example, what kinds of attributions made by victims increase or decrease vulnerability to stressors. Finally, there is considerable scope for exploring the health condition of bullies, a task begun in schools but not, as yet, undertaken in workplaces. The finding in schools that both bullies and victims tend to be highly depressed people suggests that those who are both bullies and victims are probably most at risk of serious unwellness.

Why peer victimisation induces poor health

To the satisfaction of most, if not all, who are prepared to look at the evidence for a connection between peer victimisation and poor health, it seems extremely likely that poor mental and physical health can be induced by constant bullying and harassment. There are good theoretical reasons why we should expect such a causal connection, based on the understanding of the effects of stress.

The plausibility of a connection between peer victimisation and deteriorating health becomes more evident when we consider the stressful nature of peer victimisation. A useful transactional model of stress, proposed by Cox (1995), conceives stress as arising when a person experiences a significant imbalance between the demands being made upon him or her and his or her perceived ability to cope. In this formulation, emphasis is placed in part on the person's appraisal of the situation and his or her resources, and partly upon feedback received when there is an attempt to cope.

Applied to the typical situation in which a person is experiencing peer victimisation, some or all of the following features are likely to be present:

(1)   The demands being made are seen as being in excess of the person's capacity to cope. This may be evident from an immediate appraisal when the person is first targeted by an aggressor or only evident later when the person makes ineffective responses to the situation.

- ○   The timing of attacks is unpredictable and therefore difficult to prepare for. There is considerable research evidence showing that uncontrollable events are more stressful than controllable ones.

- ○   The nature of the bullying is often ambiguous. The bully may deliberately (and effectively) confuse the victim by appearing nice one moment and nasty the next. We know that ambiguous events are often perceived as more stressful than clear-cut events.

- ○   The failure to cope is humiliating for the person who feels lowered in the eyes of other people – and feels more vulnerable to attack.

We may note here that feelings of humiliation, frequently experienced by children who are bullied, may have a direct connection with suicidal thinking. Cynthia Pfeffer (1990), an eminent authority on suicide, put it this way:

> Probably one of the most critical factors in precipitating suicidal ideation arising from interpersonal problems is humiliation – feelings of disgrace and public disparagement may shatter a youngster's healthy sense of narcissism and sense of identity, and loss of a basic sense of one's worthwhileness is a powerful force to increase thoughts of self-annihilation. (p.81)

(2)   The victimised person is in a situation in which (i) escape is difficult or impossible, and (ii) different strategies are tried and found wanting, for example, seeking help, avoiding confrontations or placating the aggressor(s).

(3)   The person may become isolated and, from time to time, suffer the stress of 'under demand' when deprived of the opportunity to interact with others.

(4)   The situation is increasingly seen as uncontrollable by the victim and the victimisation appears likely to continue indefinitely.

These are conditions similar to those suggested by Perrez and Reicherts (1992) as determinants of individual stress reactions. It is now widely accepted that the experience of such stress can alter a person's emotional state, typically producing anxiety and depression, and may also produce changes in physiological function (Cox 1995). In some individuals this may lead to a lowered immunity to infection and the reporting of a range of health complaints (Vaernes *et al.* 1991).

A complementary perspective on the stressful effects of very severe peer victimisation has been suggested by Einarsen (1999). He draws upon ideas on trauma and traumatic events proposed by Janoff-Bullmann (1992), who claims that our most fundamental assumptions are that the world is benevolent and meaningful and the self is worthy. When these assumptions are severely challenged, as typically occurs when people are hounded and harassed for no evident reason and nobody is supportive towards them, psychological collapse may well follow. There is a sense of being unable to control events and a spiralling-down of self-esteem. Whatever one does may cease to matter. This view would account for profound unhappiness, depression and suicidal thinking of individuals who have been severely bullied without the semblance of support from others on whom they felt they could rely.

Why bullies might also suffer

The low physical health of bullies is more difficult to explain, especially among those who see themselves as successful and also popular with others. It may be that some bullies at least are troubled by the effects their bullying produces on their victims. It is misleading to think of all bullies as entirely lacking in empathy or without occasional feelings of shame. We know from the work of Pikas (1989) that in one-to-one situations children who have bullied others can be 'reached' and a 'change of heart' is sometimes possible by a sincere sharing of concern for the victim. But another explanation is perhaps more plausible. The work on the relationship between home background and tendencies to bully at school clearly shows that dysfunctional families and cold, over-controlling parents tend to rear children who bully others. The poor health of children who bully – especially perhaps tendencies towards depression and suicidal thinking – may derive from the kind of parenting and home life that makes children both intensely miserable and determined to take it out on others. This, it must be stressed, is not to argue that children who bully are not individually responsible for their actions, but rather to suggest that the poor health of children who bully may often derive from a history of negative experiences at home.

Conclusion

To those who have taken a serious and concerned interest in bullying and its effects on children, what has been written in this chapter may seem obvious and indeed unnecessary. 'People suffer when they are bullied' may strike them as a thundering platitude. Yet, odd though it may seem, it has scarcely dawned upon many health professionals that bullying is a major mental health issue. Many cling to the hallowed ground of Freud and Bowlby – it's parenting, just parenting that is the trouble.

In Australia, as in many parts of the world, mental health issues relating to young people focus almost exclusively on the family and what parents do or fail to do. Last year (2000) I received a very useful publication from the Australian Early Intervention Network for Mental Health in Young People. It contains details of no less than 195 programmes throughout Australia, directed towards promoting better mental health among young people. Almost entirely it focuses upon parenting. Here is a quotation that appears repeatedly in justification of particular programmes:

> There is good evidence that solid, consistent caring, non-abusive parenting serves to build resilience – and poor parenting is linked to adverse mental health outcomes, particularly where early abuse and neglect has occurred. (p.34)

We should add that there is now equally good evidence that abuse at the hands of peers is linked to adverse mental health outcomes, particularly where bullying, physically and psychologically, and exclusion has repeatedly occurred. This perspective currently appears to be taken by only a small proportion of health workers.

Chapter 6

What bullies and victims are like

Give them power and someone or something weaker than themselves. That seems to be enough to make them torment that someone or something. Have psychiatrists ever investigated this? Have they tried to find out why something weak and vulnerable inspires compassion in some people and cruelty in others?

– Ruth Rendell (1998, pp.282–283)

Physical characteristics

Let us start with the obvious. Bullies are big hulking brutes and victims are weedy little guys. Too crude? Well, there is a bit of truth in this. Olweus (1973, 1978), who went to some pains to demonstrate this in studies conducted among boys in Stockholm, was among the first to point out the relevance of sheer size and strength.

Recently the question was raised: are short pupils at risk of being bullied more than others? The *British Medical Journal* (Voss and Mulligan 2000) published the answer following a study of 92 short, normal adolescents (shorter than 97% of people in their age group) and others (the controls) who were taller. An anonymous self-report measure of peer victimisation was used. Significantly more short pupils reported being bullied, regardless of sex, and also after controlling for social class. The short children also reported being upset more by being bullied. The most obvious explanation for the differences is that the shorter children are weaker and therefore more vulnerable. Unfortunately, the researchers did not distinguish between different forms of bullying to which students are sometimes subjected. Were short children excluded more, one may wonder? The report indicates that they had as many good friends as controls, but more of them evidently spent more time alone at recess. It seems possible from this study that shortness may indeed be a factor that leads to children being discriminated against and even bullied indirectly.

It is often suggested that children who look or sound different are more often bullied, for example, children who have red hair or spectacles; or who are skinny or obese; or children with an unusual accent. Olweus has examined this possibility and has concluded that such physical differences do not significantly increase the risk of being bullied. However, this possibility should not be dismissed too lightly. As we shall see later in the discussion of disability in Chapter 8 there is evidence that children who are disabled are bullied more than most, especially if their disability is visible and extreme. Further, some differences, for example in colour or accent, may be taken as indicators of race or social class, and in some social environments lead to being discriminated against and bullied by mainstream children.

Mental characteristics

Personality in general

It is common to attribute bullying behaviour to an individual's personality, where personality may be defined along the following lines: 'The pattern of characteristic thought, feelings and behaviours that persist over time and situations and distinguish one person from another' (Phares 1988). This formulation includes cognitive, affective and behavioural aspects of a person. It assumes that each of these is relatively stable during the lifespan and evident across a range of different situations. This does not mean that people do not sometimes have changes in mood, think differently or behave inconsistently. Rather that these variations are seen as relatively minor. It does not mean that situations exercise no control over behaviour, but such control is limited. Many have believed that bullying can be understood in the light of analyses of personality.

Nevertheless, some do not. In their examination of the responses of schools to bullying in Australia, Soutter and McKenzie (2000) are emphatic. The bully and the victim are not types of person, they maintain. Bullying behaviour, the authors go on to explain, is a consequence of a kind of social ethos in which behaviour occurs rather than being due to a personality type. It is sometimes pointed out that people behave quite differently in different situations. A child, for instance, may sometimes be an extravert at home and an introvert at school. Yet most observers do observe a degree of consistency – by no means perfect – in the behaviour of people across situations. Moreover, if the social ethos were the only determinant of behaviour it would be hard to understand why people exposed to the same social pressure behave in such widely different ways. It seems that the attention paid to 'personality' is an attempt to provide explanations for such diversity. Some refuse to recognise the influence of personality, partly, I suspect, because of a laudable reluctance to apply blame. In a recent Internet publication, 'Bullying in the Fire Service', we read: 'It is not helpful to try to draw up a stereotype of a bully or a bullied person.' Yet the very same publication points out that certain personality characteristics of the bully such as aggressiveness, sarcasm, anger and maliciousness may 'come to the fore in certain work circumstances'. Still others attribute a great deal of importance to personality.

Not surprisingly descriptions of the personality – or perhaps more accurately the character – of bullies tend to be highly negative and emotionally charged. Here, for example, is a list of terms for describing bullies proposed by Tim Field (1999):

> Vile, vicious, devious, glib, shallow, superficial, slippery, slimy, ingratiating, fawning, toadying, obsequious, sycophantic, untrustworthy, evasive, narcissistic, petty, greedy, fraudulent, arrogant, mean-spirited, selfish, insensitive, cunning, scheming, deluded, unbelievably energetic, and demonic.

Sometimes bullies are presented as vicious creatures, as in a popular book advising educators on how to bully-proof their school (Garrity *et al.* 1997). Figure 6.1 is a representation of the bully that appears on numerous pages of their book.

Figure 6.1 The bullydog

The bullydog, you may note, has a ribbon in his hair, suggesting that though he may look vicious, in reality he is really rather silly, even 'girlish'.

Another characterisation of a bully is given below. It – and several of its friends – appeared in an article I wrote for a periodical on defining the bully, swimming decoratively in and around the text. The title, 'Sharks of many shapes and colours', was not my idea, nor were the sharks. But now that they are there, they do illustrate the way people, perhaps especially editors, would like us to see the bully, that is as a sub-human, dangerous, marauding menace.

Figure 6.2 The bullyshark

It is customary to consider aspects of personality under the headings of cognitive, affective and behavioural. Let us begin with how it is thought bullies think.

Cognitive aspects of the bully's personality

A popular view of how the bully thinks is to be found in Tim Field's description of the so-called 'serial bully' whom he sees as responsible for most, though not necessarily all, bullying. It should be said that he also recognises the importance of situational factors, especially 'the recent frenzy of downsizing and reorganisation' in the workplace. But essentially he sees the problem as lying with the personality of the bully who exploits such a situation.

Field sees the thought processes of bullies as being in many ways inferior to others. Characteristically, the bully:

- lacks understanding of what is being said
- has poor judgement; cannot think ahead

- has a selective memory; perhaps chooses to remember selectively
- is paranoid
- lacks insight
- is deeply prejudiced
- appears intelligent but actually performs poorly
- holds grudges after minor slights
- is uncreative
- has a compulsive need to control others
- is obsessed with cleanliness
- is rule bound
- can't learn from experience.

In some respects this view is consistent with the social skills model elaborated by Crick and Dodge (1994). They saw aggression as resulting from social information processing biases or deficits at one or more of the following points in a five-stage process of assessing and responding to social situations: social perception, interpretation of social cues, goal selection, response strategy generation and response decisions. Broadly, an aggressive person is socially inadequate because he or she can't think properly.

It is important to see that the research suggesting that very aggressive people are generally cognitively inferior or impaired has rarely focused on the bully per se. We need to recall that although bullies are aggressive by nature, they are people who seek to take advantage of less powerful people in situations in which they can be dominant: in short, they are aggressive people who discriminate. They also engage in bullying in different ways, some physically, some verbally and some through social manipulation. It may be that generalisations about the personalities of bullies may apply to one type but not another.

The research on the cognitive capacities of bullies is relatively meagre and controversial. Some research has suggested that some bullies may be more socially intelligent than people in general. Kaukainen *et al.* (1999) in Finland have claimed that among children, those nominated as being socially intelligent by their peers are more likely than others to engage in indirect or relational kinds of bullying. This is certainly plausible. In order to manipulate others effectively one needs to be both perceptive and subtle. One needs to understand the dynamics of social situations, to be able to read the not-so-obvious social cues, and to have the social skills to systematically denigrate and isolate people one doesn't like.

Research conducted in England has suggested that schoolchildren who guess what people are really thinking despite seemingly contrary information are more, not less, likely to bully others (Sutton 1998; Sutton, Smith and Swettenham 1999a). They have, according to the authors, a superior 'theory of mind'. Put crudely, they can read minds rather better than others. One can see how such a capacity might be an advantage to someone who wants to engage in mental torture, as evidently some bullies do. Measuring theory of mind is obviously fraught with difficulty. Here is the kind of problem that it is claimed primary school bullies are more likely than others to get right.

> During the war, the Red army capture a member of the Blue army. They want him to tell them where his army's tanks are; they know they are either by the sea or in the mountains. They know that the prisioner will not want to tell them, he will want to save his army, and so he will certainly lie to them. They know that the prisoner will not want to tell them. The prisoner is very brave and very clever, he will not let them find his tanks. The tanks are really in the mountains. Now when the Red side asks him where his tanks are, he says, 'They are in the mountains.'

Is it true what the prisoner said? Yes, says the bully. Where will the other army look for his tanks? By the sea, says the smart bully. Sutton (1998) concluded: 'These results support the view that bullies may not be the social inadequates they have been portrayed as; they may in fact possess a theory of mind that is superior to their followers and their victims' (p.114).

Such research is apt to be somewhat infuriating because it suggests that bullies are in a sense superior. Sutton's report seems to have raised the hackles of some American researchers (Crick and Dodge 1999). It needed to be pointed out that socially undesirable need not be incompetent (Sutton, Smith and Swettenham 1999b).

However, when we look at Sutton's research in more detail we see that it was those children who bullied more often than others verbally that scored highest on the theory-of-mind stories. There were non-significant correlations for physical and indirect bullying. So it was the children who teased, ridiculed and called others names a good deal who were the 'smartest'. Could it be that whether a bully is cognitively smart depends on the kind of bullying he or she engages in?

Sutton (1998) recognised that more than one study was needed to upset orthodoxy. He went on to suggest that rather than use a test made up of stories, which might favour the more verbal – including verbal bullies – a visual test might be preferable, such as the 'reading the mind in the eyes test' proposed by Baron-Cohen et al. (1999). A student in Australia, Robyn Farley, took up this challenge in undertaking an Honours thesis in 1999.

The test in question devised by Baron-Cohen *et al.* – called 'the eyes task' – is a curious one. It consists of 28 photographs of the eyes of men and women of various ages. Around each photograph are four words describing mind states such as relaxed, upset, surprised and excited. The photographs are presented briefly through a projector for six seconds. The respondent is asked to say in each case which of the four mental states is depicted.

Try this one:

happy　　　　　**thinking about something**

excited　　　　　　　　　　　**kind**

Figure 6.3 The eyes task

The correct answer is 'thinking about something'. At least this is the answer about which there was a very high consensus among viewers – with no limitations on how long they can look at it. Some further validity has been indicated for this test in findings that autistic children (known to be not very good at reading facial cues) do poorly on the test.

Well, contrary to Sutton's expectations, the bullies did not do well! In fact, those who were assessed as more inclined than others to bully physically got significantly lower scores than others. Support for bully-is-an-oaf theory. For measures of verbal and indirect forms of bullying the eyes task produced no significant correlations. A nice refinement in this experiment was the inclusion of a word knowledge test which enabled the researcher to dismiss any objections that the results were due to differences in literacy. Of interest, too, is the finding that on none of the measures did bullies prove to be less literate than others. (There is no support here for the idea that bullies are handicapped though inferior literacy skills.)

Reconciling results from different experiments is a hazardous business. We have results that suggest that bullies (at least verbal bullies) are cognitively 'smarter' than non-bullies; and results that show that bullies (at least physical bullies) are cognitively 'dumber' than non-bullies. It is of course true that different tests were used, but both supposedly tested theory of mind capacities. It is also true that the subjects in the second experiment were young adolescents, those in the first, primary school children. Perhaps age does make a difference. Arguably, as children get older, those who are most perceptive tend to give up the idea that they can achieve dominance at school by physically bullying others.

We have looked at experimental approaches to studying the cognitive capacities of bullies and others in no small detail. From this we may appreciate the difficulties in making generalisations in this developing area of study, and the need for caution – and considerable scepticism – in appraising the generalisations that flow so easily and confidently from some sources.

In the list of bully attributes proposed by Tim Field (1999) we see a number that may strongly remind some older psychologists of what was widely regarded 50 years ago as the basic structure of the so-called authoritarian personality (Adorno *et al.* 1950). That formulation was intended as a characterisation of the Fascist mentality: being obedient to authority ('rule bound'); keen to control others; deeply prejudiced; and obsessed with cleanliness. This mentality is also supposedly hostile towards low-status individuals. It seemed likely that such characteristics would be found in a particular kind of bully, especially in a person who is inclined to carry out orders from a 'superior' regardless of consequences for a targeted person. We may call to mind Hitler's henchmen, those who dutifully murdered thousands of Jews in concentration camps in Germany. Experimentally, people high on authoritarianism, as measured by a personality scale, the so-called F (for Fascist) scale, were the ones most likely to carry out instructions to punish subjects for making mistakes when ordered to do so (Milgram 1965).

How do bullies see themselves? According to Field, as 'wonderful, kind, caring and compassionate'. And again, as 'invulnerable'. At the same time they are judged to be 'insecure' and 'low in self esteem'. There is then this puzzling collection of seemingly contradictory qualities. We may perhaps see the contradictions resolved in the judgement that the bully lacks 'insight'.

The suggestion that the bully thinks of himself or herself as wonderful and invulnerable would lead one to suppose that when bullies are given the opportunity to describe themselves they would choose to come over as pretty good, confident and self-assured. Unfortunately for this theory, they don't. They come out as average (see Chapter 5). Schoolchildren who bully are at least as likely as others to say, 'I feel I don't have much to feel proud of'; and 'at times I think I'm no good at all'. They are no more likely than others to say 'I am able to do things as well as most people'; and 'on the whole I am satisfied with myself' (Rigby 1997b). They are, alas for the theory, indistinguishable from non-bullies.

When we measure self-esteem we do of course rely upon the respondents giving us reliable information. Are we misguided? Are bullies liars? But if they are liars, why don't they boast about themselves more? Perhaps they really have low self-esteem and make themselves out to be average. Yet the idea that bullies really have low self-esteem is contradicted by repeated demonstrations using psychological measures of self-esteem.

Yet here for example is a recent book with the curious title *Jump into PDHPE, Book 2* by Watt, Nemec and Dawe (2000). In case you are one of the many who do not know what PDHPE is, it stands for Personal Development, Health and Physical Education. It provides a lot of information for children about health matters and includes the usual 'profile' of the bully. 'Most bullies,' the authors confidently assert, 'have low self-esteem and feel insecure' (p.78). The authors felt no need to cite any evidence.

Affective aspects of personality

Here are Tim Field's (1999) descriptions of the emotional or feeling side of a bully's nature. The bully:

- is emotionally immature
- is incapable of being intimate or sustaining intimacy
- lacks concern for others
- is often moody, inconsistent
- is quick to anger, impulsive
- has no sense of guilt or remorse.

Some of this accords with the research findings of others. For example, in a study of 11-year-old children in a South Australian primary school using both teacher assessments and self-reports of children, Slee and Rigby (1993) identified children who tended to bully others or were themselves victimised by peers. These children were also assessed for 'psychoticism' or P factor, using Eysenck's (1965) Junior EPQ personality measure. It was found that those children identified as 'bullies' scored significantly higher than other children on this scale. This result suggested that bullies tend to be impulsive, hostile, low in social sensitivity and lacking in cooperativeness. This study would suggest that young children who bully others tend to be somewhat lacking in empathy.

Empathy is generally conceived as having both cognitive and affective aspects, that is being aware of the thoughts and feelings of others and also experiencing some kind of vicarious emotional arousal by the affective state of another (Hoffman 1984). In a study of Australian secondary students aged 12 to 14 years, Farley (1999) examined the degree of empathy experienced by students who were identified through self-reports as bullies, victims and others. The measure used to assess empathy, the Interpersonal Reactivity Index (IRI) (Davis 1980), has four sub-scales assessing: (i) perspective taking; (ii) fantasy; (iii) empathic concern; and (iv) personal distress. It was found that bullies scored significantly lower than others on 'perspective taking'. For example, they appeared less likely than others to try to understand their friends better by imagining how things looked from their point of view, and when they were upset at someone, they were less likely to put themselves 'in the other person's shoes' for a while. Bullies also seemed to be deficient in empathic concern. They were less likely than others to have 'tender, concerned feelings for people less fortunate...' or to be 'quite touched by things I see happen'.

Interestingly, there was no evidence that the 'bullies' were lacking in emotion when they were in a difficult situation. In fact, they were more likely than others to say they were sometimes emotionally distressed, for example they were more likely to agree that they sometimes felt helpless in the middle of a very emotional experience and ill at ease in emergency situations. It was in the area of feeling for other people, not for themselves, that they showed relatively little emotion.

There is then consistent evidence that children who bully are relatively low in empathic regard for others. But we must be careful how we interpret this. Low empathy does not mean no empathy. We need to remind ourselves that one of the most effective ways of dealing with many (not all) bullies is through the method of shared concern developed by the Swedish psychologist Anatol Pikas (1989). This approach assumes that many bullies can be 'reached' by a credible person sharing his or her concern about the plight of a victim. This may not be easy, but it is very unwise to abandon it as a possibility.

The suggestion that children who bully tend to be emotional and helpless in some situations implies that all may not be well with the emotional life of bullies. We have seen that their self-esteem may not differ much on average from that of others, but is there any evidence of exceptional emotional distress in the make-up of most bullies? Some studies have indicated that this is indeed the case. Depressive symptoms in children are more evident in bullies than in children who are not involved in bully/victim behaviours (Rigby 1998c; Slee 1995). Bullies tend to be more depressed than average, and are like victims in this regard. More seriously, bullies, like victims, are more prone than others to have thoughts of suicide (see Chapter 5). The finding that bullies in childhood and adolescence are often emotionally troubled is rarely given much prominence. In part, this may be because it seems to be 'making excuses' for the bully. It may seem to be one step away from concluding that bullies can only be cured by comforting and kindness. It may seem to be denying that bullies have a sense of responsibility.

Behavioural aspects of the bully's personality

There are things that can be said about the bully's personality without fear of contradiction. For example, when Olweus (1993, p.34) claimed that 'generally bullies have a more positive attitude toward violence and the use of violent means', nobody could disagree. When Hazler *et al.* (1997) described the consensus among so-called experts in the field on what bullies were like he placed at the head of the list this characteristic: 'control(s) others through verbal threats and physical actions' and 'chronically repeat(s) aggressive behaviours' (p.7). In fact, such statements merely describe what interpersonal aggressiveness in general is, and this is a necessary part of any definition of bullying.

If we touch upon less obvious kinds of behaviour we can buy ourselves an argument. For example: are bullies loners who can't and don't make friends? We might like to think so, especially if we recall some of the negative qualities attributed to them. Read Tim Field's list again: vile, vicious, vindictive, etc. Recall too that bullies are sometimes supposed to be hopelessly lacking in interpersonal skills. It may come as a surprise then to find that in a large sample of over 30,000 Australian students, those who bullied most reported having more friends and being more popular than others. Were the bullies deluded? Perhaps some were. Still, the work of Olweus (1993) supports the view that bullies tend be about as popular as others and studies of peer acceptance have not consistently shown that bullies are generally less accepted by other students. Commonly bullies have a few strong supporters (Cairns and Cairns 1994) as well as some hangers-on. School bullies are generally not likely to be motivated by an appeal from a teacher who offers to teach them 'social skills' so that they can have good friends like others do.

Yet we have seen that bullies are often depressed and troubled. Is there something about their behaviour that contributes to this state of affairs and could this something if overcome lead to a happier and more socially constructive life? One suggestion is that bullies do not experience cooperating with others to the extent that others do. This hypothesis was supported in a study of Australian students, some of whom were identified as bullies, some victims, some neither. They all completed a reliable questionnaire measure of cooperativeness. The bullies turned out to be significantly less cooperative than most others across a wide range of possible cooperative behaviours (Rigby, Cox and Black 1997). Bullies were, among other things, more likely than others to dislike being in joint projects, to prefer not to share their ideas, to avoid consulting with others, and to believe that committees are a waste of time. It seems likely that for many of the bullies working constructively with others had not been a happy experience.

I will suggest a further quality that I think may distinguish the bully from others. I do this with some trepidation, for as far as I know my assumption hasn't been tested. It is that bullies are often bored. We can try to explain being bored in at least two ways. We can say that a person brings to a whole range of situations a predisposition to be unimpressed, unstimulated, irritated at the lack of anything interesting happening. We can also say that some situations are intrinsically boring. I imagine being in a sensory deprivation chamber would mark the point of extreme objective boringness. And we can say that some classrooms are boring to some children and not to others. The role played by personality may be a limited and complex one, and depend for its influence on the nature of the environment as it is perceived by a particular child.

Personality of the victim

First, an objection. To call somebody a victim (I often hear) is to disempower them. Call them, Field says, 'the target'. This makes it possible to blame the bully with greater vigour: as vile, venomous, violent, vicious, vindictive, vituperative and so on. Perhaps we should call the bully the 'targeter'. Personally, I am relaxed with 'victim', recognising that it need not imply a permanent and enduring state. And I would concede that it would be exceedingly unwise to encourage a person who is going through a period of being targeted to see himself or herself as an inevitable victim.

Just as one may wish to blacken the character of the bully – especially the serial bully – so one may wish to find sterling qualities in the character of the victim. Here is a list of positive characteristics that Tim Field (1999) sees as manifest in the targets selected by bullies:

- Being popular with people.
- Being incorruptible, having high moral standards.
- Being honest and having integrity.
- Being giving and selfless.
- Being imaginative, creative, innovative.
- Being successful, tenacious, determined, courageous.
- Standing up for a colleague who is being bullied.
- Being sensitive.
- Having a strong, forgiving streak.

Such then are some of the presumed criteria for the selection of targets by bullies. Such a list is comforting to those who are bullied and counters the tendency that many of them have to think unduly badly of themselves. Unfortunately the understandable bias in favour of victims of bullying can lead to one making questionable judgements.

First, we find that victims of bullying do not tend to be particularly popular. On the contrary, as numerous studies of schoolyard victims show, they tend to be friendless, isolated and sometimes despised. A comment made to me by a schoolboy sums up the feelings that many children, at least, have towards victims: 'I wouldn't be friends with someone who lets himself be pushed around.' They are emphatically not seen as 'successful, tenacious, determined and courageous' among their peers, much as we would like them to be. It is doubtful whether people who are continually targeted by bullies do tend 'to stand up for colleagues'. Are victims typically 'giving and selfless'? This again seems doubtful. The research with Australian schoolchildren (Rigby *et al.* 1997) suggests the opposite. The children in this study who were identified as victims were significantly less cooperative than others – and given the negative experiences with peers, who can blame them? Are they, in general, 'imaginative, creative, innovative'? Some, perhaps. But the psychological testing of workplace victims reported by Randall (1996) suggests the opposite. These victims turned out to be significantly 'less independent' and 'more conventional' than other workers.

Correlates of peer victimisation

Here is a list of characteristics that researchers have claimed are correlated with being victimised either at school or in the workplace, in some cases in both environments:

- Having low self-worth and low self-esteem.

- Being non-assertive.

- Having poor social skills.

- Being psychologically introverted.

- Being physically less strong than others.

- Being relatively uncooperative.

- Not being group oriented.

- Not being competitive.

- Being shorter then average.

- Being less stable than others.

- Lacking poise, not being relaxed.

- Having a bad stammer.

- Being lonely, isolated.

- Prone to anxiety, depression and suicide.

The correlations that have been reported have in no cases been high (usually around .3), suggesting that there are many exceptions. We may find short people (like Napoleon) who are highly dominant; strange introverts (like Isaac Newton) whose bizarre behaviour guaranteed them immunity at school; physically weak or disabled people (like Stephen Hawking), whose status nobody challenges; and so on. And we should never forget the large number of people who belong to minority social and/or racial groups, for whom individual characteristics as explanations for being bullied are largely irrelevant. These people are often the victims of social prejudice. Hence we should not be surprised that correlations with personality factors tend to be small. Nor should we dismiss them as trivial.

Tim Field does, however, include in his list some characteristics of victims that are consistent with those identified by research psychologists. In particular, he claims that victims – I mean targets – also have these characteristics:

- Low assertiveness.

- A tendency to self-deprecation, indecisiveness and approval seeking.

- A need to feel valued.

- An inability to value oneself.

- A higher than average level of dependency.

Such characteristics suggest – do they not? – a low level of self-esteem. As we have seen, numerous research papers have been written showing that victims as a rule do score lower than average on measures of self-esteem. There is no argument about that. Nobody has questioned that victims tend to have a poor opinion of themselves. But there is considerable argument about what such a finding means and what if anything should be done about it. Much hinges upon what we make of correlations between victimisation and measures of personality characteristics.

The basic problem is that correlations between two variables do not tell us anything about the causal relationship (if any) between the variables. We do not know whether A causes B or whether B causes A or whether C causes A and B to be related to each other. So that even when we have tested and retested and confirmed beyond reasonable doubt that certain qualities tend to 'go with' being victimised more than most, we have the difficult problem of how to view the nature of the relationship. We may ask, for instance, whether having low self-esteem causes one to be bullied, or whether being bullied causes one to have low

WHAT BULLIES AND VICTIMS ARE LIKE

self-esteem. Conceivably, both possibilities may be supported; conceivably neither.

In Chapter 5 we touched upon an important study by Susan Egan and David Perry in 1998, in which they posed this question: 'Does low self-regard invite victimisation?' It is worth examining in more detail as it throws light upon the role that personality – and especially self-esteem – plays in the behaviour of children who are frequently victimised. As we have seen, they were able to make use of a longitudinal research design in which they assessed a large group of children at two points in time. This was done in November and again, five months later, in April of the following year. In total, there were 189 children who took part in this study. They had an average age of 11 years. In their study Egan and Perry assessed the children's self-perceived social competence, which is one aspect of self-regard, and one that seems most likely to be related to bullying. They reasoned that children who had low self-regard of this kind were more likely to be bullied than others. Children were identified as having low self-regard if they agreed more strongly than others that they wished more children of their age liked them and that they found it particularly hard to make friends. As it turned out, according to peers, such children were more often victimised by others at school.

The researchers were particularly interested in whether having low self-regard predicted an increase in their being bullied five months later. It did, even when the researchers controlled for the fact that some children were physically weaker than others, had poor social skills, tended to be anxious, depressed or withdrawn or behaved in an aggressive or disruptive manner. They concluded reasonably that low self-regard was indeed a key factor in predicting subsequent increases in victimisation. But remember that they were talking about low self-regard in a special sense. They had in mind self-perceived social confidence, not, for instance, whether they felt good about their school work or the games they played or any other domain in which self-regard could be measured.

But did such self-regard become worse when they were victimised? The answer is 'yes'. Children who were victimised more often than others suffered a significant lowering in their self-regard compared with what it was five months earlier. So we have, thanks to Egan and Perry, good evidence that self-regard is related to peer victimisation as both cause and effect. But the question remains: how can we explain this process?

It is easy to see how one's perception of social competence would take a dive after being bullied. Low though one's social competence may be, to be spurned and treated with contempt must further demoralise children who 'wish that more children liked them'. Their worst fears are confirmed: self-regard spirals ever downwards.

Why low self-regard should precede an increase in peer victimisation is less obvious. The researchers suggest that perceived low social competence signals a kind of incompetence that more aggressive children can (and often do) take advantage of. To put it simply, they do not stick up for themselves because they cannot stick up for themselves. One possibility is that they do not feel they are worth sticking up for. They may feel that they deserve to be bullied. It has even been suggested that victimised children seek out their tormentors. This seems unlikely to me. In my experience victimised children normally do all that they can to avoid those who bully them. It seems more likely that children who report having low social competence are simply telling it as it is. They have few friends and they find it difficult to make friends. They are simply more vulnerable than others. Low self-regard is I believe normally a consequence of this fact. Rather than see the way individuals perceive themselves as the primary cause of being bullied, it is more sensible to see both being bullied and having low self-regard as the outcome of unsuccessful attempts to deal with interpersonal difficulties of the kind that lead to them being bullied by some, if not all, of their peers.

It needs to be stressed that it is not low overall or global self-esteem that has been found to be a precursor to peer victimisation. Egan and Perry actually included in their battery of tests a measure of global self-esteem and found that it was *not* such a precursor. This should not surprise us. Feeling good about one's school achievements – being top of the class in maths – may contribute to feeling good about oneself and may even provoke hostility from some children who would like to pull the high achiever down a peg or two. To repeat: it appears that the sort of low self-esteem that matters here is an indicator of perceived (and probably real) inadequacy in handling interpersonal difficulties that precedes peer victimisation.

It does not follow that the relevance of personality characteristics to peer victimisation can always be explained in such a way, that is, as a by-product of a current behavioural inadequacy. Why, we may ask, do we find, over-represented among victims of bullying, people who are introverted, non-competitive and unstable? Again, we are faced with the difficulty of identifying direction of causality. Can bullying cause people to become more introverted, less inclined to compete and more unstable? Commonsense suggests that this could happen. As well, longitudinal studies, e.g. Kochenderfer and Ladd (1996) with very young children and Rigby (1999) with adolescents, indicate that mental health can be undermined by constant bullying (see Chapter 5). But we can only speculate on how being introverted and non-competitive can place children at greater risk of being bullied. It seems likely that an aversion to high levels of stimulation, which is characteristic of the introvert, would incline such individuals to avoid rough-and-tumble situations and cope badly when forced to take part in them.

Similarly, a dislike of competition may be traced to a non-aggressive nature which inclines a child not to retaliate when attacked. As yet, these speculations have not been confirmed.

Personal and social integration

A recurring idea in the history of personality theory is that problems in personal relationships and overall happiness can be traced to how one feels about oneself and how one feels about others. It has sometimes been claimed that acceptance of self and acceptance of others are positively related, but the evidence is that they are only weakly correlated (Rigby 1986). Many people are high on one and low on the other, for example, high on acceptance of self and low on acceptance of others. Morrison (2001) suggests that these are likely to be the bullies. She sees bullies as having a lot of respect for themselves but little respect for others. A bully will agree with the statement that 'at school I am listened to when I have something to say' but does not feel pride in belonging to the school. One may say that the bully is lacking in social integration. This latter point is well supported by Rigby and Slee (1993a) in their work with Australian schoolchildren. It was found that bullies were much less likely than others to express any liking for their school.

Morrison (2001) goes on to suggest an ingenious way of describing bullies, victims, bully/victims (sometimes a bully/sometimes a victim) and others using the two dimensions of 'respect' (for self) and 'pride' (in one's wider community).

Table 6.1 Typology of school bullies, victims and others		
	Respect for self	**Pride in the school**
Bullies	yes	no
Victims	no	yes
Bully/victims	no	no
Others	yes	yes

Source: Morrison 2001, p.117

Of course one finds exceptions, but as a generalisation Morrison was able to find some empirical support for the typology among Australian primary school children. Of considerable interest, this analysis suggests ways in which children may be helped to change their status as bullies or victims or both. We are challenged to think about how bullies can develop pride in their community and seek to promote it; how victims can develop self-respect in their relations with others;

and how bully/victims can be helped to achieve both personal and social integration.

Shame

The respect that the bully feels for self is arguably made possible by a non-acceptance of an appropriate sense of shame in relation to the bullying actions he or she
has engaged in. Morrison argues that the bully typically displaces any shame that
might be momentarily experienced onto others. In effect, they proclaim: 'They
can take the blame! Not me.' By contrast the victim is seen as taking too much
blame and shame on board and unable to deal with such feelings appropriately.
He or she becomes the sort of person seeming to be 'asking' to be victimised.
Hence for Morrison – and the school of thought that values restorative justice –
experiencing appropriate levels of shame and dealing with such feelings by
appropriate restorative action is the way forward towards building a socially and
morally healthy community that can in fact be 'bully free'. It is fair to say that this
line of thinking has its critics, principally from those who believe that it is
counter-productive to induce 'shame' in anyone, even bullies, because they may
then carry the burden of stigmatisation, become alienated and desperate to strike
back. This, however, is to ignore the socially integrating effect that occurs when a
person recognises the harm he or she has done to others, and sincerely makes rep-
aration.

Pros and cons of typologising

The very fact that we use such terms as 'bullies' and 'victims' (or 'targets') reveals a
partiality for labelling. Strenuous attempts are sometimes made to avoid such ter-
minology, ending, somewhat farcically, with the claim that 'I am talking about the
sort of people over-represented in bully/victim cases, whom unenlightened
people call bullies and victims (or targets)'. At the same time, the people who
worry so much about labelling have a point. I shudder at the thought of a child in
preschool being branded 'bully' carrying the designation on through primary
and secondary like a leper with a tinkling bell. I know that some would support
such a shaming procedure. (In Canberra, Australia, a teenager caught shoplifting
was paraded round the city wearing a placard displaying the nature of his misde-
meanour to rapturous applause from the media.) We must ask ourselves the simple
question: why are we using such terms?

 The terms 'bully' and 'victim' do suggest a relatively enduring personality
characteristic. Relatively enduring, mind. We know that among very young
schoolchildren, being victimised by peers is not a very stable characteristic
(Kochenderfer and Ladd 1996). It becomes more so as children get older. We
know, too, that many children who bully others in primary school 'grow out of it'

in secondary school, as they begin to realise that there are more enjoyable ways of relating to others or even becoming dominant in socially acceptable ways. But there are certainly some people for whom there is a remarkable degree of continuity through the lifespan in tendencies to bully or be bullied (see Farrington 1993). As long as we do not commit ourselves to such slogans as 'once a bully, always a bully' or 'once a victim always a victim' we will find evidence to justify the claim that we are talking about something that can go on and on.

The danger of rigid stereotyping becomes evident when we begin to see the bully as nothing but a bully or the victim as nothing but a victim. In fact, it has long been claimed that some individuals are both bullies and victims, that is they sometimes bully others and are sometimes victimised by others (Besag 1989). We might expect these types to predominate in situations in which there is a constant struggle for ascendancy in an ethos in which might is right and the consequences of falling further down the 'pecking order' are particularly harsh. We might also find that a clever child can bully a bigger, physically stronger child intellectually, in the classroom, but not in the playground, where the roles may be reversed.

We may even find that bullying and pro-social tendencies can in some individuals go together. In a study of the interpersonal relations of Australian schoolchildren (Rigby and Slee 1993a), it was found – to the authors' surprise – that the correlation between tending to bully others and tending to give support to others were only slightly negative. We had expected that nearly all children who informed us (anonymously) that they greatly enjoyed upsetting wimps and scaring others would say they disliked sharing things and helping others. Of course, some of the bullies may have been 'having us on' or wanting to come across as good guys. (We learned later that bullies tend not to respond in a socially desirable way.) But the very weak negative association between bullying others and acting pro-socially greatly surprised us at the time.

But the more you think about inconsistencies in human behaviour the more understandable it is that pro-social and anti-social tendencies (such as bullying) can co-exist. Here are two examples. Biographies of the famous scholar and Christian writer C. S. Lewis reveal a kindly man who loved his friends and donated generously to charities. Yet his students at Cambridge describe him as an intellectual bully who delighted in demonstrating his superior knowledge before them in their one-to-one tutorials. Another man with formidable pro-social credentials is the cricketer Ian Botham. His work to raise money for children with leukaemia involved him in long and often painful walks in the UK from John O'Groats to Lands End and subsequently across the Italian Alps following the trail of Hannibal. In the world of cricket he was known not only as a belligerent batsman but also a loyal team member. Another side of his character is suggested in an autobiography written by a team mate, Geoffrey Boycott (1991). According to Boycott, Botham delighted in tormenting weaker members of the team, including Boycott. He describes how he was assaulted by Botham in the team-room.

> He jumped on top of me, pinned my arms back and started drumming with his fingers quite hard on my forehead, which hurt. I said: 'Get off. If you don't get your own way or somebody disagrees with what you say, you just try to bully them.' He carried on and tried to make light of his actions: 'It'll start to hurt soon, Fiery. The pain will dig into your subconscious.' I said: 'It already does hurt, and I repeat that you are a bully. I'm convinced of that now.' (p.109)

Such demonstrations of inconsistency in the behaviour of bullies and victims does not mean that we should discard the concepts, but they should introduce an element of wariness when we feel like rushing to conclusions.

Conclusion

Conceptions of what bullies and victims are like can matter greatly. This was brought home to me forcibly in an email from a school principal that I received a few months ago. He had been talking with a father of a child who had been continually bullied at his school. The parent had evidently been encouraged by what he had read to take a view of 'school bullies' that had troubled the principal, who wrote to me as follows:

> In my discussions with the parents of a 'serial victim', if such terminology exists, the father has produced a lot of internet 'evidence', all unsourced, which claims that bullies are always sociopaths. In your experience of schools, is this a reasonable statement or conclusion? My own experience and that of the Department behaviour support staff helping us with our anti-bullying policy are somewhat less categorical.

Mad dogs, sharks, sociopaths… There is certainly 'support' for this contention – not always, as we have seen, unsourced. But 'reasonable' it is not. Categorising people who bully in simplistic terms will never do – whether by demonising them as monsters or labelling them as psychological no-hopers, or, for that matter, viewing them as tough guys, basically OK, whom we must learn to tolerate.

Chapter 7

Why bully?

> Men are not gentle creatures who want to be loved and who at the most can defend themselves if they are attacked; they are, on the contrary, creatures among whose instinctual endowments is to be reckoned a powerful share of aggressiveness.
>
> – Freud, *Civilisation and its Discontents*

Some people are quite satisfied with explanations for bullying which identify 'personality' as the effective cause. It seems enough to say that bullies are aggressive, unempathic, cruel, impulsive etc., and that victims are unassertive, introverted, anxious, socially unskilled etc. As we have seen, there seems to be considerable satisfaction to be had from blackening and demonising the bully. But for many people such attributions to personality do not take them far enough. They want further, deeper explanations. They ask *why* people are like that.

Broadly we can distinguish between three kinds of explanations sometimes advanced for the things we do. Since time immemorial people have given credit or discredit to gods or demons that have come, often unbidden, into their lives and got them to do creditable or discreditable things. Others have rejected such supernatural explanations and viewed their actions as a consequence of the kind of biological organism they are or (through evolution) have become. Still others have seen their behaviour as a response to the environment, physical, social and cultural, in which they live and the ways in which the environment has operated upon them to condition them to act the way they do.

These views or perspectives are not necessarily mutually exclusive. A person may see no contradiction between being religious, recognising biological and evolutionary influences on behaviour and attributing actions to previous learning and the demands of specific situations. Or for that matter taking an existential position and asserting that to bully or not to bully is a matter of free will. Yet the differences in perspectives do excite controversy.

Supernature

The belief that beings with supernatural powers can and do influence human behaviour is to be found in the literature and folklore of every culture. In Western countries the notion that supernatural forces operate in people's lives derives largely from traditional Christianity. In the Old Testament God and the Devil are seen to be in competition for human souls, inspiring and corrupting by turns. The Ancient Greeks saw gods and goddesses at work everywhere; the Romans made a point of propitiating the more powerful ones. The view that people can be cursed or bewitched is less evident in contemporary society than, say, in the 17th century when the witches of Salem in North America were seen as 'possessed' and appropriately despatched. But the belief that the Devil can order people to do evil things is still not without its believers. At the trial of Peter Sutcliffe, the Yorkshire Ripper, who was found to have murdered 13 women in a year-long reign of terror in the north of England during 1980, the accused testified that he had heard voices that told him that he must seek out and kill prostitutes who deserved to die.

Aside from pathology, it is sometimes said that in their present state humans cannot avoid behaving badly, whatever resolutions they may make. As St Paul lamented: 'For the good that I would do I do not; but the evil which I would not, that I do' (Romans 7.19). According to this view, people inevitably from time to time abuse their power at the expense of others. In short, they bully. Some point to a time when people began to 'go wrong' – when Adam was tempted in the Garden of Eden and 'fell', thereby dooming successive generations to sinfulness. Whether the Fall is conceived as an historical event or as an instructional myth to explain the tendency for people to fall down on their moral responsibilities, Christians commonly claim that it is our nature to exploit our relations with others, to bully them for instance, and that a supernatural act of divine grace is needed to prevent such things from happening. The French philosopher Simone Weil has argued that in the absence of rare moments of grace humans are condemned to behave as do farmyard hens that 'peck' at those weaker than themselves. John Betjeman (1960) recalling the torments he suffered at the hands (and feet!) of schoolyard bullies seeks to explain it all as a manifestation of an evil spirit.

As certain as the sun behind the Downs
And quite as plain to see the Devil walks

To some this perspective provides a satisfying explanation for bullying conceived as evil. This view becomes more plausible when we reflect upon the nature of some malicious forms of bullying whereby an individual may continue to derive intense and seemingly incomprehensible satisfaction from the spectacle of another person being hurt without cause. To others this explanation for bullying can appear as mere superstition or even a cop-out: 'The Devil made me do it.'

Nature

Bullying may be understood as an inevitable part of the struggle that is insepara-ble from existence. In a sardonic yet light-hearted poem, Aldous Huxley (1920) describes the origin of the struggle at conception.

A million, million spermatozoa
All of them alive:
Out of their cataclysm but one poor Noah
Dare hope to survive.

He reflects ruefully on what might have been 'another Shakespeare, a Newton or a Donne – but the One was me'. He continues:

Shame to have ousted your betters thus,
Taking ark while others remained outside!
Better for all of us, froward Homunculus,
If you'd quietly died!

We live here by courtesy (or perhaps discourtesy) of the prize-winning sperm, the pre-natal super-bully, who helped to make us what we are.

A few years later on a more sombre note, Hitler pontificated thus in a speech delivered in Kalenbach in 1928 (cited in Bullock 1964).

> The idea of struggle is as old as life itself, for life is only preserved because other things perish through struggle. In this struggle, the more able win, while the less, the weak, lose. Struggle is the father of all things.

Here we see a brutal application of the Darwinian principle of the survival of the fittest. To what extent, we may ask, can we understand bullying in the light of evolutionary theory?

Evolutionary theory as an acceptable theory has had its ups and downs. Many of Darwin's religious contemporaries saw it as a threat to the supernatural, God-given order of things, and sought, largely unsuccessfully, to block its passage. Herbert Spencer, that towering intellectual and influential figure in Vic-torian England, speeded it on its way, seeking as he did so to extend its applica-tion beyond the merely biological into the social and cultural domains. Our insti-tutions and way of life were to be understood as part of the great unfolding process of evolution. In the early 20th century so-called advanced thinkers like Julian Huxley and H. G. Wells spoke glowingly of the science of eugenics as the means by which humankind could be improved by giving evolution, so to speak, a helping hand. Hitler and the Fascist movement took the idea seriously and sought systematically to bully the biologically unfit and those who on spurious racial grounds they chose to see as unfit, out of existence. Darwinism through its association with such evil practices got a bad name from which it is only just recovering. Increasing numbers of 'advanced thinkers' are innocent once again, confident that they can understand the nature of life, its genetic basis, the genome, and work wonders for the human species through genetic engineering. Evolutionary psychology is now in its pomp: witness the stream of books and articles demanding our attention. Can it help us understand bullying?

From an evolutionary perspective 'social dominance' holds centre stage. All creatures are programmed, as it were, to seek to acquire the necessary resources to survive. Because resources are limited, creatures are forced to compete with each other, as Darwin (1859) argued they must. From this perspective, bullying may be seen as one means by which more powerful creatures get what they need. Not, one should emphasise, the only means, but the one systematically employed by those we call bullies.

We cannot dispute that 'dominance' is the primary goal that the bully seeks. But we may question whether energy invested by Bully A to dominate Victim B is always, or even typically, the means by which the bully gains access to 'necessary' resources. If we look now, mundanely, at what the schoolyard bully gets out of the bullying it may turn out to be such things as lunch money, a favour, admiration from a gallery of watchful fans; maybe enhanced security as he/she rises in the school pecking order – hardly necessary resources. We might nevertheless choose to see in this behaviour vestiges of a strategy employed by those primitive ancestors who ensured the bully's survival.

Patricia Hawley (1999) in her interesting paper 'The Ontogenesis of Social Dominance: A Strategy-Based Evolutionary Perspective' argues that the kind of behaviour that we might call bullying (she calls it 'coercive behaviour') can be understood from an evolutionary perspective. She sees it as a largely unsuccessful adaptation to the conditions of modern life. There are, she suggests, other more effective ways of achieving dominance, that is, by cooperative and pro-social means. And this, she maintains, is what more complex and highly evolved organisms, such as humans, eventually (mostly) come to realise. As children grow older and more mature they begin to see that pro-social means rather than anti-social means are in fact more likely to produce the coveted goal of social dominance among their peers. Thus the aggressive, pushy, bossy, bullying toddler develops in time into the pro-social schoolboy or schoolgirl and subsequently into the even more socially cooperative adolescent.

This view has some appeal. There are indeed primitive bullies who remind us of our allegedly brutal ancestors, though we know of primitive people whose brutality, if present, seems to be carefully hidden from anthropologists (Dentan 1968). But equally there are sophisticated bullies who often do access the resources they crave (popularity, promotion, conspicuous success) – and arguably in the process do much more harm to others than mindless thugs. It is only by dwelling upon the cruder variety of bullies that Hawley's (1999) view can appear persuasive. It is true, as she says, that the more overt forms of bullying tend to decrease with age; but other forms may actually increase.

Central to the evolutionary perspective is that it is in our nature to strive to be socially dominant, bullying being one primitive expression of that need. Put simply: if our ancestors had not been dominant we wouldn't be here. We come from a long line of successful dominators. It is in our blood, our guts, our brains, our genes. If this is so, we would expect to see in every human interaction evidence of a desire or intention to become elevated relative to someone else. If we watch people even in friendly encounters, say at a party, we will doubtless often find some evidence to support this view. Notice how people introduce themselves, how they drop clues to their importance, the gossip they engage in. But if we are to sustain this theoretical position to apply to all interactions, we will need considerable recourse to paradox. We may argue – if we are sufficiently perverse – that humility is always a mask or a ploy to support a subtle form of self-aggrandisement: Christ washing his disciple's feet being a cynical means of establishing dominance through a dramatic show of self-abasement. Wedded to the position that human beings invariably seek to establish dominance in their social sphere – one way or another – we stretch credulity to its breaking point.

It's in the genes

Behavioural geneticists are constantly reminding us that a high proportion of the characteristics that guide our behaviour is inherited. They draw largely on studies showing a greater similarity in the characteristics of identical twins – who have the same genetic make-up – compared with non-identical twins. There is strong evidence that identical twins are much more similar in personality than non-identical twins even when members of the 'identical' pair have been brought up in different home environments and the non-identical twins have experienced the same home environment. Such studies have led to the claim that approximately half the variation in personality characteristics between individuals is genetic in origin. Some of what is heritable may be described as 'direct' – for example, a nervous disposition. Some can be viewed as 'indirect', as when a person is treated in a particular way because he or she is known to have a nervous disposition.

We should ask whether the kind of qualities associated with bullying others or being bullied could, to some degree, be inherited. The answer appears to be 'yes', although only one study to my knowledge has made use of twin studies to examine whether the tendency to bully is to any degree heritable. In a study by O'Connor *et al.* (1980) mothers of identical twins (n = 54) and mothers of fraternal twins (n = 33) rated their children (mean age eight years) on their tendency to bully others, using a six-item measure of good reliability. The identical twin correlation (.72) was significantly higher than the fraternal twin correlation (.42). This difference was interpreted as indicating substantial genetic influence upon the tendency to bully others.

We can add to the specific finding of O'Connor *et al.* results from numerous studies that have shown that aggressiveness is to a substantial extent inherited. Besides this, there are studies that have shown that characteristics less obviously associated with being a bully or being a victim are also significantly heritable. These include introversion–extraversion, anxiety, stability, social competence, self-esteem, cooperativeness, impulsiveness and empathy. No-one is claiming that this is all there is to it. It would be foolish, for instance, to argue that social competence and self-esteem are unaffected by experiences with others. But what is inherited, it is argued, can have a major influence on how one treats, and is treated by, others.

The environment

In common usage the environment is that by which we are constantly surrounded or the conditions under which we live. It is everything except us. But how can 'everything' be broken down so that we can gauge environmental effects of this kind or that kind on anything? On bullying for instance. Admittedly somewhat arbitrarily we will exclude the sun, the moon and the stars (to the chagrin of astrologers) and identify these aspects:

- the home environment
- the school and the peer group
- the neighbourhood.

Elsewhere (Chapter 9) I examine the possible effects of some other places or situations on the likelihood of engaging in bullying others and being bullied, for example, in prisons and in the workplace. The three aspects of the environment listed above have figured individually or jointly in an increasing number of studies of bullying and have become the foci of a number of different perspectives that will now be described and examined.

The home environment

The home is generally recognised as making the deepest and most enduring contribution to the way children think, feel and behave both in their homes and outside their homes. Commonly the word 'nurture' is used to describe this function. 'Nurture' has a positive ring about it. It has the same root as 'nourishment'. It is what helps us grow, physically and psychologically. Those who provide the nurturing are usually biological parents, mother and father, although 'caregivers' may include single parents, foster-parents, siblings, grandparents, uncles and aunts and, indeed, anybody else who may play a part in the rearing of children. Close contact tends to be more continuous and intimate with babies and very young children and for that reason is often thought to have greater impact and significance in the nurturing process. The question naturally occurs: does the way the child is nurtured really have an enduring effect on its subsequent behaviour, more especially in the way it relates to members of the family – and also to non-family members in the bigger, wider world which is entered, as a rule, when the child goes to school? Can the way the child is nurtured reduce its chances of becoming a bully, a victim or a bully/victim in later life?

The answer to the question about whether a child can be reared so as to be less likely to become a bully or a victim in the family is probably 'yes'. We know that some parents monitor their children's behaviour in the home quite carefully and seek to promote cooperation between their charges. Generally they do it simply by administering appropriate rewards and punishments, and, with persistence, manage to influence, if not entirely control, the way their children behave towards others – *in the home*.

The question of whether a child can be so reared as to reduce his or her chances of being involved in bully/victim problems outside the home is a contentious one, despite the fact that over the last ten years or so a great deal of research has been undertaken to find out. We must be careful in considering what it tells us and what it doesn't tell us.

This I think is solid and indisputable. There is indeed a link between what parents and families do in the home and the behaviour of their children at school with their peers, and that includes being a bully and/or being a victim in encounters with other children. Notice that we are talking here about a statistical relationship. There are definable ways of parenting and definable ways in which families function (more later about how these may be defined) which are significantly related to the involvement of children in bully/victim problems at school.

This is an important discovery. But it does not necessarily mean what we would like it to mean. We have discovered an association; we have not yet established to everyone's satisfaction the nature and direction of a causal relationship. We will see later that the meaning of the association is in dispute. But for the moment let us accentuate the positive. If such a relationship as I am claiming did not exist, then it would be time to quit worrying about how parenting might affect a child's peer relations. An association does not prove a cause, but it does make the discovery of a causal relationship possible. And, moreover, it does give us a clue as to which children are 'at risk' of bullying or being bullied.

The association between parenting and children's interpersonal behaviour

It is useful to examine in a little detail what the research literature tells us about the relationship between parenting and children's behaviour at school. In an examination of 83 studies conducted between 1939 and 1998 on the relationship between parenting and the behaviour of children, Schneider (2000) has provided overwhelming evidence that the two are related. Most of the studies he reports examine the relationship between parenting behaviour and childhood aggression and acceptance by peers. A large majority involve studies of the interpersonal behaviour of young children in preschools and primary schools. They consist of studies in which measures of parental behaviour, inferred through interviews with parents or through direct observations of parent–child interactions, are correlated with measures of children's behaviour outside the home, derived from reports provided by teachers, the children themselves or peers or from direct observation.

The studies show that aggressive parenting and aggressive behaviour on the part of children with their peers are related. Here are some examples:

> Sears *et al.* (1953) found that the more severely boys (aged 3–5 years) were punished for aggression by their mothers, the more aggressive they were at preschool.

> Eron *et al.* (1963) reported that children aged eight years who were exposed to high-intensity punishments behaved more aggressively with their peers.

> Larzelere (1986) found that among children between 3 and 17 years of age, aggression towards peers at school was more common among children who (according to their mothers) had been spanked more frequently, especially if 'reasoning' was not incorporated into the disciplinary action.

> Pettit, Dodge and Brown (1988) reported that children aged five years with mothers who used restrictive discipline were more aggressive with their peers.

Pettit *et al.* (1991) reported that children aged three to five years were more aggressive with their peers if their mother engaged in coercive and intrusive interactions with them.

Strassberg *et al.* (1992) found that the more parents used aggressive strategies to deal with conflicts, the more aggressively the child behaved with peers.

Although aggressive behaviour by parents is the main variable that has been reported as correlating with children's behaviour with peers, permissive parental behaviour also appears to be related.

Sears (1961) found that among 12-year-old children, high levels of permissiveness were correlated with anti-social aggression.

Levy (1966) reported that among children with ages ranging from 4–16 years, mothers rated as 'overindulgent' tended to have more aggressive children.

Some studies have focused on children with high levels of interpersonal competence and popularity with peers. Such children are rarely bullied and tend to be non-aggressive. Here again there are numerous studies that report parenting correlates, for example:

Austin and Lindauer (1990) reported that better-liked children (aged nine to ten years) were less controlling, less directive and less intrusive.

Hart, Ladd and Burleston (1990) noted that for two groups of students (aged five to seven and nine to ten years) more popular children had mothers who were disinclined to use power-assertive disciplinary methods.

Pettit *et al.* (1991) reported that higher levels of social competence among five-year-olds were found when their mothers were more responsive in their interactions with their child.

Henggeler *et al.* (1991) reported that among eight-year-olds, those children who were most popular with their peers had fathers who were most receptive to solutions to problems that they (the children) proposed.

Strassberg *et al.* (1992) reported that among five-year-olds, the more popular children had parents who use least aggression in resolving conflicts.

Although the studies summarised above do not deal with bullying per se, they do deal with qualities in children that are related to bullying, e.g. being aggressive or having low social competence and being unpopular with peers. Moreover, the bulk of these studies employed measures of parenting behaviour from one source, e.g. direct observation or interviews with parents, and measures of peer relating from another source, e.g. self-reports from children or peer reports from other children who knew them. This enabled the researchers to avoid one of the weaknesses in conducting research of this kind, that is reliance on information obtained from one source only. Admittedly, the correlations between the measures of parenting and children's behaviour are generally not high (often between .2 and .3) but the fact that there are so many studies producing consistently significant results in relation to children in widely different age groups should convince us that the association is a reliable one. Although there is plenty of room for other, non-parenting influences to play a part, we do have, I think, a prima facie case for believing that what parents do and how children behave outside the home with other people are connected in some way.

You may have noticed that research emphases have been on what mothers do. To some extent this is understandable. Generally they form closer relations with children and play a more nurturing role. Sadly, fathers are generally neglected in these studies – and it matters. A further area of concern is the common practice of not discriminating between the effects of parenting and family functioning on boys and girls. This also matters, as there are grounds for supposing that boys and girls may react differently at times to the same treatment from their families (Rigby 1993, 1994). Finally, there is a dearth of studies that are longitudinal in nature. Such studies are exceptional, but there is one. It deserves a paragraph.

In 1997 the first prospective study of early family experiences of boys who were both aggressive and bullied during their middle childhood years was undertaken by Schwartz et al. (1997) in the USA. Mothers of 198 5-year-old boys were interviewed to ascertain how the children had been treated by their parents. Some 3 years later a group of 16 children was identified as 'aggressive victims'. The researchers were able to show that these children differed from others in having experienced at an early age more punitive, hostile and abusive family treatment than other groups. Unlike studies in which measures of parenting and children's behaviour are undertaken at about the same time, a prospective study of this kind enables one to infer that the aggressive behaviour of children is not a cause of the parenting and quite possibly an effect. That the effect of aggressive parenting should show up among children often referred to in the bullying literature as bully-victims is particularly interesting, as these children have been shown in a number of studies to be the most psychologically distressed of all bully/victim sub-groups (see Zubrick et al. 1997).

Early attachment and young children

Some of the research on possible effects of parenting has been theory driven. Much of the research has focused upon the early years of the relationship between the caregiver and the child. The close attachment or bonding of mother and child has received tremendous emphasis. There was a time when not a moment was to be lost in getting the newborn baby safely, securely in its mother's arms. The theory of attachment, as proposed by John Bowlby (1969), is as follows. The attachment relationship that develops between the primary caregiver – usually, but not always, the mother – and an infant over the first few years of life lays the foundation for an 'internal working model' that continues to influence the child's future development throughout the lifespan. Needless to say, if this is true, how a child relates to its peers will be in part determined by the nature of the attachment – or the failure of the attachment – in the first few years of life.

It would seem to follow that children involved in bully/victim problems would have a different history of attachment from those who are neither bullies nor victims. There is some evidence consistent with this view. It should be explained that it is possible to categorise infants according to how they react when they are reunited with their primary caregiver after a brief and usually unhappy period of absence. Most children are glad to see her and show it. These are the securely attached. Others may ignore her, scream loudly and angrily or even push her away. In 1987 Troy and Sroufe reported that children who at 18 months had shown signs of insecure attachment, being anxious/avoidant or anxious/resistant, were more likely than others to be involved in bully/victim problems at age four to five years. Smith and Myron-Wilson (1997) have reported other studies supporting this finding, although it is fair to say that some developmentalists have come to different conclusions, for example Lamb and Nash (1989) who write: 'Despite repeated assertions that the quality of social competence with peers is determined by the prior quality of infant–mother attachment relationships, there is actually little empirical support for this hypothesis.' (Cited in Harris 1998, p.152).

One of the things that commends this line of research is that the early testing of subjects in these experiments makes it unlikely that the behaviour involving bullying (being victimised or victimising others) has been learned from the peer group. But what we do not know is how the children who acted so insecurely as infants would have acted with a different caregiver. Perhaps the insecurity was inherited. We know that anxiety is a characteristic that is to a substantial extent heritable. The crucial factor may be the inherited nature of the child, not the treatment from a caregiver. Until we partial out the genetic factor the theory must remain speculative and controversial.

It would, of course, be unthinkable to allocate babies at random to 'caregivers' who would provide or not provide the conditions likely to bring about secure attachment. The best we can do is to draw upon the experimental work of Harlow and Harlow (1962) who did in one experiment deprive baby rhesus monkeys of contact with any other animal, the consequence of this extreme treatment being lifelong social maladjustment. This is certainly consistent, up to a point, with attachment theory. But in another experiment, baby rhesus monkeys were allowed other babies to be with (no mother). Although the mother-deprived babies were distinctly unhappy, there were no signs of subsequent social maladjustment. For those who think you can extrapolate from one species to another, it would seem that the identity of the carer and even the role of the carer may not be so crucial after all.

Further implications of parent–child relationships

The general notion that unsatisfactory relationships with parents constitute a root cause of unsatisfactory relations with one's peers has been accepted by a number of researchers, including several who have specialised in the study of aggressive and bullying behaviour between children. Two main questions have been addressed: what are the parental antecedents of being bullied by peers at school, and what are the parental antecedents of bullying others at school? More recently researchers have been concerned with the question of how parental behaviour may account for some children being both bullies and victims.

A study conducted by Olweus (1993) in Sweden with adolescent schoolboys and with their parents suggested that the mode of parenting was a significant factor. The boys were assessed by a number of their peers according to how frequently they were bullied by other students. Subsequently, interviews were conducted with the mothers and fathers of the students (aged 13–16 years) included in the sample. Olweus's analyses indicated that in addition to being generally physically weaker and more passive than other students, the children who were victimised most often were: (i) overprotected by their mothers; and (ii) distant from their fathers, who were critical of them.

Some studies have attempted to describe the relationships between involvement in bully/victim problems at school as bully or as victim or as both and prior relations with parents. One instrument that appears suitable for such an inquiry is the Parental Bonding Instrument (the PBI) devised by Parker et al. (1979). This is a questionnaire in which respondents are asked to describe their parents and how they have been treated by them in the past. There are two sub-scales to the measure; one assesses the quality of care received by the respondent from a male and a female caregiver in the family (usually a mother or father) and the other the degree of control that each exercised over him or her. An example of an item to assess parental care is 'speaks to me in a warm and friendly voice'; an example of parental control is 'tries to control everything I do'.

The PBI was administered in Australia to adolescent students (769 boys and 663 girls) between the ages of 12 and 16 years, together with reliable self-report measures of tendencies to bully others and tendencies to be victimised by others (Rigby, Slee and Martin 1999). (We also included in this study measures of mental health and psychological extraversion – for reasons to be made clear later.) Our main interest here is whether the students' appraisal of their parents related to their reports on their involvement in bully/victim problems. We found that most of the correlations between measures of parental bonding and self-reports of involvement as a victim or as a bully were small but statistically significant (see Appendix 8).

Even though the correlations are small and several do not reach an acceptable level of statistical significance, they are all in a direction that suggests that parental care *may* have the effect of reducing the tendency to bully and also the tendency to be victimised by peers, whilst high levels of parental control may have the opposite effect, that is, increase the tendency for children to bully others and also the tendency to be bullied by others. There is some limited support here for the claim made by Olweus that parental control (or over-protection) of boys by mothers can increase the likelihood of them being victimised. It is also suggested by these results that over-protection of girls by fathers may have a similar effect.

Here we may pause and examine some possible alternative interpretations of these results. First, the PBI items are framed in the present tense, and it may be the case that the parents' perceived behaviours do not have a long history. Adolescence we know is a time when children are particularly critical of parents and especially sensitive to being 'controlled'. Further, it may be that negative and controlling attitudes of the parents are in some cases at least a response to negative behaviours on the part of the child. Finally, we come back to the old bugbear of research of this kind, and ask: could the actions and reactions of child and parents be determined by other factors that are attributable to a common genetic source? For example, both parents and children may share a disposition that makes them get mad at each other.

Perhaps the modest correlations can be accounted for if there are enough pairs of parents and offspring who are extraverted and also mentally distressed. Fortunately, it was possible to take this possibility into account by controlling for each child's level of extraversion and mental distress. Much as expected from previous studies, we did find that extraverts were more likely to bully and introverts to be bullied. We also found that the more mentally distressed had a tendency to be involved in bully/victim incidents. What happened when extraversion and mental health of children were controlled was that some associations remained significant for girls but not for boys. Girls who felt less well cared for were prone to bully. Girls who felt highly controlled by parents were prone to bully too, leading one to conclude that a high level of parental control combined with a low level of care may well be a recipe for bullying by girls. We should add that over-controlled girls were also more likely than others to experience peer victimisation. For boys we are left with the conclusion that parental influence – as assessed by the PBI – may well be negligible as far as peer bullying among adolescents is concerned.

Research conducted in Italy by Baldry and Farrington (1998) has contributed further to our knowledge about relationships between parenting and children's peer relations. Their work was with children between the ages of 11 and 14 years in a middle school in Rome. As in the Australian study, an anonymous self-report questionnaire was used to identify bullies and victims. To assess parenting practices a number of questions were asked of the students about their parents. Their answers led to parenting practices being categorised as 'authoritarian', e.g. if the student answered yes to this question: 'Do your parents always decide things for you?', or 'authoritative', e.g. saying yes to: 'At home do you have the possibility to say what you want?' In addition there were measures to assess how punitive parents were and the extent to which parents got along, e.g. whether they quarrelled and argued a lot.

They also found that in comparing children categorised as 'bullies' as opposed to 'non-bullies' the former were more likely to report having parents who were relatively authoritarian, punitive, not very supportive and inclined to disagree with each other. They reported that victims and bully/victims also tended to have authoritarian parents. Somewhat surprisingly, the 'pure' bully (who bullies but is not bullied in return) did not appear from this analysis to have parents with such negative characteristics. In some respects this study provides results similar to those of the Australian study, especially in suggesting that perceived high parental control is associated with being a bully and with being a victim – although it may be recalled that in the Australian study this finding applied specifically to girls. (It is a pity that the Italian results were not examined separately for boys and girls, since differences could well have emerged.)

Again, we are faced with some uncertainty in interpreting these results so as to establish causal links. Could uncontrolled genetic factors have accounted for the associations that have been suggested? As in the Australian study some factors were employed to control for other influences, some of which may have a partial genetic basis. These included self-esteem and perceived social competence, both of which have been shown to have some significant heritability. Analyses showed that with these factors controlled (as well as gender) having authoritarian parents was significant for bully/victims vs neither and for victims vs non-victims and for 'only victims' vs non-victims. Bullies vs non-bullies were distinguished by having low-supportive and highly punitive parents.

Family relationships and bullying

Some might say that we are focusing in an unduly narrow way in picking out (or picking on) parents as possible causal agents in explaining bullying. Perhaps the family may be a more appropriate unit on which to base an analysis. In England a rather ingenious method was used to examine how children categorised on the basis of peer reports saw their families (Bowers, Smith and Binney 1992). These researchers utilised the Family-Systems Test (Gehring and Wyler 1986) to assess structural aspects of families. This is a figure placement technique in which children place small wooden dolls representing family members on a chequer board so as to 'make a picture of their family' showing 'how close everyone feels to each other'. In addition, one to three blocks can be placed under each figure to show 'how powerful they are'. Unlike many questionnaires and interview procedures, this is a procedure that really engages children's attention. The subjects in their study were children between the ages of 9 and 11 years. Bullies, victims, bully/victims and controls (neither bullies nor victims) were identified by peer nomination. It was found that bullies tended to place significantly greater distance between representations of family members, suggesting a low level of cohesiveness in their families. Unlike children not involved in bullying, both bullies and victims tended to see their fathers as much more powerful than their mothers. This suggests that such children are more likely to come from families whose structure is highly patriarchal. One further characteristic of victims was noteworthy. They were significantly more likely than others to clump all family figures together, with no clear separation between any of the figures. This suggested that their families were very high in cohesiveness: arguably too high, suggesting a degree of enmeshment consistent with over-protectiveness of each other. The finding that bullies and victims, though similar in some respects, come from families differing greatly in cohesiveness is a particularly interesting one, all the more so since it was replicated in a similar study conducted in a different culture by Berdondini and Smith (1996) in Italy.

Family functioning and bullying

If a family as a total unit functions badly, individual members, it may be argued, are likely to be affected in ways that may influence how they behave outside the family. According to Roelefse and Middleton (1985) there are six major dimensions of family functioning that are of particular relevance to adolescents. They maintain that 'good family functioning' is evident when these conditions are fulfilled:

(1) There is a coherent family structure with members accepting each other according to clearly defined and consistent roles, e.g. as authoritative parents and respectful children (Structure).

(2) Within the family, individuals can express themselves freely (Affect).

(3) There is good, clearly understood communication between family members leading to them addressing problems together constructively (Communication).

(4) Control is exercised in a democratic rather than authoritarian manner (Control).

(5) Positive values such as personal honesty are transmitted from parent to child (Value).

(6) There is a sense of positive connection with the world outside the family (External systems).

We may ask whether the absence of such characteristics on the part of parents contributes to a young person becoming a bully, a victim or a bully/victim at school. This question was addressed in a study undertaken with Australian schoolchildren (380 males and 476 females) aged between 13 and 16 years (Rigby 1994). Students were categorised with respect to their direct involvement in bully/victim experiences using self-reports. In addition, students completed a 42-item questionnaire, The Family Functioning Assessment Questionnaire (FFAQ) of Roelefse and Middleton (1985). The total scale proved to be highly reliable in the sense of being internally consistent, perhaps not surprisingly as the test had been developed with data from Australian adolescents.

The results indicated that for both boys and girls the families to which bullies belonged functioned overall less well than the families of other students. The specific dimensions that showed significant differences for both sexes between bullies and students not involved in bullying were affect and communication. This is perhaps summed up best by the item on the scale that was most highly cor-related with the rest: 'We feel free to express our opinions in our family but we consider each other's feelings.'

Unlike the results for bullies, the results for victims follow a different pattern for boys and girls. Girl victims indicated that their families were functioning rela-tively badly. They showed poor structure; there was generally low affect; commu-nication was relatively poor; good values were less commonly being transmitted. In none of these or in any other areas assessed by the FFAQ were boy victims rela-tively disadvantaged compared with those not involved in bullying. This raises the unanswered question: why do girl victims tend to come from poorly functioning families, but not boys?

In general, then, knowing about a young person's parenting and family background does provide some indication of whether that person is more likely or less likely than others to be involved in a bully/victim problem at school. We may draw some confidence in this belief by noting that research conducted in different countries, for example, Norway, Australia, Italy and England, points to similar conclusions. But note too that the connections revealed by research are not strong and are open to alternative explanations. They certainly do not provide strong support for those who might lay the blame for bullying squarely on parents.

Peer group pressure and bullying

There can be no doubt that the peer group can be a powerful influence on how children behave. This can readily be observed in the way they speak, for instance. As Harris (1998) points out, the children of migrant families soon learn to speak like other kids, not like their fathers and mothers with accents they brought from their former country. They opt to wear the clothes other kids wear, not what their parents like. Their interests and hobbies are, by and large, the interests and hobbies of their peers. They have a drive to fit in, to be like the others.

For those who need convincing of the powerful influence of the peer group we have the famous experiment of the robber's cave (Sherif *et al.* 1961) conducted over 40 years ago but still cited today, remarkably enough, in social psychology texts for students. Perhaps its longevity is due to a dearth of significant studies of real life behaviour that are rigorously experimental and also revealing. In this study, boys were randomly allocated to two groups – genetic considerations thereby cancelled out – and on a summer camp allowed to develop a group identity, with a little encouragement. They were given names – the Rattlers and the Eagles – and encouraged to compete. In next to no time the group members were welded together, true believers in their destiny, which, in due course, included the vilification of their rivals. Whenever they could, they engaged in abusing members of the other group, physically and verbally. According to the experimenters, an outsider would have seen these boys as 'wicked, disturbed and vicious bunches of youngsters'. Clearly aggressiveness among boys can be stimulated and maintained through the creation of a group identity, especially if members of a group are directed towards seeing themselves as different and superior to another group. This may explain the bullying of 'outsiders'.

If we are interested in explaining individual behaviour in the area of bullying it is better to speak of 'peer groups' rather than 'the peer group'. There are groups that encourage bullying and groups that do not. Some groups glory in bullying. Several years ago I interviewed a likeable young boy of about nine years old whose background I knew nothing about at the time, who cheerfully told me that he had a gang that specialised in bullying. Each day the group identified a potential victim in the playground and gave him or her – no gender bias – absolute hell. If the child was likely to put up a serious fight, then the bullying, usually physical, was undertaken by the group. When the victim was 'weak', one member of the group was delegated to do the bullying and the rest watched. Such specialisation is rare, but the promotion of a group identity that can lead to bullying someone is not uncommon. They may or may not have some interests that draw them together, for example, a liking for a violent sort of sport that goes with a tough guy image, or an obsession with computing which can be (not always) the preserve of the more introverted, who may accordingly be labelled as 'computer nerds'. We have seen that some bullying is in fact perpetrated collectively by groups and even orchestrated on occasions by individual leaders.

But whilst we can see that peer pressure may lead children to bully others and thereby promote or uphold a satisfying image of being tough, it does little to explain how some children come to be victims. It is unlikely (but not impossible) that a child may identify with a group that is being victimised and thereby bring victimisation on himself or herself. If this happened we would be inclined to look for the unusual motivation of those who wish to suffer the fate of the oppressed, or alternatively, for signs of pathology. And it begs the question of why some children for whom the idea of being tough is attractive do not bully others.

There is as yet little empirical evidence relating to the importance of different kinds of social influences that operate on children to incline them to engage or not engage in bullying. But there is one useful study that has examined social influences affecting the tendency to bully among early adolescents in the USA (see Espelage, Bosworth and Simon 2000).

Espelage *et al.* undertook their study at a large middle school, the data being gathered using anonymous questionnaires from 1361 students in grades 6, 7 and 8. Unlike some measures of bullying tendencies the scale they used was broad in content and psychometrically reliable. The extent to which individuals bullied others was inferred from estimates they made of how frequently they had engaged in the following behaviours over the previous 30 days:

- Called other children names.

- Teased other students.

- Said things about students to make other students laugh.

- Threatened to hit another student.

- Pushed, shoved, slapped or kicked other students.

Negative peer influence was assessed by asking students how many friends they had who: (i) were involved in gang activities; (ii) had hit or threatened someone; (iii) suggested that the student do something against the law; and (iv) damaged or destroyed property.

Adult influence thought likely to discourage aggressive behaviour was assessed by asking respondents to think about adults they spent most time with and indicate how many tell them: (i) if another student hits you, hit them back; (ii) if another student wants to fight, you should try to talk your way out of a fight; (iii) if another student asks you to fight, you should tell a teacher or someone older; (iv) fighting is not good, there are other ways to solve problems.

Parental and family influence centred upon two areas in which it has been claimed that bullying behaviour may be encouraged in families, namely by parental punishment and lack of family attention and support. Respondents were asked to estimate how often they had been hit by parents for breaking rules and how much time they spent with family members and talked and engaged in activities with them.

Finally, respondents were asked to indicate how much gang activity there was in their neighbourhood and how safe they felt.

Using a statistical technique of multiple regression analysis to assess the unique influence of each of the above factors produced very interesting results. Each of the factors contributed significantly to predicting the self-reported frequency of bullying. Their order of importance, as inferred from the amount of variance in the bullying scores attributable to each factor, was as follows:

(1)   Absence of positive adult models.

(2)   Low level of neighbourhood safety.

(3)   Little or no time spent without adults being around.

(4)   Negative peer influence.

(5)   Being spanked at home by parents.

By far the most powerful influence on bullying behaviour according to this analysis was the absence of positive adult models as indicated by reports of spending little or no time with adults. This is precisely what William Golding (1954), author of Lord of the Flies, would have predicted. In the absence of adults the young adolescents on Golding's mythical island begin to engage in the most violent, and indeed lethal, form of peer victimisation. With the arrival of adults, the normal world reasserts itself again.

Physical punishment is the least powerful of the inferred influences, but its contribution to bullying was as predicted. Aggressive parenting and aggressive peer relating went together. Importantly, the study draws attention to a factor often neglected in studies of bullying, namely what goes on in the wider community, beyond the home and beyond the school: the neighbourhood. Where there is a low level of perceived community safety, there would appear to be more bullying going on among children at school. This raises the question of whether it is fair to say, as Randall (1996) has suggested, that bullying is – at least to some extent – imported into the school from the community.

We should acknowledge, as the authors do, the limitations of the study I have described. It relies heavily on student judgements of the intensity of different kinds of social influences. Respondents provided the data on how often they bullied others as well as data on social influence. It would have been good to have controlled in this study for social desirability responding. It would also have been good to have made use of independent measures of bullying tendencies (say through peer nominations) and social influences (say through interviews with family and neighbourhood members). Yet despite these shortcomings, we may be persuaded that adult influence on whether a child engages in bullying is greater than those who attribute overwhelming influence to peer pressure would have us believe.

A further study which enables us to examine the possible contributions of peer and adult pressure to bully others focused upon the degree to which adolescents believe that their peers and adults encourage them to engage in bullying others (Rigby 1997d). In that study respondents were asked in an anonymous questionnaire to indicate whether they thought nominated persons would support them in bullying someone (see Appendix 9). Those nominated included mothers, fathers, close friends and teachers. Not surprisingly, only a minority of students saw others approving of them bullying someone. There was nevertheless a big contrast between the perceptions of how they thought their close friends and adults would react. Up to 15 per cent thought that their friends would approve of at least one kind of bullying they might engage in. This is about three times the proportion who thought that adults might support them. This suggests that the influence of peers, especially close friends, may be crucial in some cases.

However, when we look at the ratings provided by students on how much they care about the judgements others may make of them if they bullied someone, we see that on average students cared more about what parents would think than what their peers thought of them (see Table 7.1). Students were asked to say on a seven-point scale from 'a great deal' to 'not at all' how much they would care about the judgements others might make about them if they bullied someone. This provided a measure of how much influence over their bullying behaviour respondents thought each of the rated persons had. Most students indicated that they cared a good deal: on average they scored above 4, the mid-point indicating neutrality. But notice that both boys and girls cared *less* about what their peers thought than about what their parents thought. Teachers were seen as the least worth taking notice of.

		Table 7.1 Mean rating of sources of influence on student bullying or not bullying someone		
	Close friends	Your mother	Your father	Teachers
Boys	4.68	5.35	5.32	4.14
Girls	5.57	5.74	5.63	4.80

We might ask whether there was any relationship between how the students thought they were being influenced by others and the extent to which they engaged in bullying others. The answer is yes: significant correlations (.34 for boys and .32 for girls) were found between a measure of self-reported bullying behaviour and reported influence from others (see Rigby 1997d, p.215, for further details).

Both the study by Espelage *et al.* (2000) and that of Rigby (1997d) suffer from a failure to control for genetic influences. A recent ingenious study conducted in Texas, USA, by Loehlin (1997) has overcome this problem, and although it did not assess bullying per se, it did examine related behaviour as indicated through personality measures. The research question was whether members of 839 late-adolescent twin pairs who shared more friends were more similar in personality than those who shared fewer friends. By comparing results for identical twins (330 pairs) with results for non-identical pairs (509 pairs) it was possible to control for genetic influence. Respondents were asked: 'Do you and your twin have the same or different friends?' They could answer by choosing one of the following answers:

(1)   All of my friends are also my twin's friends.

(2)   Most of my friends are also my twin's friends.

(3)   Some of my friends are also my twin's friends.

(4)   Few or none of my friends are also my twin's friends.

In addition, respondents completed a reliable personality test, the California Psychological Inventory. One of the dimensions assessed was of particular relevance to bullying: namely, dominance, a construct reflecting the extent to which respondents sought to act in a dominating way. (One would expect bullies to be strongly motivated to dominate.) In general, twins who indicated that they had relatively few friends in common – and were assumed to have been influenced by peers differently/have different friends – were more different on the measure of dominance. The obtained correlations (0.19 for identical and 0.20 for non-identical twins) between the measure of dominance and having different friends were small but statistically significant – and remarkably similar for the two sorts of twins, suggesting that genetic influences interacting with choice of similar or different friends was unimportant.

Second, the study enabled one to examine the possible effects of parents treating one twin in a pair differently from another. To obtain a measure of how similarly or differently parents treated the respondents, parents (usually mothers) were asked to rate their parenting of each twin in terms of the attention they paid to each and the discipline they applied. The question here was whether differences in treatments were related to differences in personality. In general the correlations suggesting parental influence were lower than those suggesting peer influence. For dominance the obtained correlations though positive were smaller (.07 for identical twin pairs and .04 for non-identical twin pairs). This result may be interpreted as giving some support for the view that by late adolescence the influence of peer group is stronger than that of the parents on dominance. Yet in some areas of personality – for example socialisation – the correlations relating to parental influence are higher than those for peer influence. Hence, it seems that parents may have more influence in some areas but not in others. The author, John Loehlin, concludes cautiously that the study gives 'mild support' for the view that peers shape personality more than parents do. But quite appropriately he calls for further research in this area. As far as bullying is concerned, it would be good to see, incorporated in such a study, a better measure of bullying than 'dominance' which, as I have argued earlier, may be achieved by non-bullying methods, especially among more mature students in late adolescence. The finding that 'socialisation' is more closely related to parental than peer influence – even in late adolescence – suggests that a relatively long-term effect on the tendency to act in a socially responsible manner is certainly possible.

Conclusion

In seeking to explain why people bully a variety of factors have been suggested. Some of the explanations are extremely general, their purpose being to explain why there is a tendency to bully in human nature. These include explanations that take a religious or supernatural view of the causes of human behaviour and posit a force for evil that we are not always able to resist. Alternatively, the urge to bully others, especially as children, is seen as implanted through an evolutionary process that has enabled us to survive. Such general explanations for bullying are difficult, if not impossible, to evaluate.

Other explanations have sought to explain why some people bully or are bullied more than others. These include explanations that attribute bullying tendencies (and sometimes the tendency to be bullied by others) to genetic factors; to the early home environment; to the peer group; and to the wider community. Evidence has been piling up in support of each of these explanations. However, because the influences alluded to above operate together, the unique effects of each needs to be disentangled from that of others. And this unfortunately has rarely been done.

As we have seen, currently we have a good deal of evidence obtained from diverse sources – the USA, England, Italy and Australia, for instance – that the involvement of children in bully/victim problems is related to the kind of parenting they have experienced and the sort of family life they have had. This has led many people to assume that inadequate parenting and dysfunctional family life cause bullying or at least constitute a causal influence. However, as we have seen, other explanations for the association are possible. Increasingly, the claim that parenting is directly responsible for a child's involvement in bully/victim problems at school is being challenged, principally by behavioural geneticists and by social psychologists who emphasise the importance of the peer group as a causative influence in accounting for the way children behave towards each other.

Despite the challenges to the view that parents may influence their children to become bullies or victims, it would be premature to abandon this viewpoint. One may concede that some children who are inclined to bully others might actually elicit cold and/or over-controlling behaviour from their parents and that their behaviour may contribute to the dysfunctionality of a family. One may concede that genetic influences on a child's behaviour may (for better or worse) frustrate attempts by parents to shape their child's behaviour. One may concede that a child's peers – and the influence of the neighbourhood – may have an important effect on how that child behaves. And yet, it is still conceivable that under some conditions parental influence on how a child relates to others, both inside and outside the home, could be important. One might expect parental influence to be greatest under extreme conditions, for example where parenting is highly abusive. It may also be the case that the effects of parenting on the way children relate to others are greatest in the early years of schooling and attenuate as the years pass by and other influences increasingly take effect.

Chapter 8

The contribution of differences

Of course we bully him. He's not normal.

– Australian Year 9 focus group member

I often hear it said that a child is being bullied at school because he or she is different, or 'I get bullied at work because I am different'. Is being 'different' per se a reason for being bullied? When one looks at the kind of differences said to cause the bullying or harassment, you find a wide array of characteristics. These include physical characteristics such as being obese, skinny, red-haired, bespectacled, wearing a hearing aid. When I have asked children whether children who look different are bullied more often than others, most children have said yes. However, research findings have been reported that throw doubt upon this judgement. The leading authority on bullying in schools, Dan Olweus, claims that children in Sweden who look physically different are not bullied more often than most. It is easy to see why it is thought that physical differences do give rise to bullying. Almost everybody has some physical idiosyncrasy that marks him or her out from others. We see a fat person being bullied and assume that obesity is the explanation, forgetting that many other bulky people are free from any kind of harassment. Yet doubt remains. The literature on disability and bullying makes it clear that some physical differences can and sometimes do give rise to bullying. Generalising about physical differences needs to be more specific.

We have seen that psychological differences can result in being bullied at school. Children who are introverted, anxious and low in social competence, for instance, are over-represented in the numbers of children who are bullied. There can be little argument about that, although, of course, we must always take into account the company such children keep. I was once told by a scout master (who happened to be a professor of psychology) that he overcame the problem of bullying in his troop, which was acute, by testing the children for extraversion/introversion and dividing his group into two: the extraverts and the introverts. With their own kind, the children were much less inclined to bully. I do not commend this to scout leaders since I would prefer children to come to terms with diversity.

In this chapter we will be examining the contribution of social differences. These are generally more easily defined than psychological attributes and are not so amenable to change. One is, with rare exceptions, born unambiguously male or female, a member of a given race or ethnic group, and having a social class ascribed to one by the status of one's family. One may be born disabled or become so to a degree that the condition is difficult or impossible to change. Ageing is inevitable, and although one may seek to hide it, people who live long enough are defined socially as 'elderly' or less kindly as 'old'. How, we may ask, does belonging to one or more of these social categories affect one's tendency to bully or to be bullied or conceivably both?

Gender

As we have seen, boys are more likely to engage in bullying more often than girls, especially using physical and direct means. In our examination of bullying in schools in Chapter 3, it was noted that although most bullying takes place *within* gender groups, boys are more likely to bully girls than vice versa (for details refer to Appendix 4 and Appendix 5).

Why do boys engage in bullying more often than girls? One answer, admittedly superficial, is that boys are generally more aggressive than girls. This is particularly true when we consider physical forms of aggression, less so for verbal forms and probably untrue of indirect forms of aggression. We should add that although being generally aggressive does not inevitably result in being a bully (since bullying involves repeated, deliberate, unjustifiable hurting of less powerful people) being aggressive obviously increases the chances of one acting in a bullying manner. If we want a more satisfying answer we have to ask the question why, on the whole, males do engage more often than females in aggressive acts. This could provide us with a partial answer to the question of why males bully others more often.

A popular explanation is this. Males are physically constituted so as to be more aggressive than females. This begs the question of what physical differences between the sexes could possibly justify such a statement. We find that studies of brain differences between males and females produce inconclusive results. For

every claim that there is a clear brain difference suggesting a biological explanation for males being aggressive, there are plausible counter claims suggesting that
the 'explanations' fail to explain. Read, for example, Moir and Jessel (1991) for an
account of how brain differences explain gender differences; then read Turner
(1994) to hear from another 'expert' that they don't. Testosterone differences
between the sexes, especially between the adolescent male and the adolescent
female, have frequently been advanced to explain why adolescent boys are so
much more aggressive (see Biddulph 1997). Unfortunately for this view on sex
differences, the role of testosterone in producing aggressive behaviour is
complex and still controversial. As Sapolsky (1997) has shown there is no
reliable relationship between testosterone production and aggressive behaviour.

All this is good news to those who would like to explain the differences as
purely the result of social or cultural influences. But wait. There is one difference
too obvious to miss. One is that males of the human species are on average bigger
and stronger than females. It may reasonably be claimed that differences in
physical strength are not inevitable. We have seen a gradual reduction in differences between men and women athletes in their athletic performances over the
last 50 years. The overlap in physical strength between the sexes is becoming
greater. Few however would predict that in the area of physical prowess equality
will in time be reached.

But how is physical size and strength related to aggression? Does it follow
that bigger people are more aggressive? Of course not. But it does mean that
physically stronger people have the potential to act aggressively – and effectively
– and with less risk involved. They can more often engage in proactive forms of
aggression successfully – in the sense that they can effectively impose their will
on others by physical means – which is a large part of what physical bullying is. It
has sometimes been argued that in domestic situations women are at least as likely
as men to engage in physically aggressive acts (Archer 2000), but the aggression
of women in these situations is typically reactive rather than proactive, that is, in
response to a situation which they see, often rightly, as intolerable. Physical
bullying of men by women is rare, but not unknown, and generally carried out by
the smallish proportion of women who are physically stronger than their partners
and capable of controlled violence. If this view is correct, one would expect that
in situations in which women were physically more powerful they would engage
in bullying their spouses physically as often as men do. As far as I know, the
relevant research has not been done.

The bullying carried out in schools, workplaces and homes is generally of a
verbal kind. Hence, the argument that physical differences account *directly* for
most bullying is quite dubious. We are faced with the more difficult question of
why boys are reported as bullying girls more than vice versa – using verbal means.

One possibility, suggested by the Finnish psychologist Bjorqvist (1994), is that the more physically powerful male is at smaller risk of suffering as a result of physical retaliation from the less powerful female. Some boys, one may suppose, bully girls verbally at school because it seems a safer option. Not always. From time to time I hear stories from women who as schoolgirls severely disconcerted boys who were teasing them by resorting to entirely unexpected physical retaliation, thereby bringing the bullying to a dramatic end.

The view that direct aggression (physical and often verbal) has a potentially greater pay-off and less risk when employed by physically stronger individuals – and therefore generally by males against females – may therefore account for some of the gender differences in cross-gender bullying. However, physical differences are much less relevant when we consider indirect forms of bullying – as in excluding people, turning people against people, spreading hurtful rumours. And here we find that the perpetrators are much less likely to be male, and as we have seen females are more likely to employ this kind of aggression against males rather than vice versa.

Although I think there is something in the argument that the greater bullying by males can in part be explained by differences in physical prowess, as can some bullying between females of different physical strength and fighting skills, I am not convinced that it explains everything, at least not as it stands. I am inclined to believe that the greater physical strength of most males led historically to the imposition of some roles on women that have in the passage of time seemed unreasonable and inconsistent with values that assert equal rights for women. What in the past would seem to most men and women merely a reasonable allocation of responsibilities and duties in an unchallenged patriarchal system has become a matter for strenuous disputation. With it the definition of bullying has changed. What was seen to be justifiable in most people's eyes is no longer the case.

Is it possible that a further, obvious, physical difference between the sexes has some explanatory value? I have in mind the fact that, even in an age of changing role expectations and radical genetic engineering, it is still females that have babies and females who generally take the major responsibility for nursing them. Does such experience – or even the potential experience of bringing young life into the world and caring for it – have implications for how one reacts towards other human beings? Psychological tests show that, generally speaking, females are more nurturing, more empathetic, more caring. It would be surprising if such qualities (which of course some men also have): (i) do not have a basis in a gender-specific life experience; and (ii) are not made more possible by a given biological nature and function.

But is there not more to it? Should we not highlight contemporary social and cultural influences to which males and females are exposed? In exploring social determinants of aggression Gilbert and Gilbert (1998) have proposed that we can add to our understanding of bullying by studying the 'construction of masculinity' and in particular the factors that give rise to its construction. They draw attention to the well-known fact that sex-based harassment and homophobic verbal harassment is not uncommon in schools. In Australia, for instance, it has been reported that some 90 per cent of children believe that sex-based harassment occurs at their school and 44 per cent claim that there is homophobic verbal harassment (Collins *et al.* 1996). (Unfortunately the survey related to children's beliefs about what is the case rather than personal experience of such harassment.) According to Gilbert and Gilbert such findings 'support the view that the construction of masculinity is a powerful component of harassment and bullying in schools, one that does not receive the attention it deserves'.

In my book *Bullying in Schools – And What to Do about It* (Rigby 1997b) I raised a question which still puzzles me. It is why bullies continue to enjoy victories over the weak when there is little or no prestige to be gained in behaving in this miserable fashion. 'Students of masculinity,' we are told, 'would explain that at least some of it can be explained as a confirmation of one's masculinity, based on the sense of power that comes from dominating others' (Gilbert and Gilbert 1998, pp.188–199).

Before we examine this view it would be well to have a clear idea of what masculinity is. The New Penguin English Dictionary defines it as 'having qualities appropriate to a man'. This source gives as an example of its usage 'her deep masculine voice'. What, we are forced to ask, are these 'masculine qualities' that are considered appropriate? I think we must admit that on this matter there is no agreed answer. What people say will vary from sub-culture to sub-culture and is continually changing. But here is a list of qualities (derived from a study of televised sport) in the UK in the 1990s that are seen as conforming closely to conventional constructions of masculinity: 'toughness, aggression, commitment, power, courage, ability to withstand pressure, timing, dexterity, speed, accuracy, concentration, flair, imagination' (Whannel 1992).

We are asked to believe that the boy whose masculinity is constructed so as to incorporate these qualities will be predisposed to bully, that is, to continually, unabatably enjoy hurting weaker people, without justification. By selecting one of these qualities – aggression – one can make some sort of a case. As I have argued earlier, aggressiveness is a necessary but not sufficient factor entailed in bullying. But we have to remind ourselves that the moral judgements we make about aggression depend very much on the context in which the aggression is applied. We have, for instance, a picture that comes down to us of the founder of the Christian religion of 'Gentle Jesus, meek and mild'. This we may think is strangely inconsistent with the behaviour of the angry man who used a whip to drive the economic rationalists out of the Temple in Jerusalem, or of the speaker who used violent language to denounce the child abuser, saying that it were better for him that a millstone were hung about his neck, and that he were drowned in the depth of the sea. It is by no means unusual for a person to perform aggressively when the situation appears to justify it, and mildly when it does not. Indeed, this is a common view of what manly people do. The view that the bully is a coward, true or false, is widely held by children and adults. If we look again at the list of masculine qualities, we see that, with the possible exception of aggression (and only then when it is linked with undesirable actions), they are qualities that most human beings, female and male, would like to have.

But are there not boys who are impressed by one aspect of what is often seen as maleness – the tough aggressive side – and distort this in such a way that it constitutes (and justifies) bullying? Could their sense of masculinity take this as its basis? Quite possibly. But I do not think that this is generally the case. As far as I know, nobody has asked boys whether they think that bullying others is what a 'real' boy would do. Somebody should try it. The nearest I have got is asking schoolchildren (2940 boys and 2508 girls) with an average age of 13 years what significant others would think of them if they bullied someone (Rigby 1997d). The results indeed showed that a much larger proportion of boys than girls believed that significant others, especially their friends, believed that people approved of them bullying others (see Appendix 9).

But this result should be kept in perspective. It turned out that only a minority of boys believed that if they bullied someone they would have the support of close friends; a much smaller percentage thought that their parents and teacher would approve. It appears from this study that about one boy in five believed that his friends would support him in 'making other kids scared'. (Subsequent analyses showed that normative pressure from all sources combined was a significant predictor of self-reported bullying for boys and for girls – see Table 5 in Rigby 1997d, p.215.) It is also clear that although some girls felt they had the support of others to engage in bullying, they constituted a much smaller minority. (Here we should bear in mind that the behavioural indices selected in this study were mainly physical and did not include indirect forms of bullying that are practised more by girls.) But the main point worth making is that 80 per cent of boys did not feel that their friends would support them in bullying others. This is clearly inconsistent with the view that boys in general feel pressured to bully others or do so as an expression of their 'masculine identity'.

Still, the data are worrisome as far as a small but potentially dangerous group of students are concerned. We found that almost one in ten boys believed that their fathers would approve of them scaring other children and that approximately one girl in twelve believed that their friends would be supportive if they got into a fight with someone they could easily beat. This suggests that there are indeed some children whose bullying attitudes towards others are being formed in accordance with how they think significant others would like them to be. Most of these children are boys, but we should not ignore the fact that a substantial proportion are girls.

Sometimes male aggression against women is seen as a means by which a man promotes his notion of what it is to be 'masculine'. I think this is so unusual as to be almost pathological. We may recall Nietzsche (1891, 1952): 'Goest though to a woman? Do not forget to take thy whip.' No doubt literary geniuses have their pathological followers, and we should be careful not to underestimate the extent of domestic violence, often a form of bullying, perpetrated by men (see Chapter 4). But a healthier and more common reaction on the part of men in domestic disputes is that described by G. K. Chesterton (1912):

> When a woman puts up her fists to a man she is putting herself in the only posture in which he is not afraid of her. He can be afraid of her speech and still more of her silence; but force reminds him of a rusted but very real weapon of which he has grown ashamed.

Perhaps with the advances in physical fighting skills on the part of women, more and more men have some cause to be afraid, but the fact remains that very few men, even with their male confidants, boast of assaulting a woman. The most common reaction to having done so is shame.

Gilbert and Gilbert (1998) discuss some of the things schools do to promote aggressiveness in schoolchildren, especially among males, which could (one may think) lead in some circumstances to gender-based bullying. In their view schools promote and/or perpetuate gender stereotypes learned in the home. They do so by adopting a 'masculine management style' – for example, through an emphasis on hierarchy and competition; by teachers adopting a teaching style that treats boys and girls differently, e.g. by using labels like 'ladies and gentlemen'; and by devising curricula that promote masculine values, e.g. abstract reasoning and morality, as against the importance of emotions and feelings. It is difficult to evaluate these suggestions. On the one hand, there is some evidence that non-competitive and group-centred approaches as practised by some schools, for example Steiner schools, may provide an ethos in which peer harassment is relatively infrequent (Rivers and Soutter 1996). Whether such an environment has a special effect in reducing the extent to which boys engage in unpleasant teasing of girls for instance is unclear.

Thus far we have been concerned primarily with the question of why boys bully more often than girls. We must now consider the question of why some of the bullying between members of the same sex is related to notions of gender. It is not easy to estimate the extent to which this kind of bullying occurs. Certainly there are frequent reports from boys that they are teased at school by boys for being or appearing gay or effeminate and from girls who are bullied by girls for not conforming to an acceptable female stereotype. Evidence on the incidence of such behaviour is mainly anecdotal or based upon quotations from what some students have said. N.Duncan (1999) provides copious examples of gender-based bullying in secondary schools, but does not place it in the context of other kinds of bullying and teasing. In a study of name-calling and nicknames among 60 primary school students (aged 8–11 years) in Wales, Crozier and Dimmock (1999) reported that some 20 per cent had experienced nasty comments and unkind nicknames on a daily basis. Nicknames commonly referred to a child's appearance or to a distortion of the child's name. The nasty comments and untrue stories contained a preponderance of derogatory sexual references. In making such references, according to Crozier and Dimmock, the intention is to hurt other children by identifying the victim with a group that is regarded in the culture as being deviant. Sometimes the label for a category is sufficient, e.g. lesbian; but most often an abusive slang term is used, e.g. 'poofta' or 'queer'. Sometimes the term may imply sexual promiscuity as in 'tart'.

Alternative interpretations for such behaviour are possible. It may be that the use of denigratory sexual language by the children relates to what they see as unacceptable and contemptible deviations from what a person should be, e.g. a sissy boy or a butch girl, and that they sense that the target will feel bad by hearing such judgements regarding their sexual identity. Or it may be that the sexual references have no clear meaning, being part of a tirade or 'bad mouthing', expressing a generalised hostility and belittlement.

Here I think the 'students of masculinity' are on firmer ground; firmer still if they are also students of femininity. I have suggested that masculine ideals that boys hold do not normally include bullying others, though they may well support expressions of aggression in some contexts, as in sport and war. But boys do normally want to be accepted by other boys – and only subsequently by girls – and they see that this is unlikely to happen if they engage in some activities seen as appropriate for girls, such as playing with dolls. For some boys this may well constitute a dilemma, for some do like playing with dolls. To be accepted by boys however this must be strenuously denied. The denial becomes more credible if as a boy one berates (or even bullies) another boy for 'sissy' behaviour. A similar, but less severe, process of gender identity formation seems to occur among girls. A girl may feel constrained to engage in 'girlish' activities that are not congenial, and to abjure activities that imply a masculine side to her nature. But the parallels are not so exact. The process is not so exacting. To be a tomboy may be a social advantage in some quarters, though to be over-butch may not.

Probably the most severe and hurtful form of bullying between boys occurs when one of their number is viewed as being in some way 'gay'. According to Agnew (1989) homophobic verbal abuse is particularly widespread in single sex boys' secondary schools, and reflects the oppression of, and fear of, gay people in the school and in society more widely.

This is so despite the general increase in acceptance of homosexuality in most Western countries as reflected through changes in the law and even the promotion of social functions and parades celebrating a homosexual lifestyle. Nevertheless, the mainstream conception of qualities that are appropriate to a man include 'heterosexual'. To the extent to which the stereotypical view of what a man is or can be prevails and is strongly and inflexibly held, it seems likely that 'poofta-bashing' – physically, verbally and indirectly – will continue. However, the fact that stereotypical and prejudiced thinking can be broken down provides us with some hope.

Is bullying gendered?

Before leaving this topic it is worth commenting upon a perspective on bullying that represents it as 'gendered'. The phrase 'aggression is gendered' or 'violence is gendered' crops up with great regularity in current literature on gender and aggression. Definitions of bullying have been proposed which include the assertion that it too is gendered. The phrase has about it a triumphant intellectual quality. But what exactly does it mean? If it means that human males are more likely than human females to be aggressive, violent and to bully, there can be little or no argument. The statistical evidence is practically indisputable. Males bully more, on average. So do some age groups. So do some ethnic groups. If it means that every male is more aggressive, more violent, more inclined to bully than every female it is clearly wrong, just as it is wrong to assume that all young adolescents bully more than all late adolescents.

I suspect that the assertion that bullying is gendered is a slogan rather than a statement that tells us anything precise about gender differences. Like most slogans it has its uses and abuses. Positively, it draws attention to social forces that contribute to gender differences in this area. There is, however, a danger at the present time that it can promote the myth that women are never aggressive, violent or bullying – and, unfortunately, to do so at a time when these tendencies in some women are becoming increasingly evident. It would appear that aggression is becoming increasingly 'de-gendered'. Barbara Ehrenreich (1997) is right in claiming that what has been seen for so long as an attribute of masculinity is now being seen as an attribute that women can also possess. She writes:

Already in popular usage, the dismissive term 'wimp' is applied almost as readily to women as to men, implying that the appropriate stance for both sexes is tough and potentially battle-ready. The division of humanity into 'masculine' and 'feminine' may persist, but these categories may have less and less to do with the biological sexes. With the admission of women to warrior status, we may be ready for the long overdue recognition that it was not only human males who made the transition from prey to predator, but the entire human race. (p.320)

Whether the television character Xena the Warrior Princess is a wholesome influence or not, it is indisputable that images of her kind are increasingly prevalent, popular and influential. If, as many believe, the media both reflects and promotes current thinking about gender roles, it seems likely that females will be influenced to become relatively more aggressive, violent and more inclined to bully, and that the link between gender and aggressiveness will become more attenuated.

Race

Although the term 'race' has dropped out of use as a precise and scientific way of describing a group of people, it retains emotional connotations that appear useful for the purposes of denouncing prejudice and discrimination against groups of people who have, or who are supposed to have, common ancestors and similar physical characteristics or a common culture. Hence although few, if any, would make out a case for, say, describing the Greeks or the Italians as a 'race', when people (apart from themselves) in Australia call them 'wogs' or 'dagos', the cry of 'racist' has become an automatic response. Hence, we will go with common usage and see 'race' as a general term that covers the old and discredited meaning, as in the Aryan race, and include what is sometimes called ethnicity.

The simplest and most common way of defining racist bullying is deliberate harmful action directed against members of a racial group, which, as we have said, implies ethnicity as well. This definition has the advantage of being particularly helpful to those who conduct surveys. As a means of quantifying the extent of racist bullying, all that is needed (it seems) is an estimate from one's survey of the proportion of people who are being treated in this way by members of different racial or ethnic groups. Estimates of racist bullying can then be made for each of the groups in a given community. Unfortunately, this approach is quite flawed.

The trouble is this. A person may choose to bully a person of another ethnic group for a variety of reasons, for example, because he or she is fat, thin, tall, short, slow, clumsy, shy, odd-looking or just plain vulnerable; in short, for reasons that are probably not connected with presumed physical or psychological characteristics of the group to which the target belongs. The problem of misrepresenting the nature of the bullying – racist or not – is especially great when one is describing the motives of individual bullies. Does this matter? After all, bullying has taken place and the target is of a different race. Yes, it does, if we are to make accurate assessments and understand the motives that lie behind different kinds of bullying.

A further problem arises when we try to make estimates of 'racist bullying' from reports on how often one has been bullied by members of another racial or ethnic group. Generally the ethnic group against which most racial bullying is presumed to be aimed constitutes a small minority in a community. There are exceptions, as in the case of indigenous Fijians who were in a majority before they were effectively dispossessed of political rights of the indigenous Fijian population. If we assume that the proneness to bully is distributed fairly evenly across ethnic groups, the chances of encountering a bully from the majority group are of course much greater. If there were no racial bullying at all the minority group would encounter more bullying from the majority group than vice versa. This does not, of course, justify a situation in which a minority groups is bullied. It merely states the obvious, but that needs stating in view of the naïve assumption that one can infer the scale of racial bullying from the proportions of people in different groups bullied by members of another group.

How then can one estimate the extent of racial bullying? Difficult though it may seem, it can best be done by establishing the motive for acts of bullying conducted between individuals from different ethnic groups. Ahmad and Smith (1994) provided useful data on racist bullying when they reported that, in their survey of over 6000 British children, of those being bullied 17.4 per cent of boys and 18.1 per cent of girls in primary schools and 12.1 per cent of boys and 6.3 per cent of girls in secondary schools reported being called nasty names 'about my colour'. Here we can see that 'racist' bullying was being defined and operationalised, though rather narrowly. 'Racist bullying' as the term is now widely used extends beyond colour. Nevertheless, it is worth noting that these figures comprise about one quarter of the percentage that had been called names regardless of presumed reason. A further limitation of this data as an indicator of 'racist bullying' is that it does not include physical bullying, nor indirect bullying such as exclusion practised on racial grounds. It seems likely that anti-racial policies that target overt expressions of racist bullying may create the impression that racist bullying is decreasing when it is possible that indirect forms of racial bullying could be increasing.

One early study of racist bullying was conducted in the late 1980s in the Netherlands (Junger 1990). The respondents in this study were students aged 12 to 17 years from four ethnic groups: Moroccans, Turks, Surinamese and Dutch. There were approximately 200 in each group, selected so as to minimise social-status differences. Dutch children, acting as a comparison group, were from the same locality (street or block) as their ethnic counterparts. Given the expectation that the mainstream Dutch group would report being bullied less than the other groups, the researcher was surprised to find that there were no significant differences between the four groups in either being bullied physically or in being verbally harassed. Subsequent research has provided similar findings; see, for example, Boulton (1995) in Britain and Losel and Bliesener (1999) in Germany. However, when respondents in the Dutch study were asked why they thought they had been bullied or verbally harassed, between 40 and 50 per cent in each minority ethnic group said it was because of their ethnic background. Among the Dutch comparison group the figure was less than 10 per cent. Clearly there was on the part of the many non-Dutch subjects a strong belief that their ethnicity was an important reason for them being bullied and verbally harassed at school.

Racist bullying experienced by indigenous Australians

We cannot of course assume that all racial or minority ethnic groups are bullied equally in all countries. But there is general agreement that among white Australians there is sometimes a degree of racism directed towards Australian Aboriginals. Its nature and the effects it can produce on Aboriginal children has been documented in a recent qualitative study of bullying that was conducted among Aboriginal students attending a large Western Australian government high school catering for approximately 1200 students (Emery, Hayes and Parlett 1999).

Of these, Aboriginal students comprised a small minority of 1.57 per cent, which happens to be similar to the proportion of Aboriginal people in the Australian population. Discussions were conducted with 11 Aboriginal students assembled in a group; these were supplemented by individual interviews. The respondents were asked to talk about their experiences of racist bullying at their school. It was established that they understood 'racism' as being devalued or disadvantaged on grounds of race, colour or culture. Examples taken from their own experiences included 'putting our race down', 'showing no respect for Aboriginal people', 'being singled out because you are Aboriginal', and 'just thinking we are all bad or something'.

With the exception of one Aboriginal in the study, all the participants had been called racist names by white students within the school environment. These included 'Coon', 'Abbo', 'Boongs', 'Nigger', and 'You black piece of dirt'. Some white children saw them as inferior, at a primitive level of evolution. 'They call you "monkeys" sometimes, or they go "oooh oooh oooh" and swing their arms.' An anonymous letter which one of the Aboriginal students received during the period of study read: 'You animals. You have no intelligence, only the cunning of low life.'

Sometimes, it was reported, an Aboriginal student would employ verbal abuse to describe a black person acting like a white person as a 'coconut', meaning white on the inside. Aboriginal children who were not dark-skinned (as is the case with some Aboriginal people) were sometimes derided by white children as 'imports'.

The respondents were angry at the high level of negative stereotyping they had to endure, implicit in such statements from students as 'You crowd are a mob of dogs', 'You're the ones who stole my TV and video' and 'Dirty Abbo'. But not only from students, as this account suggests

> One time I went on an excursion with the school and we went to this kitchen. Everyone was touching stuff, the food and everything. I lifted up this lid on this box and looked at this chocolate that was in there. The teacher yells at me, she yells, 'Don't touch that!' They're really into hygiene here. That teacher carries on as if Aboriginal people have got disease or something. Everyone was touching stuff, all the white kids. She was getting at me.

Repeatedly the Aboriginal children complained of the unfair way in which teachers handled conflict in which they became involved with white children. Whether a physical blow was struck and by whom were the sole criteria for attributing blame and, in some cases, carrying out suspensions. This is how one Aboriginal student saw things.

> When an Aboriginal kid gets called names, there's nothing they can say back. We don't go around just making up names just for white people, just to get at them and make them feel small. So we fight them. That way they are too scared to say anything.

According to my Aboriginal informants, the culturally appropriate response of the Aboriginal child when verbally harassed is to respond physically, which happens to be culturally inappropriate in a school run predominantly for the 98.43 per cent white children. And, one may add, it is easier for teachers to apply a simple rule than to address the root of the problem, which as Emery *et al.* in their report correctly see as racial prejudice.

One may reasonably question whether the seemingly high level of racial bullying described by Emery and *et al.* is to be found only in exceptional schools in Australia. The large-scale Australian study using the PRQ (Rigby 1997c) suggests that indeed Aboriginal students are bullied more often than other students. This study was based upon data from 86 schools where students completed the questionnaire between 1993 and 1998. Aboriginal students comprised 2.0 per cent of the sample of 38,487 respondents. Statistically significant differences in reporting 'being bullied' by other students were found for students identifying themselves as Aboriginal in each of five different ways (see Table 8.1).

Table 8.1 Aboriginal and non-Aboriginal students reporting being bullied at school 'often': Percentages reporting		
	Aboriginal	**Non-Aboriginal**
Being teased in an unpleasant way	12.4	10.2
Being called hurtful names	15.9	12.0
Being left out of things on purpose	10.7	7.3
Being threatened with harm	8.1	5.1
Being hit or kicked	8.7	5.7

Whilst both Aboriginal boys and Aboriginal girls reported being more frequently bullied than others, the differences were more pronounced for boys, for example among boys being called hurtful names (the most common form of bullying in schools) was reported as happening 'often' by 17.4 per cent of the Aboriginal boys.

Typically Aboriginal students comprise a small minority in any school and their being victimised to some extent may be a consequence of their minority status. In the very few schools where Aboriginal students are in a majority I hear complaints from white children that they are being bullied by Aboriginal students, often intimidated physically. Obviously, the risk involved in bullying members of a minority group is much smaller than is the case when a targeted person can call upon many other children to help or to retaliate.

It has also been suggested that the members of some ethnic groups are more vulnerable than others, being less tough and aggressive. According to Sullivan (1998) Asians are perceived as relatively unaggressive and an 'easy target'. Maoris have a reputation for being physically tough. In Fiji, although Indians generally were good at business and able to wield economic power, they were no match for the stronger, more aggressive, sport-oriented, indigenous people who bullied them out of their political rights.

Sometimes a distinction is made between institutionalised and non-institutionalised racist bullying (Sullivan 1998). An institution may have rules or act on principles that disadvantage one group at the expense of another. For example, in Nazi Germany in the 1930s Jews could not hold political office and indeed in many cases they did not have the right to live. The consequence was that they could be bullied with scarcely any risk or impediment. Ethnic groups in many parts of the world are still similarly, if generally less severely, disadvantaged, their members suitable candidates for the most overt and atrocious bullying.

How far to extend the notion of 'institutional racial bullying' is a problem. For example, should it be applied to government policies that promote 'assimilation' of ethnic groups into the mainstream of a national culture as opposed to providing the means for independent or autonomous development with distinct representative political institutions? When educators allocate proportionally more resources for teaching a mainstream language in a multicultural community are they guilty of 'racist institutional bullying'? Is the absence of affirmative action in favour of an historically disadvantaged group also an indicator? Should there be special consideration given to indigenous ethnic groups as opposed to late-coming immigrant groups? These practical questions are raised, and answered in different ways, when we think about racist institutional bullying.

Disability

Although it has been claimed that physical differences apart from size and strength make little or no difference to the likelihood of being bullied (Olweus 1993), where the differences are such as to constitute 'disability' the situation may change. There is accumulating evidence that disabled individuals are often more likely than others to be bullied.

Because the term disability covers a wide range of specific kinds of impairments to which some individuals adjust better than others, defining disability is not easy and identifying the disabled is controversial. Probably the most widely accepted definition of disability, proposed by the World Health Organisation (see Broome and Llewelyn 1995, p.62) is as follows:

> Disability refers to a stable and persisting physical or psychological dysfunction at the personal level, by necessity again confined to the individual; this dysfunction stems from the limitations imposed by the impairment and by the individual's psychological reaction to it.

When we speak of 'dysfunction' we have in mind how a person should function and what constitutes a significant deviation from what is 'normal functioning'. Although the notion of disability is grounded in objective impairment, there can be, and sometimes are, differences of opinion about whether some individuals should be categorised as 'disabled' and also how one should react to disabled people. Probably most people react towards those they see as disabled with sympathy and concern. Not everyone though. As we have seen, in 1996 Holzbauer and Berven coined the term 'disablement harassment' and gave numerous examples of its operation. They described a case (taken from Wright

1983) of a child whose legs were congenitally deformed and how he was treated on the first day of school.

> My sister Terry took me to school the first day. Clutching her hand, I hoisted myself up the steps of the schoolyard. It was crowded with children… I heard loud laughter. 'Hey, Louie, look at the ape man.' Three big boys came toward me… The crowd of jeering boys had grown. One of them came over and shoved me. I shoved back against his knee. 'Oh, you want to fight, kid?'…'I want to go home.' I hung on Terry's arm, tears rolling down my cheeks. 'Sissy, sissy.'

This account makes it clear, as do many others describing the treatment by peers of disabled children, that something other than 'verbal behaviour as distinguished from physical violence or force' may be involved. I propose a broader category of 'disablement bullying' (modelled on that of Holzbauer and Berven 1996) to cover such experiences more adequately.

> Disablement bullying is defined as the unwelcome bothering, tormenting, troubling, ridiculing or coercing of another person related to the disability of that person and may be composed of verbal, non-verbal (as in gestures), physical (as in pushing or striking) or indirect behaviour, as in exclusion from activities in which the disabled person could take part. The bullying behaviour is typically repeated and often takes place in a social context with the bully attempting to gain power over the disabled individual.

Reference to indirect forms of bullying is particularly important in examining ways in which disabled people may be treated, since their exclusion from activities in which they could take place is common and most hurtful.

Much of the research on the connection between disability and bullying has been done with children. The large majority of cases concern children with congenital impairment. It has been estimated that up to 2 per cent of all children have some degree of such disability. The most common form is cerebral palsy, a condition that is often associated with epilepsy and severe problems related to hearing, seeing, learning and feeding. Other relatively common physical disabilities include spina bifida and muscular dystrophy. Learning difficulties associated with chromosomal abnormalities or defects in the central nervous system are experienced by about 4 children in 1000. A relatively common form of disability is Down's syndrome. This is commonly associated with both problems of learning and social difficulties due to facial appearance. In addition, many children are severely handicapped by specific difficulties in seeing and hearing. Less severe disabilities include having limb deformities, such as club foot, speech impediments, as in stammering, poor coordination and clumsiness; cognitive and/or emotional difficulties, as in mild autism and Asperger syndrome and attention deficit disorder. All these and more can bring about unwelcome attention from peers.

Children with disabilities are nowadays often described as children with 'special needs' and, where possible, integrated in schools with mainstream children but with some special facilities made available to assist them in ways deemed appropriate according to the nature of their disability. There are presumed advantages in such integration – for special needs children who can learn to cope with situations and people they will encounter in the 'real world', and for mainstream students who can learn to understand, and treat with understanding, people different from themselves. It had been confidently predicted in the 1970s that with increased contact between the disabled and other students the stigma of disablement would vanish (Wolfensberger 1972). Sadly this did not happen. The research evidence is clear that children with special needs are bullied in such contexts far more frequently than other children (Dawkins 1996; Martlew and Hodson 1991; Nabuzka and Smith 1993; Whitney, Smith and Thompson 1994; Yude, Goodman and McConachie 1998). Whether they are more damaged psychologically by being in mainstream units than in more protected or sheltered situations is a contentious issue for which evidence has been provided in support of both sides of the question.

Some reports have assessed the degree of difference between the proneness of disabled and non-disabled children to be victimised by peers. It clearly depends in part on the nature and severity of the disability. Nabuzka and Smith (1993) reported that of the children at two schools in England, where they conducted their research, special needs students with moderate learning difficulties were significantly more likely than others to be selected as victims of bullying. Of these disabled children, some 33 per cent were nominated by students as frequently victimised compared with 8 per cent of other children. In a further study in which special needs students were matched for school year group, age and gender with other children, the results showed that the former had between two and three times more risk of being bullied. They were also at more risk of bullying others!

It appears that the visibility of the abnormality is an important factor. It was found that when 5–11-year-old children were asked to indicate how much they liked or disliked other children as presented in photographs, they rated children in wheelchairs much more negatively than those with hearing aids or spectacles (Maras and Brown 2000). Dawkins (1996) found that among children attending hospital clinic, those with visible abnormalities, such as an unusual facial appearance and/or unusual gait, were more than twice as likely to be bullied at school than other paediatric patients. The risk, she reported, was greater among disabled children who had few friends, played alone at playtime, required special help at school and were male. In another study, children aged 9–10 years, with hemiplegia (paralysed along one side), were found to be bullied more than matched controls. The difference was not accounted for by teacher-estimated IQ or behaviour. The authors surmised that the observed difference may have been due to either neurologically determined deficits in appropriate social skills on the part of the victims or, alternatively, the prejudices of children without disabilities. Both factors could have operated.

It does not follow that all people with a similar disability have an equal likelihood of being victimised by others. In a study of adults with mental retardation in South Australia, Nettelbeck *et al.* (2000) were able to identify 31 who had over the last 12 months been victims of a personal offence and 32 who had not. They found that those with the lowest IQs and those with eccentric mannerisms were no more likely to have been victimised than others. The distinguishing feature was the higher tendency of those who were victimised to respond to potentially threatening situations with hostility and aggression. The non-victims were more likely to withdraw quietly. Here we see that although being mentally retarded may increase vulnerability to being bullied, how the target was inclined to respond to threatening situations constituted an additional risk factor – and one which individuals might learn to overcome.

In some cases the bullying of disabled children may take the form of teasing and mocking. This is often so with children with a speech impediment. In a retrospective study in England of 324 adults who stammer, it was found that 83 per cent of them had been bullied at school (Hugh-Jones and Smith 1999). No fewer than 71 per cent reported that they had been bullied by peers at least weekly and 18 per cent every day. This is far in excess of what is normally found among children. The main form of bullying was ridicule and name-calling. The researchers ascertained that in 97 per cent of cases the stammering preceded the bullying, that is, it was a likely cause rather than an effect. Children with more severe stammering were bullied more often and especially when they had few, if any, friends. Most of the respondents believed that as a result of the bullying they had lost confidence in themselves, their self-esteem had suffered, they had become more shy, nervous and depressed. Some felt ashamed of themselves and experienced difficulty in making relationships with anyone. Sadly, some 33 per cent reported that the effects still persisted.

The reactions of disabled people to being bullied may sometimes lead to an intense desire for revenge. Vash (1981) describes the case of a disfigured young man who as a child had been severely bullied and had became a 'whipping boy' for his poor alcoholic and dysfunctional family. Nearly every evening his parents, two siblings and two cousins would get drunk and make vicious fun of his disfigurement. One evening when the group had been more abusive than usual, he systematically lured each inebriated individual into a different room of the house, bludgeoning each one of them to death. A different reaction was observed in another case. This concerned a German who had lost a leg in an accident. One afternoon after school had ended for the day, his wife saw boys harassing her husband, spitting on him and saying repeatedly: 'You live off our taxes. You'd have been gassed under Hitler.' According to his wife 'he was so sorry that I had to find out about it. But he added, I shouldn't be sad. It wasn't new to him. He said it was the first time for me, but it had happened to him often, and it didn't matter.' Shortly after this incident the man committed suicide. He wrote to his wife that people with disabilities do not have a chance in this world and that he would now personally 'destroy the cripple'.

Why are disabled people so often the target of bullying? One's first reaction is likely to be one of incredulity and disbelief. Most people think it right to respond empathically to those less fortunate than themselves. But clearly many do not. It has been suggested that disabled children are often unpopular with their peers because they lack valued qualities or abilities such as attractiveness, intelligence and athletic ability; that they are often rejected by peers because they are socially incompetent and prone to depression (Schneider 2000).

Another suggestion is that severely disabled people constitute a group whose members one rarely encounters and the imagination runs wild about the kind of people they are. In fictional books and films they are often depicted as thoroughly (not specifically) abnormal, either as sinister or depraved, as in the case of Frankenstein's monster, Long John Silver and Captain Hook, or unusually good or saintly as with the Hunchback of Notre Dame, Cyrano de Bergerac and the Phantom of the Opera.

It has been suggested that some disabled people may be bully/victims and that they may, at times, engage in bullying more than others do, despite their opportunities being more limited. Among those who become disabled later in life by accident or through the ageing process, adjustment to loss of faculties may take the form of first denial, then anger and generalised hostility, then depression, before there can be a final adjustment. Such mood swings, though understandable, could at times give rise to them wishing to hurt others and engaging in acts of bullying. However, these speculations as yet lack empirical support.

Social class

Studies of the relationship between children's involvement in bully/victim problems and the socio-economic status of their parents have provided mixed results. Some have suggested that social class makes a difference. In a study conducted in schools in and around Sheffield, England, a largely industrial area, it was found that involvement in bully/victim problems was significantly more likely to occur in schools in relatively disadvantaged areas (Whitney and Smith 1993). In Scotland Mellor (1999) found that children of parents with professional and managerial jobs were less likely to be bullied, whilst those whose parents had skilled manual jobs were more likely to be victims – and also more likely to be bullies! Research conducted in the Netherlands suggests that bullying is more common among children from socially disadvantaged and inner-city areas (Junger-Tas 1999).

As against the above findings, Olweus (1999) claimed that among boys attending Swedish schools bullying was unrelated to social class (indicated by indices of parent income level and length of parent education). In neither Spain nor Portugal was bullying found to be related to social class (Almeida 1999; Ortega and Mora-Merchan1999;). In France a study of the relationship between the bullying behaviour of 77 students (aged 15 years) and the social class of their adoptive parents (the children were all adopted before the age of 3 years) concluded that there was no significant relationship (Duyme 1990).

The reasons for such inconsistency in the results from studies of social class and bullying may, in part, be due to cross-national differences in the psychological characteristics of members of higher and lower socio-economic status groups. For example, there is evidence that whilst people whose occupations may be categorised as 'lower class' in England tend to be relatively pro-institutional authority, the opposite is the case in Australia (Rigby, Metzer and Ray 1986).

But perhaps more importantly, in assessing bullying tendencies and their relation to social class, we should distinguish between the ways in which bullying may be expressed. Some research has focused on the expression of physical aggression and claimed that acting aggressively in a physical way is more characteristic of children from families who are economically disadvantaged. For instance, according to Dodge, Pettit and Bates (1994) in the United States physical aggression on the part of children arises as a result of harsh discipline, lack of maternal warmth, exposure to aggressive adult models, maternal aggressive values, family life stressors, mother's lack of social support, peer group instability, and lack of cognitive stimulation. All these, they suggest, are more common in families of low socio-economic status.

But what of other forms of aggression and bullying such as verbal and indirect bullying? A recent Australian study of schoolchildren attending seven schools differing widely in socio-economic status (Rigby and Bagshaw 2001) provided evidence that students attending the secondary school in a catchment area with the lowest social status indeed had the highest level of physical bullying, but students in the different schools did not differ significantly from each other on measures of verbal and indirect bullying.

The elderly

The elderly have some of the characteristics of young children. They tend to be less powerful mentally and physically than many of those with whom they interact on a daily basis. We sometimes speak, rather unkindly, of the elderly as entering a second childhood. It would therefore be surprising if chronic imbalances of power did not result in them being bullied by those who choose to abuse their power over them. Cases of elderly abuse are often reported, as in the following example from Minaker and Frishman (1995):

> With good health and a sizeable pension, 76-year-old Mary T. should have been enjoying a comfortable retirement. But in fact, her life was made miserable by a seemingly endless barrage of threats, insults and indignities from her live-in son. A habitual gambler and drug user, the son was merciless: he spat at Mary, brandished a knife in her face, stole her money, and sold her possessions. After several emergency room trips and two hospitalisations, social workers convinced Mary to move out and join a support group with other elderly people abused by their loved ones. With a new apartment and understanding friends, Mary finally had some peace. But her son found her, and feeling a mother's guilt and shame, Mary took him back – and opened the door for another round of heartache. (p.1)

Some of the issues that arise when we consider schoolyard bullying seem to apply when we consider bullying and the elderly. Just as there are provocative victims among schoolchildren, we may suspect that there are elderly people whose petulant demands and periodic tirades elicit bullying from their long-suffering, exasperated carers. Quite so. But the research is clear that it is the characteristics of the abusers that are the more powerful predictors of family violence, not the characteristics of the victims (Pillemer and Finkelhor 1989). Moreover, in general (they claim) it is not the stressed-out care-givers who are mainly to blame, but rather relatives (especially spouses) and acquaintances with their own histories of problems, such as mental illness and alcoholism.

Cases sometimes come to light of adults who force an elderly parent to give them money to support a drug habit and of adults who have for many years carried a strong sense of resentment towards an ageing parent whom they can, at last, abuse with impunity (Shapiro 1992). Financial and psychological abuse is often directed towards elderly women by their adult children whilst long-term physical abuse is more likely to be practised by their husbands on whom they are dependent for companionship (Henderson 1996).

Assessing the extent of elderly abuse is difficult. Bruises that suggest physical abuse may result from falls; accusations by elderly people of being emotionally abused may sometimes reflect paranoia. On the other hand, many elderly people who are being abused do not want their 'shameful secret' incriminating their children to get out. Some may fear recrimination if they tell, and fear that they will not be believed. Not surprisingly, figures on elderly abuse have been disputed. According to Shapiro (1992) claims that in the USA there are some two million reportable cases of abuse each year are exaggerations. His more cautious estimate of half that number nevertheless indicates that it is a major problem. In Australia it has been estimated that as many as 5 per cent of the population over the age of 65 are subjected to some form of mistreatment from someone they trust (Kelly 1992).

Mistreatment of the elderly is commonly categorised as physical abuse, psychological abuse, financial abuse and neglect. A study by the National Center for Elderly Abuse (NCEA) in Washington DC of cases reported in 34 American states indicated that the most common form of abuse was neglect, followed by physical abuse, then financial exploitation, emotional abuse, sexual abuse and other. Table 8.2 gives the percentage figures (from Minaker and Frishman 1995, p.3).

| Table 8.2 Elderly mistreatment: Percentages reporting ||
Kind of abuse	Percentage
Neglect	58.5
Physical	15.7
Financial	12.3
Emotional	7.3
Sexual	0.4
Other	5.8

The statistics provided above relate to the main kinds of abusive treatment reported in particular cases. To some extent, this may be misleading as an elderly person may be subjected to a number of different kinds of abuse, for example both physical and emotional. Physical abuse may include slapping, bruising, burning or any other action that involves the deliberate infliction of pain. Emotional abuse consists of any non-physical action that produces mental anguish; this is commonly demeaning behaviour in the form of threats, insults and name-calling. Because elderly people have often accumulated wealth and property over which others may want control, financial exploitation is not uncommonly practised by other family members. This may include forcing an elderly person to sign over property and other assets or taking money that is intended for the person in their care. Neglect may be seen as a failure to fulfil care-taking obligations, such as not providing food or health care when it is needed, leaving an elder isolated or abandoned, preventing access to necessary aids such as spectacles or hearing devices, keeping elderly persons uninformed about matters of great concern to them. Do all these treatments constitute deliberate 'bullying'? Not always. Neglect may sometimes be unintentional and due to ignorance. However, where the power is being systematically abused – as it sometimes is with elderly people towards whom there is on-going hostility or even enjoyment at seeing them suffer – we can identify it as malign bullying.

Finally, whilst cases of elder abuse occur mainly in homes, there is increasing evidence in Australia of bullying directed towards older people who have opted to remain in the workforce. Even though their experience is highly relevant and advantageous to the firm, repeated disparagement and intimidation had led many of them to discontinue their employment (Bulbeck 2001). Criticism of elderly employees is sometimes defended on the grounds that they are not familiar with new technologies, but often it appears to be due to ageist prejudice.

Conclusions

We have seen that involvement in bully/victim problems, as perpetrator or victim or both, may be associated with membership of a given social group or category. Generalisations are in fact difficult to sustain in this area. In some social contexts, one's gender, membership of a racial or ethnic group, social status or disablement may each have significant and serious implications for how one is treated by others or how one is prone to treat others. By and large (we have seen) males appear to be more likely than females to engage in bullying behaviour, and minority ethnic or racial groups are more likely than others to be victimised, as are people with conspicuous mental or physical disabilities. But there are many exceptions. Moreover, conclusions must be qualified by statements about what kind of bullying is involved.

Explanations for the associations between membership of social groups and victimisation draw upon a variety of sources. These include theories purporting to explain how social prejudice and discrimination arise and notions of how members of certain groups, such as males, come to have conceptions of self which lead them to bully others. Some explanations simply point to the fact that members of some social groups are more vulnerable to attack than others and constitute a low risk to the potential bully, and are accordingly more often victimised.

For some the focus on the relevance of social categories is so intense (and blinkered) that they practically ignore everything else. As we have seen, bullying has actually been defined so as to include, as an essential feature, being 'gendered'. I have noticed bitter conflicts between those who wish to access funds to stop sexual harassment and those who want to address bullying – as if the two were in competition! It has been seriously argued that the term 'bullying' should be dropped from analyses of social problems because it somehow conceals or minimises the overwhelming importance of countering racism (Loach and Bloor 1995). Such viewpoints may derive from an intense emotional concern and commitment over a practical issue. It is unfortunate when it obscures awareness of the total picture.

When a narrow view of bullying becomes part of educational policy the consequences may be serious. I recently discussed anti-bullying policy with a leading education department official in Australia and learned, to my astonishment, that she believed that anti-bullying policy could be covered entirely by three considerations: gender, race and disability. Bullying on 'personal' grounds did not exist, she said. Hence there was no need to recognise it in promoting educational policy. There appear to be several reasons for this view being held by some (by no means all) educational authorities. There are powerful pressure groups that seek understandably to promote their own special agenda to which government bodies are sensitive. Their aims are laudable. The groups whose interests they promote, females, people of non-mainstream ethnicity or race and the disabled, may need their support. But the effects in pushing aside other interests can be – to say the least – unfortunate. They are also, as social groups, conspicuous, unlike children who are shy, introverted, small, anxious, or unassertive, unable to defend themselves. These are people who are being bullied for being – or seeming to be – the kind of people they are, not because they are part of a group against which there happens to be some 'stupid' prejudice, and from whom they can gain support. Our sympathy and support must go out to all people who are victimised because of their membership of a group that, on average, endures more victimisation than others, but we must be careful not to neglect the rights of others.

Chapter 9

Places and situations

There, but for the Grace of God, go I.

— A comment attributed to John Bradford,
a 16th century chaplain,
on observing criminals being taken for execution

Some places and some situations are more conducive to bullying than others. Children know this. If they feel vulnerable they stay away from danger spots as long as they can: toilets for instance. They may stick around grown-ups, and in an emergency seek asylum in the school library. Adults who feel vulnerable stay away from drinking bars where there are strangers. When they go to a football match they choose the specially reserved viewing enclosure that caters for fans who support their own team. On rag day a nervous college student may decide to stay at home rather than get caught up in rowdy student behaviour.

We have seen that 'aggression' is a necessary but not sufficient condition in producing bullying behaviour. Aggression can be discharged in a large number of ways, not always anti-socially. In the schoolyard some children do indeed feel that they should only 'pick on somebody their own size'. But it is reasonable to expect that where and when aggression is stimulated, more bullying will take place. Hence, as a first step, we can review the conditions in which aggression is typically aroused.

Proposed as long ago as 1939 by John Dollard *et al.*, the notion that aggression results from being frustrated has been widely accepted as a reasonable explanation for most, if not all, expressions of anger and aggression. This simple theory has needed to accommodate subsequent observations that: (i) we feel frustrated not so much as a result of absolute deprivation, but rather because we are not getting what we expect and think we deserve to get; (ii) seeing other people act aggressively and get what they want is an incentive for us to act aggressively; and (iii) the threshold for acting aggressively can be lowered under some circumstances, for example when we are intoxicated by alcohol, lose our inhibitions through attendance at mass rallies, or are stimulated by violent and/or erotic videos. Hence we should not be surprised to find people acting aggressively under the following conditions:

- Crammed in the back of a bus, trapped in slow-moving freeway traffic or living three to a room in a college dorm (from Myers 1999).

- Feeling irritable on an unpleasantly hot or humid day.

- One's favourite team has lost the match that decided the championship.

- Attendance at a Ku Klux Klan hate rally.

- Viewing a violent video. Say, one showing a man forcing himself on a woman. At first she resists and tries to fight off her attacker. But then as she becomes sexually aroused her resistance melts. Now she is in ecstasy pleading for more (from Myers 1999).

- News that an unworthy colleague has been promoted over you.

These and similar experiences may prime some individuals to act aggressively and lead them to bully. Let us look now at what is known about the places where bullying typically occurs, starting with what we know most about – where children are bullied.

Where children are bullied

Some answers are suggested if we examine the situations in school where children are more often bullied. The results of an Australian survey are shown in Table 9.1.

Table 9.1 Student perceptions of where and when bullying occurs: Percentages reporting having seen bullying taking place in different settings		
	Respondents' age group	
	8–12 years n = 9,216	13–18 years n = 28,428
At recess	80%	93%
In the classroom	65%	81%
On the way home	49%	56%
On the way to school	19%	37%

Source: Rigby (1997c)

Why is it that recess should be the scene of most bullying, despite the fact that children spend more of their schooldays in the classroom? One's first thoughts are these. Recess time is when there are more opportunities to bully because: (i) there are more vulnerable (younger) children around than in the classroom; (ii) there is much less adult supervision; and (iii) activities are less structured, indeed they are often quite unstructured.

These conditions, one might think, would be universal in schools. One would predict that bullying would be greatest in the breaks between classes everywhere. Several years in discussion with a noted Japanese authority on bullying, Professor Yohji Morita, I was astonished to find that in Japan the class-room, not the playground, was where bullying happened most. The explanation appears to be that at break times Japanese children typically stay in their class-rooms – unsupervised by adults. In Australia and, indeed, in most countries they go out at what is still called in most schools 'playtime'. Bullying evidently takes place where there is least adult supervision. The end result of extreme adult absence is arguably what we see in Golding's (1954) *Lord of the Flies.*

This last conclusion fits in well with observations made by Dan Olweus (1993) in his study of bullying at recess and lunch time involving some 40 primary and secondary/junior schools in Norway. He reports a clear negative relationship between relative 'teacher density' during break time and the amount of bully/victim problems. He comments: 'This result indicates that it is of great importance to have a sufficient number of adults present among the students during break times...' He goes on to qualify this somewhat: '...probably on con-dition that the adults are willing and prepared to interfere with incipient bullying episodes' (Olweus 1993, p.26).

Recently there has been some, albeit limited, experimental support for the view that the presence of adults monitoring playgrounds at recess can diminish bullying. In a study conducted at a US elementary school, increasing the number of staff supervisors at recess time was one of the interventions designed to reduce 'problem behaviours' which included verbal and physical forms of bullying, such as name-calling, threats and physical attacks on other students. In addition, the staff sought to develop in students appropriate social skills, drawing attention to relevant school rules each day prior to each break. Although it is not clear which component of the intervention was effective, the outcome was clear. There was a substantial and significant drop in 'problem behaviour', especially during times when student activities were unstructured (Lewis, Calvin and Sugai 2000).

When do children bully?

In his study of aggressive fighting among British middle school children, Michael Boulton (1993) made an interesting observation about when bullying was at its most intense and serious. He noticed that there was more conflict during the last quarter of recess. Why should that be? My suggestion is that for many children as time passes the absence of structure and (with it) interesting things to do during recess becomes more and more frustrating and intolerable. Some turn to bullying as a means of breaking the monotony. We know from a number of studies that the setting-up of adult-organised games can reduce the occurrence of aggressive and unruly behaviour (Murphy, Hutchison and Bailey 1983).

It has been observed that the incidence of bullying in schools rises appreciably when children transfer from a primary to a secondary school. There may be several reasons for this: the new school is usually bigger and more impersonal than the old one; less attention is paid to individual children; there is more concern with what the children need to know and less with what children need to be. Moreover, in the new school there are many more children who are more powerful than the incoming children.

For many children the first few weeks, sometimes months, in a new school are particularly challenging. There is, among other things, a new 'pecking order' to be established. Among children and young adolescents this is often a matter of physical domination among boys and social domination among girls. Hence for a time there is likely to be for some children a period of instability as children vie for status. This drive to establish one's position in the hierarchy is also often found among adults. The means used are usually more indirect and more subtle. Not always, however. In organisations in which the use of force is highly salient, as in the armed forces and the police force, the use or threat of physical means to establish dominance is not uncommon. Initiation procedures may serve the purpose of identifying those who are 'not up to much' and are to be consigned to the lower end of the hierarchy. The period of 'testing out' during which bullying is rife may be of relatively short duration.

My own experience as a naval rating in my teens can be divided into two periods: a short one of sizing up others (and being sized up) and establishing where one was in the order of things – bound for elevation or definitely not officer material; and a later, less strenuous time, when there was growing trust and friendships were formed as the perceived need to bully or be bullied subsided.

Roles

My introduction to the professional bully was in the form of a chief petty officer on the parade ground. He saw his role as to identify the personality weaknesses in individual ratings and to do his best to terrify those he could. Theoretically this was to desensitise them to concern over the enemy without. It helped me to understand how so many NCOs (non-commissioned officers) were shot in the back by their own men when hostilities began. In practice, it was an opportunity for officers to engage in play-acting and showing off, and for the most part it seemed to do little or no harm. Yet I am not sure that for many of us it did not provide a model of how to behave when you wanted others to do as you wished. I reflected on my early days of teaching and whether my predilection for raising my voice to command attention could not be traced to those traumatising days on the parade ground.

The experimental literature in social psychology is replete with examples of how the adoption of a role can lead to serious bullying. One of the best-known is a study of the behaviour of students who volunteered to spend time in a simulated prison constructed in an American university psychology department (Zimbardo 1972). Some were randomly allocated roles of guard, others as prisoners. The former were dressed in guard uniforms and equipped with clubs and whistles. Others were locked in cells and made to wear humiliating outfits. Before long, the guards began to take their roles seriously, continually disparaging the prisoners and devising cruel and degrading routines. Bullying was rife. The situation was plainly getting out of hand. According to the experimenter, there was dangerous confusion between reality and illusion, between role-playing and self-identity. The experiment had to be aborted. It was as if the faces of the young men in the experiment actually changed to fit the masks they were asked to wear.

A study of the behaviour of security men or 'bouncers' at drinking bars shows that some, but by no means all, people whose job it is to be ready to use force to control people go to excess and feel justified in bullying others. The researchers, Wells, Graham and West (1998), observed naturally occurring aggression among young people at twelve young people's bars located in a Canadian city and interviewed participants where possible afterwards. Under the influence of alcohol, aggressive incidents were numerous and security men or bouncers frequently intervened. They were categorised by the researchers according to their modus operandi as: the 'good' – those who intervened to prevent aggression through identifying problem situations and reducing provocative behaviour; the 'neutral' – those who failed to anticipate problems but dealt firmly with aggressive behaviour when it arose; the 'bad' – those who showed poor judgement and acted unfairly or inconsistently; and the 'ugly' – those who were described as actually bullying or harassing patrons, provoking aggression and being physically aggressive. Of the 84 interventions by security staff, some 29 (35%) were categorised as 'ugly'. An interviewee who had been engaged in defending himself during a fight with three others described one such ugly episode (recorded verbatim):

> ... They grab me, the bouncers start beating me up. Like I mean you know on top of all my problems with these other guys the bouncers start working on me too, so I'm being pushed through the crowd, I'm still bent over, I see the occasional fist come, I look up and they're taking me out the back door. The only thing is they don't open the door first, they threw me right into it; it's this big oak wood door; it weighs a ton; it's closed. Head first right into it. I thought I broke my neck, right. So this time though they pull me back, I'm going towards this door, all of a sudden one of them pulls it open and they just sort of threw me off the steps. There were about five steps; I hit the ground... (p.827)

Here it would seem the role had given the bouncers permission – or so they thought – to bully. Examples from the behaviour of police officers and military personnel and even school teachers are not difficult to find. Given the role, given the situation, for some, the bullying behaviour would seem to follow, naturally.

Obedience

Bullying may occur when you are in a situation in which you are asked to carry out orders designed to hurt people less powerful than yourself. We may think that the real bully is the person who gave the orders, not the compliant executioner. This is a moot point. You may remember Lieutenant Calley, the soldier in the Vietnam war who fired on and killed numerous defenceless Vietnamese civilians. Well, he was not saved from judgement by the plea that he was only carrying out orders, any more than Adolph Eichmann and other war criminals were spared for their part in carrying out orders to exterminate Jews in Nazi Germany. We are inclined in our rush to judgement to attribute the bullying behaviour of these people to their personalities or characters, rather than to the situations in which they found themselves. It is easy in fact to underestimate the situational pressure that seems to force individuals to act obediently and carry out inhuman orders, as experiments by Stanley Milgram (1965) have demonstrated.

In the situation devised by Milgram, subjects were asked to administer electric shocks to another person as part of an experiment on the effects of punishment on human learning processes. Although in fact no shocks were given, the subjects were led to believe that the learner would be receiving shocks of ever increasing magnitude with each successive failure to give the correct answer in the learning experiment. The remarkable thing was that many of the subjects continued to 'deliver' shocks of increasing strength at the experimenter's request even when they reached a level of potentially lethal intensity.

From the viewpoint of the subject, it must have appeared that the 'learner' in the experiment was being bullied in the sense of being the target of a systematic abuse of power. That many subjects felt that the actions they were executing were unjustified is evident from the descriptions provided by Milgram of how they behaved in this situation. When the learner was heard to scream as if in severe pain and to protest that his heart was bothering him, subjects typically became indecisive, anxious and even upset, but as a rule continued nevertheless. There had never before been such a powerful and dramatic demonstration of the power of a college professor (no less) to command authority.

Grant for a moment that the learner was being seriously hurt, his life threatened by what was happening to him – for failing to answer correctly some trivial-seeming questions in a psychological experiment. Who then were the bullies? We might identify two: the experimenter who was bullying the subject with assertions that 'the experiment requires that you go on', turning a deaf ear to the concerns of the subject; and the subject who was delivering the seemingly life-threatening shocks to the innocent learner-victim. Two bullies and two victims, perhaps three bullies and three victims if we include those who joined together to denounce the study as 'unethical' and Milgram, who came to think of himself as the real victim.

This study of Milgram's impressed researchers and public alike. It provided results that were surprising. Milgram had quizzed a bunch of psychiatrists on whether they thought the subjects in his experiment – ordinary people from all walks of life – would obey the inhuman orders they were to be given. They unanimously thought they wouldn't. He impressed researchers because he was able to specify conditions that affected how far subjects would go in carrying out the experimenter's requests. He reported that the more remote the victim appeared (not visible and with no voice feedback) the more ready was the subject to act as potential executioner. The comparative lack of pain experienced by those releasing missiles on Baghdad during the Gulf War became easier to understand. He reported also that the salience of the experimenter to the subject was important:

the closer, the more distinctly present, breathing down your neck, as opposed to being present only in a pre-recorded message, the more powerful and irresistible the command.

The awful implication to be drawn from this study is that the systematic abuse of power is considerably facilitated by the readiness of people to be coerced by situations in which an authority is present and is seen as having some kind of legitimacy. Milgram commented in 1979:

> If a system of death camps were set up in the United States of the sort we had in Nazi Germany, one would be able to find sufficient personnel for these camps in any medium sized American town.'(Cited by Myers 1999, p.219)

We should add too that the authority who calls the shots may be quite cushioned from reality. The connection between pressing a button in Washington and producing a chain reaction of human destruction may be psychologically obscure. Hence the need to minimise situations in which power can be abused – and the development of enough imagination to enable the consequences of actions that devastate to be foreseen.

Institutional pressure

It is sometimes difficult to appreciate the pressure coming from the institution to which one belongs and with which one has identified. The film *A Few Good Men* begins with a scene of two young marines entering the room of a sleeping comrade and violently assaulting him, leaving him for dead. Standard bullying situation getting out of hand: the explanation, Code Red. We learn that Code Red is the unwritten code that requires marines who let the side down to be taught a lesson. 'Good' marines who had internalised this code had no option but to bully. Their dead comrade had not only proved to be a weak link in the regiment, breaking down under stress conditions, but had committed the most unforgivable of crimes. He had informed on one of his regiment who opened fire on the 'enemy' without permission, and therefore had to pay for it. We come to see that the bullying was not an act of personal malevolence but rather one undertaken from a misconceived sense of duty, reinforced by an order from a superior officer.

Threats to personal survival

We cannot ethically examine the effects on bullying tendencies of highly threatening situations experimentally, but we can draw on the experiences of individuals who have been placed in such situations. Perhaps the most extreme circumstances in which life has been continually threatened were those endured by the men, women and children in Hitler's Germany who were rounded up and placed in concentration camps to await execution. These were ordinary people from many walks of life who happened, for the most part, to be Jewish. Accounts of how they behaved under these extreme conditions have been provided by the psychiatrist Victor Frankl, who was imprisoned between 1942 and 1945 in four Nazi death camps including Auschwitz. He wrote:

> On the average, only those prisoners could keep alive who, after trekking from camp to camp, had lost all scruples in their fight for existence; they were prepared to use every means, honest and otherwise, even brutal force, theft and betrayal of their friends, in order to save themselves. (Frankl 1964, p.15)

Some of these, we are told 'the most brutal of prisoners', were selected as Capos and embraced the role of carrying out orders from the Nazi guards to further oppress and humiliate their own people.

On a less extreme scale, the prison environment in every country is seen as a threat to survival by many inmates. This is largely because there is little or no opportunity to escape from other people, many of whom are seen as dangerous types. In some prisons prisoners are too scared to leave their cells. The perceived danger is particularly high when the rate of turnover or transiency of a prison population is high, and consequently there are repeated challenges to the structure of the prison hierarchy. Survival skills are at a premium, and bullying is a way of life embraced by some as a means of getting through. High moral values appear to be dispensable.

The reality of prison life and how it can affect the moral judgements of prisoners became disturbingly clear to a group of Harvard psychologists headed by Roger Brown (1986) in the 1970s who, following the theorising on morality proposed by the eminent developmental psychologist Kohlberg (1984), sought to raise the level of moral thinking of prisoners by exposing them to reasoning on moral matters at a somewhat higher level than that to which they had grown accustomed in prison. What had proved to be a successful method with college students was dismally unsuccessful with prisoners. Brown concluded that the comparatively low levels of moral thinking which justified bullying others when it paid – and often it did – was adaptive to the prison environment and not at all amenable to manipulation by his team of psychologists.

Less extreme still, but nevertheless influential in raising the level of bullying in the workplace, are circumstances in which workers are under pressure to keep their jobs when policies of 'downsizing' are being applied. Survival needs may come powerfully to the fore – especially if it is unlikely that another job will be available if one is dismissed. Pressure to 'bully people out of work' may be seen to be at the initiative of middle managers who have to deal directly with employees, and gather, or fabricate, evidence to justify a dismissal. In reality the middle manager may be between 'a rock and a hard place' responding to pressures from above and, at the same time, seeking to avoid alienating the employees with whom he or she must get along. The stress experienced by the 'downsizers', or, as Bowie (2001) describes them, the 'reluctant executioners', is extreme. We are reminded here of the subjects in Milgram's experiment, though some, the latter-day Capos, seem to take to it well enough.

Competition

Does being in competitive situations engender bullying? Some people think so and believe that if we could produce less competitive or more cooperative environments bullying would be greatly reduced. There are several angles to this question, some of which have been satisfactorily researched whilst some have not.

Olweus (1993) raised this question in the context of his study of bullying at school: is bullying a consequence of competition at school? What he had in mind was whether aggressive behaviour of bullies could be attributed to experiencing failure and consequent frustration in their school work. His inquiries in Greater Stockholm convinced him that there was no support for the claim that lower grades obtained by bullies (they did in fact obtain lower grades than average) were a contributory cause of their bullying behaviour. This is one aspect of the question, but there are more.

For many children competition for marks in classwork or exams is not of much concern, especially so among junior students amongst whom bullying occurs more often. Status lies elsewhere. For boys it is more likely to lie in sporting prowess; for girls, being attractive and popular. Looking good, looking trendy, having the right footwear, telling the best jokes, 'scoring' with the opposite sex – all these at times for many children come before being top in geography. Being a nerd, an outsider, looking 'uncool', appearing 'goody goody', the teacher's pet or mummy's boy – these constitute greater disasters than failing French. Indeed, seeking honourable oblivion near the bottom of the class is for some 'a consummation devoutly to be wished'.

In addressing the influence of competition on children's interpersonal behaviour, the appropriate unit of analysis is probably the school. There are schools where competitiveness is strongly encouraged and others in which cooperativeness receives greater emphasis. An example of a type of school with a non-competitive ethos is the Steiner or Waldorf school. Steiner schools seek to promote a set of values that embrace a view of the natural and social worlds as a single interacting community with nature as a focal point (Henry 1992). In practice, the education provided is group-centred rather than individualistic. The child at school is encouraged to feel very much part of the school community by the way he or she is treated. For example, the school day begins and ends with every child shaking hands with the teacher, a person who maintains close contact throughout the child's school career. The school staff are also seen as equally valued – there is no staff hierarchy and all are paid the same, including secretaries and groundsmen.

Rivers and Soutter (1996) investigated the nature and incidence of bullying among students attending 3 classes of 30 students at a Steiner school in the south of England. They reported that, unlike other schools where bullying has been assessed, there were no reports of any physical bullying, although there was some teasing and indirect forms of bullying. The overall level of bullying behaviour was unusually low. The authors suggest on the basis of this study that bullying is a 'situational problem' rather than one that is due to there being bully-prone personalities. Drawing conclusions from this study about the influence of competitiveness is not easy because other features were present and also contributed to the school ethos. We might question whether the children attending the Steiner school were not from homes where parents were attracted to the Waldorf philosophy and had engendered peaceful attitudes among their offspring, although we should note that some children in the aforementioned study had been taken away from schools where they had been bullied. More studies of this kind are clearly needed before we can be entirely convinced that a non-competitive school ethos can substantially reduce bullying.

Further questions should be asked about the effects on bullying of being in competitive situations. For example, are the effects of academic competition and the effects of competition in sport similar or different? Are the effects (if any) influenced by cultural factors? It is sometimes suggested that in Japanese schools competition over school achievement in academic subjects can have extremely disturbing emotional consequences for those who are unsuccessful. As we have seen, there is some evidence that having low self-esteem, thus induced, can invite aggression. In Australia, it is not uncommon for failure in sport on the part of a national team to be described in the media as a 'tragedy'. Parents who come to 'barrack for' their children at football matches appear to show more animation and concern over their children's success in this arena than in any other. Are there reliable differences in how boys and girls are treated for succeeding or failing, and how they feel afterwards? In Australia girls are now reported as investing far more effort and achieving more success in academic achievement than boys; for boys achievement in sport appears more important.

Sport is often given a bad name for encouraging bullying. Whether playing a lot of sport does lead to more bullying is, in fact, a complex question. To some extent, it may depend on the sport – whether it is intensely physical and combative as in rugby, football and martial arts, or whether it is a non-contact sport such as swimming or jumping, where the aim is often to enhance one's own performance. In addition, the philosophy that goes with the sport can be important. Where martial arts is taught with an emphasis upon respect for one's opponent and consideration for others, one would expect less negative, perhaps even positive, consequences. Further, the learning of self-control can be an integral part of coaching children who play competitive sports, as can the development of team spirit and cooperation. Rather than inquire into whether involvement in sporting situations is conducive to bullying, we need to ask more specific questions about the nature of the sport and how it is taught.

Cooperativeness

Being cooperative is often seen as the obverse of being competitive. This can be misleading. Competitive activities may and often do involve cooperation between team members, if not between members of one team and another. Competitiveness does not invariably lead to disparagement of one's opponents, though steps may need to be taken to prevent this from happening. On the other hand, cooperativeness typically entails pro-social interactions with others that are incompatible with bullying them.

Johnson and Johnson (1991) describe what teachers are prone to say to promote the kind of environment they like:

- I want to be able to hear a pin drop.
- Don't copy.
- I want to see what *you* can do, not your neighbour.

Such an environment does not necessarily produce competitiveness, though it may; but it certainly does not prepare the way for cooperation.

The link between cooperative learning and low levels of bullying has been suggested by Olweus (1993). In discussing methods to reduce bullying, he commends cooperative learning, as described by Johnson and Johnson (1991) as a means not only of promoting more effective learning of schoolwork, but also as a means of improving peer relations. Central to this approach is engaging children in tasks which enable them to share the success of achievement brought about by them working together. In this way a sense of mutual positive dependence is engendered.

Unfortunately, attempts to demonstrate that participating in cooperative learning situations leads to less bullying have thus far not been successful. Probably the best planned study of the effects of cooperative learning on the incidence of bullying in a school was conducted in three intercity middle schools in England (Cowie *et al.* 1994). The staff from each of the schools were trained in how to apply cooperative learning methods to provide what was termed cooperative group work (CGW). Measures were taken of the prevalence of bullying before and after the implementation of the new teaching methods which were continued over two years. There was no evidence that children who had participated in cooperative learning liked each other more. The numbers of children perceived by children as bullies did not change. There was a slight but inconsistent trend towards fewer children being identified as victims. The authors believed that 'the overall impact of CGW on social relationships must, in this project, be accounted a failure' (p.197). They go on to suggest possible explanations. Some teachers were not fully committed to trying out the method, which they felt could result in them losing control once 'the lid was lifted'. Often inexperienced teachers had to cope – not always successfully – with particularly difficult children. The situation in which this intervention was done appears to have been particularly challenging. However, another explanation is possible: cooperative learning of schoolwork might not have beneficent effects that generalise beyond the classroom – to the playground jungle for instance.

Bystanders

Although bullying may indeed take place between two people with no-one else present, this appears to be exceptional. There is usually a group of people around, watching or not watching. According to the observational studies of Pepler and Craig (1995) in Canadian primary schools, peers were present in 85 per cent of bullying episodes. Where spouse abuse takes place, again bystanders, in the form of children, are often present. In a phone-in conducted by a domestic violence task force in Queensland, Australia, some 88 per cent of the respondents reporting violent encounters in the home stated that a dependant had been present on occasions.

Commentators on bystander behaviour have repeatedly been struck by the fact that bystanders tend not to intervene when they witness people being abused by others. In the USA one now famous case is often cited. This was of Kitty Genovese, a young woman who in 1964 was raped and murdered by an assailant as she was returning home at night to her New York apartment. This was despite the fact that her repeated cries for help were heard by no less than 38 of her neighbours, none of whom came to her assistance. In Britain the abduction, torture and murder of an infant, James Bulger, aged two years six months, by two ten-year-old boys made a similar impact. The abduction was captured on closed-circuit cameras at a shopping centre. Subsequently the infant was marched around Liverpool for approximately two and a half hours before finally being killed alongside a railway line. There were 39 witnesses to the abduction, many of whom subsequently reported that the infant bore signs of having been struck in the head and was crying. None had sought to intervene to save his life.

The failure to act in such cases is astonishing in view of the abhorrence people express when they reflect on such events. They typically say that they would intervene. When primary school children in Australia were asked what they would do if they saw somebody being bullied at school, a large majority replied that they would do something to stop it (Leane 1999). Yet in the Canadian study of children's behaviour in the playground (cited above), when bullying was observed in only 11 per cent of cases did peers intervene in any way.

The work of the Canadian psychologists has provided some highly specific real-life data on bullying and bystander reactions among elementary school children. On average, they report, when bullying occurred there were four other children present besides the bully or bullies and victim. After viewing video recordings of such episodes, bystander reactions were categorised according to whether they: (i) gave some support to the victim by intervening, distracting the bully or otherwise discouraging the aggression; (ii) passively reinforced the bullying by watching without joining in; and (iii) actively reinforced the bully by physically or verbally joining in the aggression. Over 53 recorded episodes, the average duration was 79 seconds. The amount of time spent by bystanders in reacting in one or other of the three ways is shown in Table 9.2.

Table 9.2 Time spent by bystanders in engaging in different kinds of behaviour during bully/victim interactions

Bystander reaction	Time spent
Giving active support to the bullying	20.7%
Giving passive support to the bullying	53.9%
Giving active support to the victim	25.4%

Source: Pepler and Craig (1995)

The researchers noted that the longer the episode lasted, the more peers were present, suggesting that bullying tends to attract more and more bystanders the longer it goes on. The general conclusions reached by the Canadian researchers are well supported by studies in which children have been asked to describe the roles that other students play when they witness bullying at their school. In studies conducted in Finland and in England it has been found that students who witness bullying tend, for the most part, to watch passively or support the bully rather than intervene on the side of the victim.

It should not be assumed that all bully/victim bystander cases are alike. Situations involving bystanders may differ from each other in a number of ways, and the kind of bullying that is observed may elicit different reactions. The main factor so far that has been researched is the numerical size of the group of bystanders. It has been found, somewhat paradoxically, that the greater the number of bystanders present when help is needed, the less likely it is that any intervention will take place (Latane and Darley 1970). One might have thought that when a large number of bystanders was present there would be a better chance of somebody translating their good intentions into purposive action. However, in numerous experiments it turned out that the opposite was true. Latane and Darley suggested that with increasing numbers there is a diffusion of responsibility such that no-one feels a sufficiently strong obligation to do something. It is also possible that the failure to act when so many people are present is seen as evidence that the situation is either not serious or that the victimisation was in some way justified. The desire on the part of bystanders to believe that 'this is a just world' in which one can feel secure – if one does nothing wrong – may also lead people to see the event as requiring no action on anybody's part (Lerner 1980).

Apart from studies demonstrating a negative association between the numbers of bystanders present and the likelihood of action being taken, there has been relatively little examination of factors that could explain bystander inaction. It appears to have escaped attention that the kinds of situations that seem to require bystander action are often qualitatively different. In bullying research, as we have seen, a distinction is now commonly made between direct physical bullying, direct verbal bullying and indirect bullying. Reactions bystanders give to each of these kinds of bullying have rarely been examined. An exception is an exploratory study undertaken by Leane (1999) in an Australian primary school. In this study 90 children with a mean age of 11 years were read three stories, each of which illustrated a different kind of bullying situation (involving direct physical, direct verbal and indirect aggression) that may be encountered in schools. The respondents were asked to record anonymously in a questionnaire how they thought they would respond to each situation. These are the stories:

Physical bullying

Tom is 11 years old. He is a short child who doesn't have many friends. Quite often he is called a teacher's pet and this sometimes makes him cry. William, who is about the same age as Tom, is quite a bit taller. He is captain of the school footy team and has a lot of friends. One day Tom was waiting in the canteen line counting his money and deciding which lollies he should buy. All of a sudden William came running around the corner and deliberately rammed into Tom. Tom started to say it hurt, when William yelled: 'What are you going to do about it?'

Verbal bullying

Susie and her best friend, Jane, are ten years old. They share the library monitor's job because they both love to read so much. They only ever play by themselves at lunch time, because they don't get on very well with other students. Mary hangs out with about four other girls and they are all best friends. They don't like Susie and Jane because they think they are nerds. Mary always says that Susie and Jane wear uncool clothes. One day when Susie and Jane were playing two square in the quadrangle, Mary and her friends saw Susie miss the ball. She yelled, 'You're hopeless at sport. You are a big fat book worm!'

Indirect bullying

Sandy likes to read books about horses. She doesn't have any friends because she is new to the school. Being shy means that most lunch times she sits on the oval reading a book by herself. But on the oval there is a big group of friends. The boys and girls all get along really well, and everyone calls them the 'cool group'. One day Sandy decides that she will ask them if she can join their group to hang out. But when she does ask, they all laugh at her and say, 'Get real, no square is going to join our group!'

Children in classrooms were asked how they personally would react to each situation if they saw or heard what was happening. They could support the bullying; ignore what was going on; or act so as to support the person(s) who were being treated badly by speaking up against what was being done or by telling a teacher. The percentages of respondents who indicated they would actively support the victim are given for each situation in Table 9.3.

Table 9.3 Junior students indicating that they would support the victim(s): Percentages reporting			
	Type of situation		
	Physical bullying	Verbal bullying	Indirect bullying
Boys	79%	57%	43%
Girls	88%	91%	74%

One can see that most of the students felt that action was needed to support the victim(s), although in view of the observations made earlier of children's actual behaviour in bystander situations, it seems unlikely that there would be such high percentages of children acting on their intentions. Nevertheless, the results suggest that primary school children do differentiate between situations as to whether supportive action is justified. Generally, action was seen by more students as justified in more direct bullying situations compared with the one in which there was a strong element of excluding as is found in indirect bullying. We may notice, too, that there were gender differences, particularly where verbal and indirect bullying were involved. Girls felt more inclined to intervene. More research in differentiating between situations is needed if we are to understand bystander reactions better. For instance, in one situation help may be seen as sorely needed and this may motivate more bystanders to want to help; but the situation may involve considerable risk to a person who intervened. We need to know more about how bystanders are affected by such considerations.

Situations may be viewed according to our perceptions of the relationships that exist between the people involved. In his examination of why none of the 39 people who witnessed the abduction of James Bulger by two older children, leading to the killing, intervened, Levine (1999) has suggested that instead of concentrating on the numerical qualities of the bystanders – and the consequent diffusion of responsibility – it would be more relevant for us to consider how the bystanders perceived the relationships between the three children. From the evidence given by witnesses at the trial it is clear that the children were seen as brothers and what they were doing was a family matter. This analysis draws our attention away from numbers to how we categorise people and the normative pressures that lead us to act towards people in perceived categories. Consistent with this view is the commonly made observation that bystanders are much less inclined to intervene in a row between a couple who are married and a couple who are not in such a relationship. The bystander's relationship with one or other of the people involved in a conflict may also affect his or her perception of the situation. In the area of peer aggression, Tisak and Tisak (1996) have reported that young adolescents believe that a bystander is much more likely to become involved in helping a sibling than helping a friend in a struggle with another person, and believe that it would be 'wrong' not to do so.

Most of the attention given by researchers to bystander behaviour has centred on bystander reactions to people in conflict situations. It is less often asked how those directly involved in the conflict are affected by the presence of others. In the school environment it appears that bullies are commonly reinforced by the positive encouragement they are given, supplemented by seemingly passive acceptance by others of what they are doing. The bully may under these circumstances seek an audience. Yet it is not possible to generalise to all situations in which bullying is being observed. Where the bullying is extreme and legal proceedings might well be taken against the bully or bullies if these actions are reported, bystanders will not normally be welcome. But does bullying within the law generally evoke popular support? Sometimes it is not clear. In the national television debates as part of year 2000 presidential election in the USA, Vice-President Gore was seen by many, if not most viewer-bystanders, as coming over as a bully in exchanges with the more laid back and mannerly President-to-be, George W. Bush. Bullies need to judge their audiences.

Situation, person or both?

In their reflections on the relatively low levels of bullying at Steiner schools, Rivers and Soutter (1996) express the view that bullying is primarily a 'situational phenomenon rather than a result of personality factors as Olweus suggests' (p.364). This is rather unfair on Olweus (1993), whose recommendations for reducing bullying include the development of a warm, caring school environment. In the review of situational factors in this chapter, it should be evident that situational factors are of great importance. We know that some environments are much less likely to give rise to bullying than others. But an explanation for bullying exclusively in terms of situational factors does not explain differences between individual propensities to bully or for that matter the likelihood of being bullied. We know that people who are exposed to the same environments, or, more specifically, the same situations, may act differently. This applies to bullying as it does to other forms of behaviour.

We know that people who behave one way in one situation sometimes behave differently in another. Harris (1998) has argued that such inconsistency is typical of children who may be well behaved at home and little devils at school, or vice versa. But is this so? In fact, there is some evidence of a degree of consistency on the part of children who bully or refrain from bullying at home and at school. In a study of peer bullying at school and sibling bullying at home, R.D. Duncan (1999) reported a study of children who bullied in one or both of these contexts. Of those children with siblings who were categorised as bully/victims (sometimes a bully, sometimes a victim) at school, some 76.7 per cent reported that they bullied their brothers or sisters at home. Some 56.5 per cent of school bullies bullied their siblings at home. By contrast a much smaller proportion of peer victims (33.2%) and those uninvolved in bullying (32.1%) at school reported that they bullied at home. Clearly some bullied in one context only, but the majority of those who bullied at all did so both at school and at home.

The debate over whether behaviour is elicited by situations or is a consequence of personality is an old one to which some old and persuasive answers have been given. Perhaps the simplest and most sensible formulation of behavioural determinants can be summed up in Lewin's (1951) simple statement: $B = f$ (P.E) – where B is behaviour seen as a function (f) of the person (P) and the environment (E) as apprehended by the person. Where there are very strong forces at play – as, for instance, in the situation in which a legitimate authority is demanding that you perform an aggressive or 'bullying' act, or when such behaviour seems necessary for survival – the P factor (the personality bit) may seemingly lose its power to influence events. Yet if we look again at those demonstrations that have been used to convince us of the immensely powerful coercive influence of situations, such power turns out to be not entirely absolute.

Take for example the situation that Milgram (1965) used to demonstrate how bullying behaviour could produce an obedient response to authority. What is little known is that the subjects in the authority experiments were first subjected to personality testing by one of Milgram's co-workers, who reported that results from the California F test of authoritarianism (see page 134) did differentiate between the more obedient and the less obedient subjects in the experiment. Those who bullied – or more accurately facilitated the bullying by accepting the orders most – scored significantly higher on the so-called F scale. (It was called the F scale because it was supposed to identify Fascist tendencies.) Elms (1972), the personality tester, wrote: 'It does look as if those researchers in the late 1940s [those who developed the test] had something which can be translated from abstract tendencies into actual authoritarian behaviour' (p.133). Similarly, in the prison simulation experiment of Zimbardo (1972), higher scores on the F scale were found among the subjects whose behaviour was directed more aggressively towards the 'inferior' prisoners.

In real life situations, we have seen that not all bouncers were 'ugly'; many of them were classified by the sociologists who observed them as 'good'. On the other hand, even in the worst and most dehumanising of all situations, in the Nazi concentration camps, there were those who turned their backs on exploiting others in a way that might increase their slim chances of survival. Having described the appalling effects of incarceration in the death camps, Frankl (1964) posed the question: do the prisoners' reactions to the singular world of the concentration camp prove that man cannot escape the influences of his surroundings? Does man have no choice of action in the face of such circumstances? He answers that such questions can be answered from experience as well as principle, thus:

> The experiences of camp life show that man does have a choice of action. There were enough examples, often of a heroic nature, which proved that apathy can be overcome, irritability suppressed. Man can preserve a vestige of spiritual freedom, of independence of mind, even in such terrible conditions of psychic and physical stress. (p.75)

Chapter 10

Attitudes and beliefs

It fills me with grief and misery to think what weak and nervous children go through at school – how their health and character for life are destroyed by rough and brutal treatment.

– Extract from a letter to Thomas Hughes
in the Preface to *Tom Brown's Schooldays*

We must not assume that the evil of bullying is a new discovery. When Thomas Hughes (1857/1968) wrote his now famous (though fictional) account of life at Rugby Public School, England, in the mid-19th century, it drew from many of its readers a storm of protest directed against bullying between schoolboys at school. Many identified with the victim.

> The fact is that the condition of a small boy at a large school is one of peculiar hardship and suffering. He is entirely at the mercy of proverbially the roughest things in the universe – great schoolboys, and he is deprived of the protection which the weak have in civilised society; for he may not complain; for if he does he is an outlaw – he has no protector but public opinion; and that a public opinion of the lowest grade, the opinion of rude and ignorant boys. (Hughes 1857/1968, p.10)

We hear similar things being said today. Here is an extract from the letters page of *The Australian* in 2001.

> Bullying is serious. It is extremely serious. There is a high suicide rate in Australia and a high rate of depression among young people. Has anyone

thought to look at what goes on in schools, where young people spend the majority of their time, in an effort to redress the issues? (Stephen 2001)

Now, the answer to this question is 'yes'; indeed there are in many countries government-directed campaigns to stop bullying in schools. In the UK, for instance, every school must have an anti-bullying policy. In Australia, two of the seven states or territories have made this a requirement in the state-managed schools. Many private schools have developed their own policies and practices. Editorials in newspapers constantly speak out against bullying. If Thomas Hughes were alive and came to Australia, some 150 years after the publication of *Tom Brown's Schooldays*, he could be forgiven for believing that the sympathy that he had awakened for the victims of school-based bullying had indeed borne fruit. We are all, it seems, on the side of the angels. Yet the grim reality of bullying, not only in schools but in all walks of life, continues to confront and oppress us.

What then is sustaining this sorry state? Is the public opposition to bullying something of a façade? What do people really think about bullying? In this chapter we will examine the evidence and the attitudes and beliefs about bullying that people really have today.

Research evidence on the attitudes of children

The first of the systematic studies of children's attitudes to victims of school bullying was conducted by Rigby and Slee (1993a, 1993b). This study was carried out in Australian schools with 314 boys and 353 girls between the ages of 8 and 15 years. We asked the students 20 questions relevant to bullying. By and large their answers suggested that they were supportive of victims (see Appendix 10).

Generally, boys are somewhat more negatively inclined towards victimised children than girls. But the differences are not large. There is only a 3 per cent difference in the percentages of boys and girls agreeing that they would not be friends with kids who let themselves be pushed around.

In a further study we sought to examine the responses of children towards victims using a qualitative approach in which children were asked to complete a sentence beginning 'Children who complain about being bullied...'. These children were from Australian secondary schools and were aged 12–15 years. There were 82 boys and 82 girls who provided sentence completions that could be coded as: (i) supportive of victims of school bullying (51%); (ii) neutral (21%); and (iii) negative (28%) towards victims. These results reflected a split in the student sample in the attitudes of children towards those who take the step of complaining about being bullied at school. Once again there was a tendency for girls to be more supportive of victims, but only by a small margin. Here are some of the things that the supporters of victims, gender (m = male; f = females) and age in parentheses, had to say about those who complained about being bullied:

> Those who complain are 'very sensible' (m,13); 'all right' (m,12); 'smart' (f,12); 'strong' (m,13); 'pretty courageous' (m,12); 'good' (f,13); and 'normally nice inside' (f,13). Their complaining was seen as justified. 'Is fair enough because you would if you were being bullied' (f,12); 'is good or it will keep happening' (m,12); 'are usually telling the truth, I feel sorry for them' (f,13); 'are trying to protect themselves' (f,14); 'something should be done' (m,15); 'need to be helped to have their self-confidence restored' (m,14); 'should be listened to and believed by people who will do something about it' (f,14); 'should have the bully stopped' (f,12); 'should be helped by you' (f,13).

> A number of those approving of 'complainers' insisted upon the rights of victims. 'They have a right to complain to people if they are bullied' (m,14) and 'shouldn't feel scared to do so' (f,14). Rights mentioned included 'the right to speak up' (f,13); 'the right to be listened to' (m,13; f,13); and the 'right to be protected' (f,14). 'Complaining,' commented one, 'is not dobbing' (m,13). 'No child should be bullied' (f,14) added another. Some provided positive advice. 'Should go and tell someone to help stop bullying' (m,14); 'go and tell a teacher' (m,12); and 'should tell their parents or teachers and then they can deal with it' (f,13). Some expressed a personal readiness to help: 'I help as much as possible' (f,14); 'I would go and help them' (f,13).

Thus it would appear that about half the children in this sample between the ages of 12 and 15 years were supportive of children who complain about being victimised. But clearly many had reservations about helping victims, especially those who complain. Some simply expressed contempt. This is how some were described:

> 'losers' (m,13); 'wimps' (f,12); 'poo dicks' (m,15); 'pussies' (m,15); 'stupid' (m,13); 'a pain' (f,12); 'people who often complain too much' (m,12); 'have little self-respect' (f,14); 'little kids who don't know anything' (m,14); 'normally ask for it' (m,12); 'bring it on themselves usually' (f,15); 'are often wimps trying to get other people in trouble' (f,14); people who 'should take it with a grain of salt' (m,14).

For some children, complaining was seen as simply counter-productive. They were seen as people who:

> 'are stupid because they just get bullied more' (m,14); 'get bullied more for whingeing' (f,15); 'get teased' (m,12); 'often get into more trouble from the bullies' (m,13).

Some students thought that the victims who complained should find better alternatives.

> 'They should look to themselves to see if they can do something to prevent it' (f,14); 'not tell the teacher but find another way to deal with it' (m,14); 'go to self-defence lessons' (m,15); 'at least do something about it other than complain' (f,15). Some saw fighting back as clearly preferable. Complainers should: 'stick up for themselves and not let themselves be pushed around' (f,14); 'face up to the people bullying them' (m,14); 'bully the bullies back' (f,13).

Not only was there division between students in the opinions and attitudes held towards victims but there was evidence that some students had mixed feelings, sometimes inclining them to be sympathetic in their attitudes, sometimes indifferent, sometimes even contemptuous, as these examples show.

> 'I feel sorry for them, but sometimes they deserve it' (f,12); 'sometimes they're over-reacting and want attention and maybe sometimes some kids need help with this' (f,14); 'are sometimes right and sometimes want to get other kids in trouble' (f,12); 'I pity them but laugh with everyone else' (m,12); 'are people I feel sorry for, although I hate to admit that sometimes I just don't care and I'm glad it's not me' (f,14).

Attitudes to bullies and bullying

A complementary approach to understanding children's attitudes to bullying is to focus upon the feelings children have towards what bullies do. The survey described above contained some questions which were concerned with this aspect (see Appendix 10).

Clear approval for the bullying actions among children turned out to be relatively low, but by no means negligible. For instance, some 22 per cent of boys and 16 per cent of girls thought it was 'OK to call some kids nasty names' and some 19 per cent of boys and 10 per cent of girls agreed that 'Kids who get picked on a lot usually deserve it'. Here the gender differences are somewhat larger, with boys more approving of bullying, but it is clear that the act of bullying is not without supporters from both boys and girls.

A more direct approach to assessing attitudes towards the act of bullying was subsequently undertaken with another sample of Australian students from 12 primary and 8 secondary schools (Rigby 1996). The sample in this study was quite large, comprising 2940 boys and 2508 girls between 9 and 18 years, each gender group having a mean age of 14 years. One of the measures employed consisted of an attitude-to-bullying scale. Respondents to an anonymous questionnaire were asked to say what they thought the consequences would be of engaging in specified acts of bullying, using a 7-point scale with categories ranging from very unlikely (scored 1) to very likely (scored 7). They were also asked to say how important the consequence would be to them, again using a 7-point scale, this time from 'not important' to 'very important'.

The results helped us to see what students thought the consequences of bullying others would be. As one might expect, students differed a good deal in what they saw as the 'pay-off' from bullying. I have listed in Table 10.1 the percentages of students who saw particular outcomes as 'likely' (rated as 4 or more on the 7-point scale).

Table 10.1 Expected outcomes of bullying someone: Percentages believing that selected outcomes were more likely than not if you bullied someone		
Outcome	Boys	Girls
Makes others scared of you	66.3	63.1
Makes you feel better than them (the victims)	43.1	37.7
Makes you ashamed of yourself	42.2	55.1
Shows you are tough	38.0	31.7
Prevents you from being bullied	33.6	25.9
Gets you admired	21.3	13.8
You feel good about yourself	13.1	8.5

Notice that the order of perceived likelihood of consequences is similar for boys and girls, although more girls appeared likely to feel shame if they bullied someone and fewer girls felt they would be admired and feel good about themselves.

How important to the students were these consequences? Although many students saw bullying as having the potential to make others scared of you, to feel better than those you victimise and to show you are tough, most students did *not* rate these outcomes as important to them. By contrast, avoiding feeling ashamed *was* important to most students; so too were feeling good about oneself and getting admired, which only a small minority thought would come from bullying someone.

This work suggests that an inclination to bully is partly a result of expecting certain outcomes: others will be scared of me; I will feel better than others; I won't feel ashamed; nobody will bully me; I will be admired; and I will feel good about myself. But only partly. To have a pro-bullying attitude these outcomes must also be important. Hence in evaluating attitudes to bullying it is reasonable to weight each perceived outcome by its perceived importance to the individual student, as suggested by the attitude theorists Ajzen and Fishbein (1980).

Normative pressure to bully others

As we have seen in Chapter 7 (see also Appendix 9) some children report that they are influenced by their peers and to a lesser extent by some adults (parents and teachers) to bully others at school. It has been often observed that we can be pressured into doing things by others contrary to our own wishes or attitudes. For instance we may be personally disinclined to act tough yet feel that acting tough in some situations is expected of one. Friends, parents and even teachers may be seen as expecting tough behaviour – and you may accede to such perceived pressure.

When respondents were asked to say whether they thought they would be supported by others if they bullied someone at school, most students did not think there would be any support for them bullying someone, but a substantial minority did. For instance about one in five boys thought that their close friends would approve of them if they got into fights with kids who were easy to beat and made other kids scared of them. Perceived support for acts of bullying from other sources was much less: fewer than one in ten thought they would be supported in their bullying by their mother, father or teacher. But there were some boys (approximately 10%) who thought their father would approve of them making other kids scared of them.

As we have seen in Chapter 7 (Table 7.1) it was parental approval for what the respondents did in the area of bullying that mattered most, mother slightly more than father. Close friends came next; teachers last. Hence, following Ajzen and Fishbein (1980) in order to get an improved measure of overall normative pressure I weighted the judgements of what the students thought significant others would think of them by the importance they attached to such judgements. It then became possible to examine how normative pressures might change over the years of schooling for boys and girls.

AGE TRENDS FOR BOYS AND GIRLS

As we have seen, attitudes in the area of bullying tend to be different for boys and girls. They are also different for age groups. For every age group between 9 and 18 years we find that Australian girls are more sympathetic of victims and less supportive of bullying than are boys. But the age trends are fairly similar. Let us examine first the mean scores obtained for age/gender groups on the pro-victim scale, that is the measure that shows how sympathetic children are towards victims.

What is most noticeable is that there is a marked decline in sympathy for victims of school bullying as children get older, that is until the age of 14 or 15, a year earlier for girls. After that age, attitudes to victims become more positive (see Figure 10.1).

Age trends for pro-bully attitudes follow a complementary trend. As we can see in Figure 10.2, they become more supportive of bullying until the age of about 14–16 years, then become less supportive thereafter. Again girls are overall less supportive of bullying and the tendency to become less supportive begins earlier than for boys.

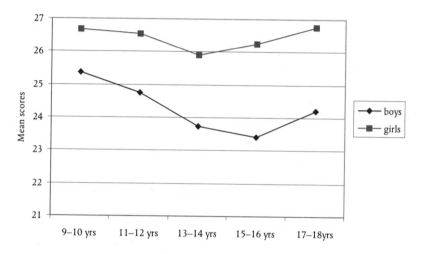

Figure 10.1 Mean scores for Australian students on the pro-victim scale

The results for the total subjective norm scale are for the sum of all pressures from the four sources: close friends, mother, father and teachers, weighted by how much notice each student reported taking of their opinions on bullying. These are given in Figure 10.3. We find a similar trend to that found for attitudes to victims, that is increasing pressure to bully up to 14 or 15, followed by a stabilisation or, in the case of girls, a reduction, thereafter.

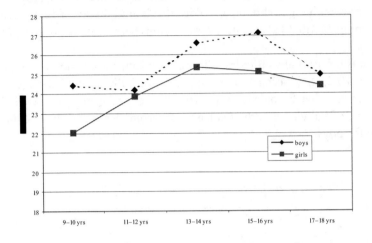

Figure 10.2 Mean scores for Australian students on the pro-bully scale

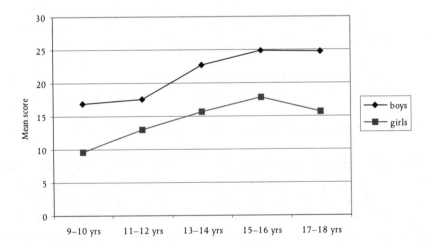

Figure 10.3 Mean scores for Australian students on the total subjective norm scale

The results from Australian students indicate that in general, primary school children are more supportive of victims, less supportive of bullies and under less normative pressure to bully than are children in lower secondary schools. This appears to be different from the situation in Italy, where it has been reported that older children in secondary schools are more sympathetic towards bullies

(Menesini *et al.* 1997). However, the authors of that study did not distinguish between younger secondary students (under 15 years) and those older. The age distribution of children in the Italian secondary school samples is not known. The Australian study suggests that this distinction is essential. It also makes good commonsense. We know that many children who engage in bullying in lower secondary grow out of it by the time they reach their senior years. One would expect that with increasing maturity children become more understanding of victims and less admiring of bullies, and that is what one finds in the Australian studies, especially in the findings about attitudes to victims and attitudes to bullies.

The question naturally arises: do the attitudes to victims and bullies and the subjective norms really make any difference to actual behaviour? As yet, we have no definite answer. Ideally we should assess attitudes and perceived normative pressure before we seek to measure bullying behaviour, and we should use more objective measures than self-reports. What has been found so far suggests that attitudes and norms do matter. The pro-victim scale has turned out to be the best predictor of self-reported past bullying behaviour, followed by the pro-bully attitude measure, followed by the total subjective norm – and these predictions were each significant for boys and girls. When we add the perceived ability to bully others (a weak but significant predictor) and control for age, we find the combination of factors accounts for about 42 per cent of reported bullying behaviour (see Rigby 1997d, p.215).

Attitudes of parents

We have seen that few children think that parents are supportive of bullying. They seem to be right. Eslea and Smith (2000) found this was so in a survey they did of the attitudes towards bullying on the part of parents of primary school children in England. How parents responded to statements about bullies and victims in an anonymous questionnaire is given in Appendix 11.

Here we may observe that whilst few parents were ready to justify bullying along the lines that it may toughen one up or that it can provide amusement, about half of the parents felt that children should act resolutely when they are bullied and not seek others to protect them. Many parents want their children to be resilient or even tough.

The use of differently phrased items for parents and children unfortunately did not allow Eslea and Smith to discover whether parents and their children differed in their attitudes. Parents were asked to consider this statement: 'There will always be bullying in schools, it's just human nature.' Some 50 per cent of them agreed with that statement – implying by their answer that there was no likelihood that bullying would ever be reduced to zero. Children were asked to consider this statement: 'Some kids will always be bullies, there's no point schools trying to stop them.' Some 27 per cent of students agreed with that statement, implying by their answer that there was no point in trying to stop bullies – a somewhat different proposition from that considered by their parents. Not surprisingly, given the different sets of questions (and the low reliabilities of the scales that were formed by the items), there was no correlation between the assessed attitudes of the children and those of their parents. Such an absence of correlation would appear to give considerable support to the view, promoted by Harris (1998), that parents have essentially no influence outside the home on what children think or do. However, we need better evidence than this to throw aside the commonsense notion that parents can and sometimes do influence the social attitudes of their children when they are at school.

But are parents more opposed to bullying than their children are? Curiously enough this question has rarely been asked and empirical evidence is largely lacking. We can only refer back to what I reported earlier: that is, in general children see less pressure coming from their parents than from other children to bully others. No doubt there are parents who wish that their child was more aggressive and more dominating at school and who would greatly prefer their child to be a bully rather than a victim of school bullying. But it is probably the case that parents usually seek to discourage their child from bullying others. Whether they do so effectively – and, if so, how – is a question of major importance, alas still unanswered.

Some support for the view that parents are overwhelmingly opposed to bullying is evident in the results obtained from the parent version of the Peer Relations Assessment Questionnaire (PRAQ) in Australia over the last five years. In a study focusing on the views of parents of 687 children (aged 8–17 years) some 90.7 per cent of parents agreed that the school should have written policy against bullying. One parent elaborated:

> The only way to ensure students have a right to a safe and bully-free education is to have a definite written policy. All parents should have to sign a form that they have read the policy with their children and that they understand it and understand that the rules and conditions will be abided by or strict consequences will follow.

One of the interesting things about asking parents to complete anonymous questionnaires about bullying and to return them to the school is the high response rate, sometimes in Australian studies as high as 80 per cent – which demonstrates the high degree of concern parents commonly feel about the issue of bullying. Most respondents are strongly opposed to bullying:

Everything should be done to stamp out bullying and give those who are bullied the skills to cope.

Bullying of any description should be stopped immediately.

Bullying needs to be on every school agenda – children are suffering unnecessarily. This is an important issue and needs to be addressed at a high level in all schools.

Differences tend to emerge, however, on how bullies should be treated. Some are highly punitive:

I cannot tolerate bullying in any degree and feel that punishment is definitely in order.

Publish their names and shame their behaviour.

On the other hand:

I don't think punishment would work. The bully should receive counselling as well as self-esteem building and communication skills.

I don't believe a bully wants to behave in that manner. They want to look big in their own eyes because they lack confidence and self-esteem. I believe that if they can be made to feel better about themselves their bullying will cease.

Some are critical of teachers:

It would be helpful if a teacher when told of a bullying incident did something about it instead of laughing and ignoring the complaint.

Some staff engage in bullying and seem to get away with it. Why?

Teachers should be trained in handling bullying to lift their skills.

My impression based upon questionnaire responses and frequent discussions with groups of parents is that more than any group of people they are strongly opposed to bullying in schools and, with few exceptions, want to see action taken to stop it. Like many others, like children and teachers for instance, they are often divided in how schools should go about it. The major area of difference lies in whether punishment or counselling or both (and if so how they can be combined) provide the best means of countering the problem. Strangely enough, few parents suggest different approaches with different kinds of bullying and different kinds of perpetrators.

What teachers think

What teachers think about bullying is of central importance in countering bullying in schools. Unless there is a general consensus on the part of a school staff to counter bullying it is unlikely that plans made and implemented by a handful of committed staff members will be successful. On the surface, at least, it looks as if teachers are right behind the anti-bullying movement.

In a survey of 200 teachers at 3 Australian coeducational secondary schools (Rigby 2001b), some 99 per cent saw bullying as a matter for all staff to address, 97 per cent of teachers believed that teachers and students should work together to stop bullying and 91 per cent believed there should be a policy specifically about bullying at their school (8% were unsure).

In another study some 95 Australian teachers from 4 primary schools and 7 secondary schools answered an anonymous questionnaire assessing their attitudes towards bullying (Rigby and Keogh 1997). Nearly all of them (98%) were sympathetic towards victims and disagreed that they usually deserved what they got. Most (but not all) teachers appeared committed to working against bullying in their schools. Some 81 per cent saw it as part of their job to intervene in bullying situations. Most felt optimistic about efforts to reduce bullying. Some 85 per cent disagreed with the statement that 'you can't stop it' (10% were unsure). We see here that about four teachers out of five are ready to take action to stop bullying and feel optimistic about the problem being lessened; however, a substantial minority appear uncommitted and sceptical about what can be achieved.

These results should be seen in the context of a social and political ethos today in which there is considerable pressure on schools to adopt anti-bullying policies and to take effective action against bullying. Education departments are constantly encouraging schools to develop anti-bullying and anti-harassment policies. Those who are critical of the anti-bullying movement are now 'politically incorrect' and run the risk of having 'inappropriate attitudes'. It seems likely that the true proportion of teachers who are sceptical, to put it mildly, about schools taking on bullying may be considerably larger than 15 per cent.

You can appreciate the reasons why some teachers are not being supportive of anti-bullying when you look at teacher responses to some of the other questions on the Rigby and Keogh study. Some 26 per cent of the teachers felt that they needed more assistance to deal with bullies. Some 32 per cent indicated that bullies made them feel personally intimidated. Results from the 200 teachers indicated that 89 per cent felt that some training is needed for teachers to deal with bullying. Such uncertainty about being unable to cope with the problem is reflected in results provided in another survey conducted in England by Michael Boulton (1997) with 138 teachers in which he concludes that a vast majority indicated that they would appreciate more training' (p.231).

Why are some teachers ready to actively oppose bullying in their school and some (a minority) clearly not? Craig, Henderson and Murphy (2000) addressed this question with a sample of 116 prospective teachers in Canada. The results of her study suggest a number of possibilities. The first is that some teachers are much less likely to take action when bullying is reported to them than when they actually see it happening. Some teachers discount children's reports, others are inclined to believe them. We know also from several studies that some teachers rarely see bullying happening. Even as far as physical bullying (arguably the most conspicuous kind) some teachers report that they see it happening rarely, if at all, while others at the same school see it happening fairly often or very often. For the less overt forms of bullying, such as deliberate exclusion and cruel teasing, it is not uncommon to find a school's staff equally divided between those who see bullying of this kind happening 'often' at their school and those who see it happening 'rarely' or 'occasionally'.

In part, the differences in the perceptions of teachers may be explained by differential exposure to year groups, with those teaching predominantly in the first two years of high school, for instance, being faced with more cases of bullying than those teaching in the most senior years. In addition, some teachers have their classes under such control that bullying in their classrooms is rare; others whose control is more relaxed or lax would observe more. Yet normally all staff take a turn in yard duty and are physically present in places where bullying occurs most. There is evidently more to seeing bullying than meets the eye. In fact there are marked individual differences in awareness and sensitivity as to what constitutes bullying.

Craig *et al.*'s study suggests that teachers who are relatively low on empathy tend not to see negative interactions between children as bullying or if they do they minimise its seriousness. Empathy is related to perspective taking. Evidently some teachers find it difficult to see things from a child's point of view. Empathy is also related to helping behaviour. Some teachers are clearly not motivated to help. We need to find out more about such teachers. One wonders whether they are so subject-oriented that they tend not to see children as individuals; whether they are people who never encountered bullying problems when they were children; or perhaps have become cynical and indifferent to the interpersonal difficulties that children have. Craig *et al.*'s research enables us to discount one plausible hypothesis. They are evidently not people who are inclined to blame victims for their predicament.

Is the tendency of some teachers not to be committed to opposing bullying in their school connected with their conceptions of 'masculinity'? The work of Craig *et al.* (2000) suggests otherwise. The tendency to display so-called masculine qualities, such as being tough and assertive, was unrelated to attitudes towards bullying. So, too, was being male or female. I found this surprising because Australian research had suggested that female teachers were more sensitive to issues of bullying in schools. When I hold seminars on bullying there is invariably a large preponderance of female teachers present, even when teachers are drawn from secondary schools where the gender balance is fairly even.

Another possibility is that teachers who are relatively uncommitted to anti-bullying activity in school conceive bullying in a different way from others. There is certainly some disagreement between teachers over what may constitute bullying. There is more disagreement in some areas than others. According to a study in England by Boulton (1997) verbal threats, acts of physical aggression and forcing people to do things were identified by more than 90 per cent of teachers as 'bullying'. Name-calling, spreading nasty stories and taking another's belongings were classified as bullying by 70–80 per cent of teachers. 'Leaving people out' was seen as bullying by only 48 per cent of teachers. It seems possible that one reason that some teachers do not 'take on' bullying is because they do not recognise its scope as clearly as others do. Many do not see that a massive amount of harm results from indirect and covert forms of bullying. If they did, perhaps they would take bullying much more seriously. Generally, teachers see physical bullying as by far the most serious form of bullying, much more so than verbal bullying (Craig et al. 2000). As we have seen, for about half the teachers who have been surveyed, what some call indirect, social or relational bullying is not seen as bullying at all.

Some studies have compared teachers' and students' attitudes to bullying. This is a difficult exercise because there is some evidence that they see bullying in different ways. In Boulton's study, pupils also answered the same questions as the teachers about what behaviours constituted bullying. It turned out that teachers tended to see behaviours as bullying much more often than students did. For example, taking another's belongings was seen by 76.8 per cent of the teachers as bullying; but only 59.4 per cent of pupils saw it that way. We are left wondering whether teachers are more sensitive to bullying or whether students are more discriminating – and more ready to refuse to label a behaviour as bullying when the context is not made clear. Boulton did not stipulate that the behaviours were occurring in a context in which there was an imbalance of power.

Rigby and Keogh (1997) examined the question of whether teachers or students were more sympathetic to victims by asking teachers the same questions as those answered by 676 students in a previous study by Rigby and Slee (1991). The results suggested that teachers were more sympathetic. All 95 teachers in the study disagreed with the statement that 'kids should not complain about being bullied'. In the student sample 17.5 per cent of boys agreed with the statement and 20.4 per cent were unsure; 12.2 per cent of girls disagreed with the statement and 27.8 per cent were unsure. Clearly for many students, but not teachers, the notion that one should *not* inform had taken a hold. Similarly 98 per cent of teachers disagreed with the statement that 'kids who get picked on usually deserve it' (2% were unsure). Among students 50 per cent of boys and 50 per cent of girls disagreed with the statement (about 35% were unsure). Here then we do get evidence of a divergence of viewpoints between many teachers and many students. Not surprisingly, teachers continually press to 'make this a telling school' and many students persist in believing that telling tales is deplorable (or unwise) and that those who are bullied may very well deserve what they get.

Not knowing what to do about incidents of bullying may also lead some teachers to deny or underrate the problem. Questionnaires answered by teachers in Australia show that teachers are often divided or unsure as to what is the best course of action. Consider these results from 51 teachers attached to a school catering for children between the ages of 7 and 17 years. They were asked to indicate what they thought about ways of dealing with children who had bullied someone:

Table 10.2 Australian teachers' views on dealing with bullying: Percentages responding			
Treatment	**Agree**	**Unsure**	**Disagree**
Some form of punishment should be applied immediately and automatically to students found to have bullied others.	61	22	17
Students found to be bullying another person should first be counselled, not punished, and given the opportunity to put things right.	51	24	25

These results reflect the large amount of uncertainty about what to do about children who bully others. In part, the uncertainty may have been elicited by my not specifying the kind of bullying. One could reasonably employ counselling first for one kind of 'offence' and punishment first for another. However, in numerous discussions with groups of teachers I find a division between those who on the whole favour punishment and those who favour counselling as a general approach.

There is generally a high level of agreement among teachers that teachers should talk with students in class about bullying and seek their cooperation in stopping it. At the same time many of those who approve of the practice say they have not tried it. When they are questioned further it becomes clear that doing so is often fraught with difficulties. This is especially so with classes of young teenage boys. Those who have tried to do so tend to report mixed success. Teachers are usually aware that if the matter is handled badly it could be harmful to children who are being bullied. Promoting a constructive discussion on the topic seems to be beyond the competence of some teachers. It may be that some dissonance in the minds of some teachers is reduced by treating the problem as one of little importance.

In summary, we find that nearly all teachers are sympathetic to victims and supportive of steps to counter bullying, seemingly more so than students, though they too, on the whole, deplore bullying and would like to see it stopped. But we have to bear in mind that teachers are under considerable pressure to support anti-bullying policies and initiatives and that the amount of opposition to commitment to act against bullying has probably been underestimated. This is a very important issue because effective whole school policies depend upon a consensus among staff members and a positive commitment. Exploring reasons why some staff members are reluctant to support anti-bullying initiatives is a matter that requires much more attention.

Attitudes to bullying in the workplace

This is an area ripe for systematic research. Unlike the school situation, we have currently little more than case studies and anecdotes. Some writers on the workplace berate the management for allegedly denying the problem; for example, in a project conducted by Andy Ellis at Ruskin College, Oxford, senior managers are described as being in denial about bullying. Ellis writes: 'The unfortunate truth is that many of these managers have entered senior management positions straight from university and have therefore never experienced or witnessed bullying while at work' (website: www.worktrauma.org/foundation/research/andyellis.htm). He adds that some managers believe that bullying is largely a justifiable attempt to squeeze the last drop of extra performance out of the employee, and this goes largely unnoticed by the workers. On the other hand, some observers believe that the situation is changing. According to Ellis, Mr McDonnell of the Institute of Personnel Management (UK) has stated: 'What might be seen as a rite of passage in the past has no place in the modern workplace.'

The emphasis is generally on what attitudes towards bullying ought to be rather than what they actually are. There is little empirical evidence. We may surmise that adults in the workplace, like children in school and like teachers and parents, are divided in their attitudes. As in many areas in which writers feel strongly on a social issue, there is little attempt so far to provide a balanced judgement on what attitudes people actually hold on the issue of workplace bullying.

Attitudes to bullying in the home

In Chapter 4 we saw that a great deal of what may reasonably be called bullying goes on in the home. Often this is described as domestic violence; some of it constitutes sexual abuse or rape. We know from social surveys that some men hold beliefs that appear to justify violence against women. The best predictor of male violence against women appears to be what has been termed 'adversarial sexual beliefs'. According to Burt (1980) such beliefs imply an 'expectation that sexual relationships are fundamentally exploitative, that each party to them is manipulative, sly, cheating, opaque to the other's understanding, and not to be trusted' (p.218). Men who verbally and/or physically abuse women are more likely than others to agree with these statements: 'Women are usually sweet until they've caught a man, but then let their true self show' and 'In a dating relationship a woman is largely out to take advantage of a man' (Hastings 2000, p.2). Such beliefs may be seen as deriving from a failure to process social information realistically. Socially relevant information is ignored and ambiguous social situations typically misconstrued.

Most studies of the attitudes and beliefs of aggressive males are very general. There has been comparatively little research into specific beliefs held by males about acts regarding the justifiability of aggression towards female partners under specified circumstances. To state the obvious: much depends upon the circumstances. There is one study undertaken with a sample of Australian secondary school students that has addressed the question of what circumstances appear to justify male aggression against females (Rigby, Whish and Black 1994). The students were asked to say whether they thought actions taken by a husband – speaking sharply to his wife, yelling or shouting at her and hitting her – were justified in response to actions a wife is presumed to have taken. The results are summarised in Appendix 7.

As we expected, support by students for husbands who abused their wives depended largely on what the students thought was justified; for example, relatively few respondents thought that a wife swearing at a husband provided justification for him hitting or yelling at her, though 12 per cent of boys and 6 per cent of girls in fact did think so. At the other extreme, a large majority thought that if a wife physically abused a child, the husband was justified in reacting aggressively, verbally or physically, towards her; indeed more than 20 per cent of boys and 20 per cent of girls thought that the husband would be justified in hitting the wife under those circumstances. When we counted the number of respondents who thought that hitting a wife was justified under at least one circumstance, it amounted to 40.5 per cent of boys and 27.5 per cent of girls. Clearly a minority, but nevertheless substantial numbers of students (girls as well as boys) indicated that physical violence by a man against a woman was justified under some circumstances.

Whether the violent actions endorsed by the students would amount to 'bullying' is not easy to answer. One criterion would generally (though not always) be met: that is, the husband would be physically stronger than the wife. In some circumstances, most people would see a violent reaction to a partner's behaviour as clearly unjustified, e.g. her lying to his friends about him or flirting with someone after being asked by him not to do so. Were the husband to act violently under these circumstances – and to do so repeatedly – the behaviour would arguably amount to bullying. It is hard not to conclude that a predisposition to bully in the area of domestic violence is present in a minority of young people well before they reach the age at which they might marry.

Of further interest in this study, more than one in ten adolescent males approved of physical violence on the part of a husband in relation to either of these wifely 'indiscretions'. As subsequent analyses showed, support for male aggression in interactions with their wives was predicted by the respondents' reported interactions with peers at school. Both children who bullied and children who were bullied at school were more likely to endorse acts of aggression by adult males directed towards partners.

Conclusions

Attitudes and beliefs about bullying are important. They help to guide the actions of people, whether these actions are directed towards bullying others, helping or not helping those who are being victimised; or, more generally, bringing about or sustaining an ethos in which people are encouraged to act aggressively and to bully others, or alternatively to act constructively and protect those who are most vulnerable to harm from others. What this chapter has shown is that although most people appear to deplore bullying, there are large individual differences, with some people prone to finding justifications for acts of aggression that can reasonably be labelled as bullying. It is true that nearly all the work I have been able to review on attitudes to bullying relates either to views held by young people or views held about young people. More work is clearly needed to understand the attitudes of older people. Yet it is fair to say that it is the attitudes of young people that are going to play the major part in determining the extent to which power will be abused in the systematic pursuit of dominating others in the years to come.

Chapter 11

What is to be done about bullying?

For every complex problem there is an answer that is clear, simple, and wrong.

– H. L. Mencken (1880–1956),
prominent American newspaperman,
book reviewer and political commentator

As we saw in the chapter on attitudes towards bullying, people are often divided about what (if anything) should be done. Among schoolteachers, some view bullying between schoolchildren as occurring with sickening regularity; others hardly notice it or think it is unimportant. Some complain that it is yet one more chore being imposed on them in the pursuit of political correctness and self-advancement of aspiring bureaucrats, making a mountain out of a molehill. For their part politicians are beginning to realise that anti-bullying initiatives, particularly in schools, are popular, especially with parents of young children who constitute a large part of their electorate. Concern about bullying in other places similarly divides people, for example, some writers believe that bastardisation and hazing among personnel in the armed forces are evil practices; others think it is laughable to worry about how these tough guys treat each other, since it goes with the territory.

But the drift is unmistakably towards increasing concern about bullying. The media has become energetic in drawing attention to the problem of bullying. It can readily be sensationalised; it sells newspapers, is a boon to talk-back radio and attractive to television documentary producers. The effect is to get us to focus almost exclusively on the violent end of the bullying continuum and virtually ignore the day-to-day verbal and relational forms of bullying to which far more people are subjected, sometimes with equally or more devastating consequences for health and well-being.

Because of this preoccupation with the more overt and violent aspects of bullying, not surprisingly authorities sometimes view bullying as a crime for which legal responses are the most relevant. This is unfortunate, because only a quite small and limited amount of bullying is of direct interest to the law – principally bullying which results in grievous bodily harm. Preoccupation with legalistic or quasi-legalistic responses to bullying has led to a reliance on tribunals and 'bully courts' to bring bullies to account, to punish them and 'send a message' to other potential bullies.

Nevertheless, some authorities see the emphasis placed upon methods of behavioural control, such as we see in many schools (and prisons), as misguided and even counter-productive. What matters, it is sometimes argued, is promoting positive ways in which people treat each other. If individuals can come to see that respecting others and co-operating with others is the best way to behave, there will be little or no need for behaviour management through the stipulating of rules and the imposition of consequences for those who break them. Hence, much argument and ingenuity is being directed towards developing alternatives to the use of threats and punishment, which are the traditional methods of controlling bullying behaviour.

These two perspectives on what to do about bullying are central to the current debate. It is a debate about both ends and means. One sees the desirable end as achieving constructive, respectful behaviour between people; the other as the elimination of hostile, aggressive behaviour between people. Disputes often arise about the effectiveness of means, with one side urging that positive improvements in behaviour between people can be brought about through instruction, persuasion and modelling of respectful behaviour; the other that we can best proceed by identifying and punishing behaviour we wish to stop. These are of course diametrically opposed positions, and in practice we see some compromises, depending upon situations (e.g. school versus workplace) and the form of bullying behaviour encountered (e.g. teasing versus serious assault). Nevertheless, the perspectives I have described do in no small measure determine what people think should be done and what people in authority in schools and in other contexts actually do.

Another way in which people concerned about bullying differ is in their views on what sorts of bullying matter. For some people bullying only matters when someone is seriously hurt physically. Others are more sensitive – or perhaps even over-sensitive. I have met teachers who feel that all teasing is wrong and must be stopped. I was asked once at a workshop by a very serious young man:

what possible good does teasing do? I found it hard to answer on the spot. When I hear gusts of good-natured laughter between friends who are teasing each other, I like what I hear. Some people can see nothing wrong with someone being left out of things completely. 'Serves them right for not being acceptable to the others. They are social misfits.' Sensitivity and capacity to identify with another's plight is a personal matter – but it can be more than that. It can determine policy.

An important difference among those who may make policy is in their conception of the breadth of the problem. For some educational authorities, I am sorry to say, the problem of bullying is all – and only – about protecting nominated groups who are seen as particularly vulnerable to being bullied or harassed by others. Hence an organisation may 'address the problem' by denouncing discrimination and victimisation on the grounds of sex, race or disability and seek to promote more enlightened behaviour towards people who are gay, female, of minority ethnicity and 'differently-abled'. Whilst such concern and calls to cease treating people in such categories badly on account of their membership of such categories is certainly laudable, this view on what bullying is misses out on so much. It ignores what may be called 'personal bullying' for which no convenient sociological category – and no accompanying pressure group serving its interests – can be found. People in this 'non-category' are by far the most numerous.

Finally, there are differences between those who advocate what may be termed a 'systemic approach' to countering bullying and those who see countering bullying as a matter of identifying 'problem people' and changing them. No-one can reasonably object to a systematic approach to stopping bullying in the sense of actions to prevent and deal effectively with bullying incidents being planned and coordinated rather than improvised. But one can question particular systems that may be proposed. Further, whilst conceding that what happens between people in any organisation depends to a large extent on how the organisation as a whole functions, it can be questioned whether concern with the 'system-in-general' leads people to overlook the fact that most bullying is carried out by a relatively small number of individuals who demand special attention. To the educational administrator concerned with 'the big picture' and responsible for many schools, the danger of focusing on individuals and labelling them as bullies and victims, rather than attending to the conditions that result in bullying behaviour, understandably looms large. It can lead to the conclusion that work at the micro-level with individual people is a distraction and perhaps even counter-productive.

Education about bullying

It is generally agreed that those who make decisions about what is to be done about bullying should be 'educated' about bullying, and that there should be a 'policy' about bullying. Among those concerned with bullying in schools, the mantra is 'whole school approach'. But behind the (sometimes) mindless repetition of this slogan there is often good sense. There has to be a general recognition of the problem. There has to be a united and common response.

Who needs to be educated? In what should the education consist? What is the most sensible and effective way of conveying the necessary information and developing understanding of the problem? These questions are now being addressed at different levels. Increasingly, we find that over-arching bodies such as education departments, trade unions, parent bodies and occupational health and safety organisations are examining for themselves the problem of bullying, and providing information and advice on how bullying can be countered. At grass-roots levels – at individual schools, kindergartens, universities, factories, offices etc. – efforts are being made to access, disseminate and apply existing knowledge about bullying in their own areas of concern. Sometimes these levels are fruitfully connected, sometimes not.

There has emerged a demand for detailed knowledge of what is actually going on between people in an organisation that can be termed 'bullying'. We find that this demand is being addressed in a number of ways. Members of a workforce sometimes get together to pool their perceptions and judgements of how people in their organisation are treating each other. Alternatively, members may be invited to inform about any bullying they have observed in their workplace or have experienced themselves. To this end, a 'bully box' may be provided into which complaints may be put. A 'hot line' may be opened to report incidents. Another way of obtaining information of this kind may be through the use of anonymous questionnaires. The information received in any or all of these ways may be used as a basis for discussion and planning what to do next. The great advantage of this approach to educating a workplace or school community is that it can be based upon a realistic appraisal of the situation to be addressed, rather than upon statistics and generalisations derived from samples of respondents whose experiences and responses could be quite different from one's own. (It is extraordinary how often schools are encouraged to make plans to counter bullying on the basis of survey results obtained from respondents in cultures quite different from theirs, for example, results from extensive studies in Scandinavia in the 1970s and 1980s.)

There are divergent views on the acceptability of gathering data on bullying using particular methods. A concern often expressed is that people should not feel under pressure to inform on others, to 'dob in' others as Australians say. 'Ethics committees' in Australia, acting as gatekeepers for researchers, are inclined to turn down research proposals that involve students naming other students as bullies or victims, though research based upon 'peer nominations' is approved in many countries and contributes to high quality research. Some people object to the use of the anonymous questionnaire on the grounds that it is more open, honest and 'manly' to state and stand by one's judgements of others, an argument much favoured by early 19th-century landowners in opposing the secret ballot in the UK. In Australia the use of anonymous questionnaires by schools to identify the prevalence, nature and consequences of bullying is now common. For instance the Peer Relations Questionnaire (PRQ) and the Peer Relations Assessment Questionnaire (PRAQ) have been employed by hundreds of schools and over 50,000 schoolchildren, teachers and parents. Some non-school organisations, such as UNISON, a UK union, have also made use of questionnaires on bullying (see Chapter 4) – but until now these have been used predominantly to research the situation in workplaces-in-general rather than to address the problem of bullying in a specific workplace. Whatever information exists about specific workplaces is likely to have been obtained through individuals making use of grievance procedures, which unfortunately do not provide a comprehensive knowledge base about what is actually happening.

The use of comprehensive questionnaire-based data has a further advantage. It has the potential to bring closer together people who have different perceptions of the work situation. Some workers will have minimised the problem; others exaggerated it. Some will have seen one kind of bullying or harassment only; others will have a broader picture. To the extent that the questionnaire is seen as providing reliable and credible information – and people are prepared to abandon or modify pre-existing positions – the opportunities for a well-supported policy are there.

But statistics from questionnaires are not the only, or, for some people, most persuasive, kind of information. Often people are much more likely to appreciate a problem by attending to stories that they are told. Reading what children have written about their experiences at the hands of bullies at school is far more enlightening for some than the most carefully gathered and nicely presented statistics. Hence I have strongly advocated that teachers – all teachers in a school – actually read what their students have written about bullying rather than wait for someone, often the school counsellor or the school secretary, to summarise results of school surveys for them. (This is a habit hard to break!)

Bullying is a topic that is frequently raised at a teachers' staff meeting, commonly at the end of the day when everybody is tired, watching the clock and wanting to go home. When staff members on such occasions are passive recipients of information and exhortations, not surprisingly, they are inclined to 'turn off'. By contrast, if teachers can only be induced to tell each other stories about bullying, describe how they felt about it, what they did, and what came of it, the situation can change dramatically. It is curious how the simple principle of pedagogy, whereby people learn and are motivated through sharing experiences, is disregarded when pedagogues meet.

Policy

It remains true that conceptions of the nature of bullying may remain comparatively unaffected by the results from questionnaires or other forms of data collection or by sharing impressions. For example, where bullying is conceived as 'deviant behaviour' that must be 'stamped out' a policy may emerge that relies entirely on rules and sanctions and zero tolerance for rule infractions. Under these circumstances, there is typically a resolve to treat minor and major violations of rules in much the same way. On the other hand, where bullying is seen less as a matter of 'deviance' and more as a matter of unsatisfactory ways of relating to others that can be rectified by psychological and social means, some, if not all, instances of bullying may be treated as 'non-crimes' and sanctions will be seen as not always necessary. Hence, even when there is a common perception of what is happening between individuals in a social environment where an anti-bullying policy is needed, views on what kind of policy is appropriate may well diverge.

Differences may also have to do with whose responsibility it is to counter bullying. At one extreme, there may be authorities who set the rules, identify the bullies and impose the penalties. At the other extreme, members of the whole community may be expected to play a part in developing a plan to stop bullying and also in implementing that plan. A broadly based policy of this kind adopted by some schools (see Rigby 2001a) is shown in the box facing.

Such a policy may be seen as applying to schools rather than to other workplaces, in particular the involvement of parents normally applies only to organisations that cater for children. But many of the principles, for example emphasising the rights and responsibilities of all members of an organisation, may be incorporated into policies made elsewhere. So too can the foreshadowing of the kinds of actions that may be taken, for example counselling (normally as an initial step) to be followed (if seen as necessary) by sanctions.

Elements in an Anti-bullying Policy for Schools

(i) A strong statement of the school's stand against bullying.

(ii) A succinct *definition* of bullying.

(iii) A declaration of the *rights* of individuals in the school community – students, teachers, other workers and parents – to be free of bullying and (if bullied) to be provided with help and support.

(iv) A statement of the *responsibilities* of members of the school community: to abstain personally from bullying others in any way; to actively discourage bullying when it occurs; and to give support to those who are victimised.

(v) A general description of what the school will do to deal with incidents of bullying. (For example: the severity and seriousness of the bullying will be assessed and appropriate action taken. This may include the use of counselling practices, the imposition of sanctions, interviews with parents, and, in extreme cases, suspension from school.)

(vi) An undertaking to *evaluate* the policy in the near and specified future.

Prevention and intervention

When an intervention takes place – especially if it involves sanctions being applied to bullying behaviour – it is normally seen not only as 'deserved' but also as likely to act as a deterrent and prevent further bullying. Where subsequent surveillance is practicable (and we must remember that with some forms of bullying, rigorous surveillance is extraordinarily difficult to maintain) bullying may well be stopped. Applying sanctions will then have had a preventative function. However, it is widely recognised that controlling bullying behaviour by sanctions alone is practically impossible. Hence considerable efforts are being made, especially in some (not all) schools, to promote pro-social ways of behaving that are incompatible with bullying others – and where possible to employ methods of intervention that aim at changing the desire to bully others rather than inducing behaviour change through the fear of consequences. It is generally admitted that changing the desire to bully in a person who seems to be profiting from bullying others is far from easy. But if it can be done, the great advantage is that the difficult and time-consuming practice of maintaining surveillance becomes unnecessary.

There has been a great deal of literature aimed at developing the kinds of attitudes and social skills that produce positive social relations and thereby prevent bullying from occurring. Some of this literature has focused on the home. It is sometimes assumed that positive parenting and good family functioning will result in children being uninvolved in bully/victim problems. Let us look more closely at what it is claimed that parents can do to prevent their children from being bullied at school.

Parenting the non-victim

Numerous writers have argued that children can be protected from being bullied by the efforts of wise parents (Berne 1996; E. Field 1999; Zarzour 1999). Parents are understandably often extremely interested in the advice provided in such books, since they, more than others, are deeply concerned about how children, especially their children, will cope if they are victimised by peers at school. Books with titles like *Bully-Proof Your Child* (Berne 1996) promise to deliver.

We can distinguish several themes in the advice currently being offered. Prominent among these are: (i) the need to develop in children high self-esteem; (ii) training in social competence; and (iii) learning to act in a pro-social way.

High self-esteem is seen by many as the core quality that can prevent a child from being bullied. Sue Berne (1996) writes: 'Self-esteem is the single most important factor in determining whether your child will grow up to be happy and successful' (p.107). She quotes approvingly the words of Stephanie Marston, an American psychologist: 'Self-esteem is the real magic wand that can form your child's future.' Berne defines self-esteem simply as 'how you feel about yourself'. She adds: 'High self-esteem means you can say: "I'm OK just as I am – always"' (p.108).

She gives an example of a child with such self-esteem – a little two-year-old girl called Natalie that she meets on a suburban railway train:

> I smiled at Natalie and said hello. She gave me a big smile. In return I asked her how she was. She looked me straight in the eyes and said confidently: 'I'm gorgeous.' The older girls [whom she was with] laughed and said Natalie always said that. (p.107)

We may take this as an example of a child who has been 'bully-proofed' by wise, nurturant parents.

If we recall the research evidence on the connection between being bullied and self-esteem, we find that, indeed, victims of school bullying do tend to have below average self-esteem (see Chapter 5). As we saw, there are alternative explanations for this association: being bullied commonly reduces self-esteem, and having low self-esteem invites bullying. Both statements are probably true. However, existing research does not support the view that high global self-esteem or high esteem in general can 'bully-proof' a child, but rather it is that aspect of self-esteem relating to social competence that may do the trick. And further, such self-perceived social competence is probably a reflection of actual social competence which, as a result of repeated encounters with others, a child knows he or she possesses and can be applied in situations that might otherwise lead to being bullied by a peer.

We have also to take on board the warning that Harris (1998) has made much of, which is that what has been learned in the home situation may not readily transfer to quite different contexts, for example with a peer group at school. In their early days at kindergarten or school, one can imagine children trying out what has been learned from well-meaning parents about relating to others, only to find that saying 'I'm gorgeous' in front of peers, charming as it is with parents and sympathetic strangers on the train, may not work at all. Indeed, one can imagine it actually inducing teasing – and having to be rapidly abandoned.

Of course self-esteem is not a simple concept and what passes for high self-esteem may on occasions result in a person actually bullying another. Harris (1998) writes: 'Violence appears to be the result of threatened egotism – that is, a highly favourable view of self that is disputed by some person or circumstance' (p.339).

It may be that the value of what one may call solid or justified self-esteem may derive from how well a person takes the knocks to which he or she is exposed. If self-esteem is fragile and the child is inclined to see himself or herself as worthless, the merest hint of criticism or non-acceptance can be demoralising. Arguably, self-esteem is most valuable to a child if it produces resilience.

What can parents do to promote stable self-esteem? Writers often emphasise the giving of praise. E. Field (1999) writes: 'Any time is a good time to praise your child. When you see them behaving in a confident manner with their grand-mother or younger sibling or on holiday or at the Scouts, point this out to them' (p.149). This suggests an indiscriminate use of praise to be delivered as long as the child is behaving confidently, assertively; even, one may surmise, when the child is bugging grandma for more sweets, ordering little brother around again, just pleased at not having to go to school or tying a reef knot the wrong way at Scouts.

Seligman (1995) in his book *The Optimistic Child* takes rather violent excep-tion to the claims that have been made on behalf of self-esteem. And also the means by which parents are being urged to nurture this precious commodity. He argues that there are almost no findings anywhere showing that self-esteem causes anything. Rather, he argues, one's level of self-esteem is a by-product or consequence of success or failure. This does not mean that parents should not praise their children or that praise will not on some occasions actually raise self-esteem, especially when it comes as a confirmation that he or she has advanced towards a higher level of competence. The praise, he suggests, should

be directed towards encouraging children's efforts towards laudable achievements – which could include asserting themselves in such a way as to deter others
from bullying them – and not simply reinforcing everything a child does in the
vain hope of developing an impregnable feel-good state. Seligman concludes his
discussion of self-esteem as follows:

> America has seen thirty years of concerted effort to bolster the self-esteem
> of its kids. The movement would be justified if it worked and self-esteem
> were on the rise. But something striking has happened to the self-esteem of
> American children during the era of rearing children to feel good. They
> have never felt more depressed. (p.36)

Feeling good without anything to show for it, as Seligman would say, puts one in
a highly vulnerable position. In behavioural terms, one has been reinforced for
doing everything and anything. As long as one is with infinitely laudatory
parents the feeling is good, but when the continuous positive reinforcement
abruptly ends, as it may do when peers see nothing so wonderful in the little
things you do, the consequences can be devastating. Serious depression may then
follow, and act as a signal for peers to bully you and deepen a sad condition from
which it is difficult to recover.

When books give advice on the development and reinforcement of skills that
are relevant to countering bullying and harassment they are on firmer ground. In
Bully-Proof Your Child Berne (1996) identifies a number of skills that parents can
teach their children to help them become more socially competent. These include
being able to approach people sensitively and to gain acceptance, communicate
clearly, make friends, act cooperatively and to negotiate and resolve interpersonal
difficulties. Where parents are able to both encourage the development of such
skills and, most important, to model them through their interactions with others,
children appear more likely to be able to interact positively – and more safely –
with peers at school. But, as Berne correctly points out, children need other
children with them continually if they are to learn to become socially competent
with peers and not merely good at role-playing with mother. The steadily
growing research showing a reliable association between non-involvement in
bully/victim problems and the quality of home life, as indicated by positive
family functioning and good child–parent relationships, provides some basis for
the belief that parents can affect the ways in which children interact with others at
school, although – yet again – we cannot discount the possible influence of
heredity.

It must also be admitted that indicators of social competence that are relevant
to family situations, especially those involving adults, may have diminished relevance when a child is being harassed in the school playground. Children rarely
shake hands and introduce themselves politely when they meet, nor do they gen-

erally inquire about each other's health and begin conversations obliquely by making observations about the weather. There are clearly limitations to what social manners can be transferred from one situation to another. However, parents can, if they will, listen to their children when they want to talk about what happened at school, and react sympathetically to accounts of what went wrong. We know that having someone to turn to when one is bullied can greatly reduce the distress one feels (see Rigby 2000). Further, parents can do a number of practical things that can help to prevent a child from being picked on by other children. They can see to it that, as far as possible, the child looks right, wears the right (peer approved) clothes, has the right haircut. This may seem a trivial point almost, but the rules of conformity can be used cruelly and begin a cycle of violence that could with foresight have been avoided.

Parenting the non-bully

Considerably less attention has been paid to the question of what parents can do to prevent their child from being a bully. (Some parents appear not at all displeased if their child is lording it over others.) Most people who want to see bullying stopped seem to believe that good parenting can play an important part. Again we find that the means are often disputed. Some emphasise positive means. The child is to be brought up by loving, caring parents who teach him or her to respect others; the parents model respectful behaviour. At the same time they do not over-protect the child. They help the child to develop good social skills, to meet people and make friends. They avoid as far as possible frustrating the child through over-control and by constantly punishing him or her. On the other hand, others emphasise the need to focus on inappropriate behaviours; in particular, they believe in reprimanding or punishing the child whenever he or she bullies someone. It is probably fair to say that most parents seek to inculcate respectful behaviour in their children by a combination of praise when they act considerately and admonition when they act inconsiderately. However, there is scarcely any research on the effectiveness of parenting behaviours on children bullying in contexts outside the home that is not open to dispute. As we have seen, the correlations between reported or observed parenting styles and children's behaviour at school are low and open to alternative interpretations.

Actions to promote non-bullying behaviour

Some schools have sought to develop in children ways of relating to others that make bullying less attractive to them. These include the promoting of cooperative learning. Here the assumption is that the gains of working constructively and cooperatively with others will outweigh the gains that could come from dominating others by a show of force. Many teachers however see competition between children as a means of maximising educational achievement, and also fear that the introduction of cooperative learning tasks will reduce their ability to control what is going on in the classroom.

Some schools seek to develop in children specific skills that will enable them to resolve conflict peaceably rather than through resorting to force. Conflict resolution skills and mediation skills are taught and practised through role-play. To the extent that bullying arises when individuals are in dispute over something and would like to see, or can be brought to see, the value of an amicable solution, one would expect the exercise of such skills to reduce bullying. But one must bear in mind that there are many cases in which a conflict does not arise from an unresolved dispute, but rather from the desire and capacity of a person or group of persons to impose their will on a targeted person who would like to have nothing to do with them. Such cases are generally not amenable to resolution by mediation.

Some schools seek to develop in children skills that are useful to prevent them from getting bullied. It is clear that some children are severely deficient in this capacity and can benefit from expert training. Others have the necessary social skills and it may seem unnecessary – and indeed wasteful of time – to teach everyone assertiveness skills. Whether schools have the resources to provide the specialised help that easily victimised children need is a contentious issue. Sometimes it is argued that bullies too need help to develop social skills. This may be true of some, but the evidence is that many of them are socially skilful; indeed, some are more skilful than average and can bully others socially because they have such highly developed skills.

Some educators have proposed that *all* children can be helped in schools to develop skills and qualities that make bullying less likely. A team of research/practitioners at the Australian National University has for several years been providing a series of workshops designed to promote more constructive and healthy behaviours among Year 5 school children in Canberra (Morrison 2001). They believe that how children relate to others, for better or worse, depends largely on how they deal with any feelings of shame; that is, positively, by either acknowledging their responsibility and seeking to repair the damage they have done, or negatively, by denying responsibility and blaming others for what has gone wrong. Activities with children are designed to promote better 'shame management'.

Much of what is done here is reminiscent of old-fashioned moral education. Children are reinforced for showing respect and consideration for others and for participating cooperatively in group activities. The Canberra team's evaluation of their workshops with children suggests that bullies who desist from bullying are more likely than others to acknowledge responsibility for their actions and handle shame by repairing damage. Victims of bullying appear to be helped as well in that they tend to become more resilient as a result of the training and less often picked upon.

Whilst the measures taken by schools to develop pro-social behaviours appear inappropriate when applied in other contexts, the problem of producing a pro-social ethos in which individuals prefer not to bully each other needs to be addressed in every context in which people regularly interact. The principles of respect and consideration for others appear to be as relevant in the workplace and in the home as among children in school.

Actions to stop the bullying

Various solutions – or ameliorations – have been suggested to stop bullying from taking place. Different perspectives are taken according to whether the focus is on the victim, the bully, the bully and victim together, or the wider circle of people that could include peers and/or parents.

Focus on the victim

It will be recalled that an essential element in defining bullying is the existence of a power imbalance between a potential target and a would-be perpetrator or perpetrators. Logically, remove the power imbalance and there is no more bullying. However, it is unrealistic to expect power imbalances of one kind or another to disappear, ever. The best we can hope for is the reduction of power differences, such that bullying becomes harder to sustain because the target has become tougher or more resilient. How can this be done? A good deal of attention has been given to what a potential victim (usually a child) can do when he or she is actually in a situation in which there is a threat of being bullied.

Advice to victims or potential victims is plentiful in the form of books, e.g. Stones (1993), E. Field (1999), Miller (1999) and Zarzour (1999), and may be found on various websites and instructional videos. Unfortunately they are not always consistent in the advice they provide. But let us begin where there is least inconsistency, that is, in descriptions of the way in which a targeted person should face the bully or bullies.

E. Field (1999) proposes that the victim looks the bully in the eye; puts on a friendly-looking face; stands straight – no jiggling; speaks clearly and calmly; and is prepared, not scared (p.163). Zarzour (1999) in general agrees but adds: 'Give him (sic) a stony-faced stare – look straight through the bully' (p.98). Romain (1997) neatly sums it up pictorially (see Figure 11.1).

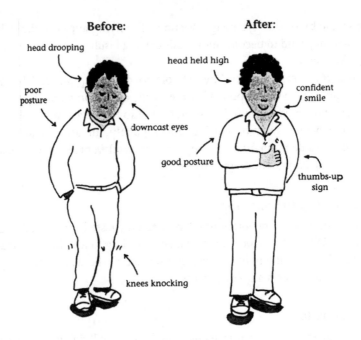

Figure 11.1 Before and after becoming assertive

An excellent website from New Zealand (http://www.nobully.org.nz/) draws on the wisdom of the Maoris: *Kia baha* meaning 'stand tall'. By all means, stand tall. The problem is how to do that in the actual situation when one is frightened or upset. Some offer further advice, beginning usually with: first practise before a mirror or (if possible) role-play with friends or members of your family. Then, when it happens – take a deep breath. Field advises 'fake it' until it becomes automatic. Given that most victims are rather timid, shy and introverted, one can see that isn't going to be easy.

Ignore it. This is sometimes suggested as the first thing you should do if somebody tries to bully you. Not everybody agrees. Miller (1999) writes: 'While kids are making fun of you, one of the worst things you can do is to pretend to ignore them in the hope that they will lose interest and stop. They won't. They know you can hear them, and if you act like you can't, they'll take that as a challenge and keep at you' (p.15). She adds: 'Even though you do not look at them or speak to them, your non-verbal reactions – clenching your teeth, staring straight ahead, frowning, etc – gives them enough proof that they are upsetting you. This is all the encouragement they need to continue' (p.19).

Zarzour (1999), who believes that acting assertively can be a first step, concedes that assertiveness may not always work, and that one might then go on to talk to the bully 'in a friendly manner'. If this fails, she says, one may calmly walk away – remembering 'to hide your fear'. This way of reacting to bullies does not appeal to many people. Parents typically would like to see a more positive or even aggressive response from their children. Children who see a child walking away following uncalled-for insults, hiding (or more probably *trying* to hide) their fear, are liable to deride the victim as a coward.

Many writers suggest that he or she should hit back verbally but not physically. The reason for differentiating between the two modes of reacting is sometimes unclear. The assumption is made that physical aggression is somehow worse than verbal aggression and, regardless of the situation, more culpable. Yet it is misleading to assume that physical aggression is always more reprehensible than verbal aggression. If we are concerned about the 'hurtfulness' of the two kinds of aggressive acts, then we need evidence that physical aggression is more hurtful than verbal aggression. In fact, in a recent study with 14-year-old Australian schoolchildren (Rigby and Bagshaw 2001), students rated 'name-calling' as more hurtful to them than a slap across the face. I think the real objections to physical counter-aggression when bullied at school are two-fold: first, the victim is likely to get the worst of it, in particular if he or she is outnumbered or confronted by a stronger person; and second, that physical aggression is seen as particularly objectionable by schools. Conspicuous violence, especially if it escalates, is always a major concern for schools.

In discussing how victims should or should not respond to bullying, we should make it clear in whose interest the advice is being given. Pepler, a Canadian psychologist who has specialised in addressing problems of bullying in schools, is quoted by Zazour as having this to say about victims hitting back: 'I can't argue that it's not effective in some situations. It may well be…' In short, it is recognised that in some situations it may be in the best interest of the individual child to hit back. Pepler continues: 'It is not a positive way to solve a problem' (p.96). But we need to ask again, from whose point of view is it not positive, the individual's or the school's? To the child who has got the bully on his or her back the outcome is very positive, if they successfully hit back. To the school, understandably concerned about its reputation, the totality of violent incidents are what concerns it most.

Rarely do we think about 'hitting back' from the point of view of the victimised child. Recently I came across an analysis of what victims should do from a young man who had just left school and posted his comments on the internet. He makes the very obvious point, curiously neglected, that it would be foolish not to distinguish between an extremely dangerous, even life-threatening situation, as when one's assailant is brandishing a knife or a group is intent on beating you up – in which case it is wise to 'play ball' or run like hell – and a situation in which a milder kind of bully is 'trying it on'. He goes on to point out that a countering blow struck in anger may on some occasions be the wiser option, even though one might subsequently pay for it by losing a fight or even a tooth; preferable maybe to being chased round the school for years to come by a rabble of insensitive kids who see you as a pushover who will not fight back.

Being assertive is widely seen as the answer, but how? It is often recommended that the victim states how he or she feels, as in: 'I don't like what you said then', followed by steady eye-contact. Or 'I don't think that's funny', when one has been deliberately insulted. Or more simply: 'I would like you to stop doing that.' If the bully is sufficiently empathic to care about the victim's feelings or opinions, the bullying may end. But many a time the bully or bullies will simply be receiving welcome, explicit confirmation that the barb has gone home as intended.

Some writers have spent considerable time and applied considerable ingenuity in devising the sort of 'come-backs' that can put the bully on the back foot and even back off for good. These tailor-made retorts vary in degree of offensiveness.

E. Field (1999) provides numerous examples of verbal tricks and questions that a victim may use. Some involve asking questions designed to put the pressure back on the bully.

> Bully: Hey homo…
> Reply: Could you explain that to me, I'm only a lay person
>
> Bully: Hey, fathead…
> Reply: Did you call me fat or obese. What is the difference?
>
> Bully: You're such a bitch
> Reply: Shall I go back to my kennel now or later?

Such a display of verbal dexterity is intended to convince the bully that he or she will surely lose in a battle of wits, in which case there is no verbal imbalance of power in the bully's favour (in this regard power has been equalised or maybe tilted the other way). Perhaps the bully would be advised to try a different medium of aggression. One is reminded of the mythical encounter that supposedly took place between two men on a narrow pavement in 18th-century London. The swaggering bully blocks an oncoming pedestrian saying: 'I never give way to a villain.' 'Oh,' says the other, stepping neatly aside, 'I always do.' Collapse of the real villain.

It is possible that some children who might otherwise be victimised could learn such tricks, but as I think the examples show, what they are asked to say must all too often appear unnatural and suggest a precocity that could afford further grounds for tormenting the child. A further problem is that such tricks are not easily learned or 'pulled off' by children who are naturally introverted and not verbally quick, which unfortunately is often the case among children whose peers ridicule them. Field recognises this problem and concludes: 'They (victims) should only say something when they can do it naturally and automatically' (p.185).

In her advice to parents, Field advises: 'Your child should always appear polite and respectful.' Never 'rude and aggressive'. Not all advisers agree. Miller (1999) sees bully and victim engaged in a desperate struggle where desperate measures may be taken. 'Brace yourself for a power struggle,' she writes, 'and be ready to stand your ground. Don't give up when ridicule seems to get worse' (p.16). Here are her examples of insults and comebacks:

Insult: You're so ugly
Comeback: Then I must be like you

Insult: You look like a witch
Comeback: That's really funny coming from a hag

Insult: You're such a skinny freak
Comeback: Thanks fatso

Insult: You're so stupid
Comeback: So few brain cells. Don't waste them on speech.

With the possible exception of the last one, these have the virtue of lacking any sort of subtlety.

At a loftier level, Fuller (2000) has suggested that children learn to deflect or 'deconstruct' insults from bullies, thereby reducing their hurtfulness. Here are his examples: if you are called a slut, point out that a slut really means 'a woman of untidy domestic habits'. A clever response, he suggests, would then be: 'How do you know I haven't done the dishes?' If you are called a faggot recognise that a faggot is an English meatball. Hence the smart answer to being called a faggot could be: 'What makes you think I'm an English meatball?' One wonders on how many schoolyard bullies this display of erudition would be rather lost. Fuller adds that among his favourite responses to the jibes of bullies are 'snotgobbler' and 'weasel breath', said with gusto and determination – and (I should think) at least a 50-metre start.

Telling

'Make ours a telling school' is a catchcry of many schools that have adopted an anti-bullying policy. As we have seen in Chapter 3, although most children at some stage in their lives have told others that they have been bullied at school – and sometimes received effective help – many children prefer to keep it to themselves, either from a sense of pride or a sense of fear. There is for some children – and some adults too (for example in the armed forces) – a stigma attached to 'informing on your mates' or showing that 'you can't take it'.

From the perspective of organisations, 'telling' seems desirable. It is a means by which the authorities can find out what is going on. If it is out in the open, they reason, they can deal with it.

Hence, a great deal of pressure may be put on children to tell. For instance, here is how one school authority, the John Kelly Boys' Technical College in England, has put the arguments for telling

> Telling is the first and most important step to stop bullying Bullying will continue because the bully thinks that he or she can get away with it.
>
> - You will continue feeling sick and miserable
> - You wouldn't want to go to school
> - You can't concentrate on your work
> - You will continue feeling scared and insecure
>
> So go ahead and tell someone! Get your courage together and let someone share your fears. Before telling someone, you should understand that whatever happens from now, you will be sharing it with someone (From website: http://www.jkbtc.co.uk)

From the viewpoint of the individual child the picture may be different. As described earlier in Figures 3.7 and 3.8 (pages 68 and 69) approximately 10 per cent of children in schools report that 'telling' led to matters getting worse – and with increasing age no improvement is evident. One can understand why many children, especially older children, are reluctant to ask others for help when they are being bullied. Telling everybody may be a recipe for disaster. Some will be glad to hear the news – and join in with the bullying. Limiting the 'telling' to people who can be trusted is an important proviso. As we have seen, school counsellors normally have a much better record of being helpful than others. But it is important for school authorities to recognize that from the perspective of individual children it is not clear whether it is in their interest to take risk of informing. Hence, if school authorities are going to encourage informing on bullies as a matter of school policy, they need to assure children that the risk is non-existent or, at worst, minimal. They need to ensure that children who tell are well protected.

Taking action on behalf of the victim

What action and when? Authorities – whether teachers, parents, counsellors or managers – are often undecided as to what kind of action they should take and under what circumstances the action is justified. Most are agreed that it is best for victims to solve the problem themselves – if this is possible. The lift to self-esteem in overcoming a bullying problem oneself is remarkable. Hence, it is generally advisable to spend time exploring what can be done by the victim, without involving the authorities. In any case, often the victim does not want the authority to take direct action on his or her behalf, and, as we have seen, he or she may have grounds for suspecting that the situation could be made worse. Persuading a hesitant victim otherwise or over-riding the victim's wishes should obviously be done only in extreme circumstances, for instance when the victim's life or health is seriously threatened. It is known that in many cases the victim simply wants to be heard and receive moral support – and that such support can reduce the stress that is being experienced and lessen negative health effects (Rigby 2000). But there certainly are cases in which it would be desirable and sensible to provide more positive help. Where a child or older person has become traumatised by a severe bullying experience, professional help may be needed, and knowing how a relevant referral can be made is important. Where intervention on behalf of the victim is seen as necessary, a guiding principle must be to reduce the likelihood of that person being further victimised as a result of informing. This means providing adequate protection – which is sometimes not easy to do. It may be that on occasions effective action can be taken on the basis of information that cannot be traced back to what the victim may have said. The Method of Shared Concern, as developed by Anatol Pikas (1989) (see pages 256–257), suggests ways in which this may be achieved.

Focus on the bully

What can be done by parents to prevent a child from growing up a bully? Zarzour (1999) declares – and some others agree: 'Bullies are not born: they're created' (p.57). The jury in fact is still out (the jurymen and jurywomen of different persuasions – behavioural geneticists and developmental psychologists – are still arguing fiercely about the verdict). But in the meantime it would be foolish not to try to produce the conditions that we know are statistically associated with the home backgrounds of non-aggressive children. And we know the sort of families in which bullies do not usually thrive. They are non-authoritarian (also non-permissive); they are caring, accepting; they are places where children are happy rather than resentful (see Chapter 7). But more specifically, what if the child behaves aggressively, as children invariably do from time to time? Here viewpoints diverge. For example, Zarzour argues that when children act aggressively, regardless of circumstances, parents should tell them that they are upset about it, and ask them whether they could not have handled their feelings better. However, parents are generally *not* upset when their children stand up for their rights; as when they persist and push away another child who would take things from them. Most parents would see such counter-aggression as a legitimate use of force, not to be confused with bullying.

A further issue upon which there are alternative views is whether children should be exposed to violent media presentations. It is sometimes argued that the media is one thing and real life another, and that the former does not affect the latter. We may see violence as mere entertainment. Sometimes the argument is that viewing violence can have a cathartic effect and enable us to discharge aggressive feelings vicariously through fantasy. The research on this issue is now quite extensive. The verdict is not unanimous, but the drift is certainly towards believing that viewing high levels of media violence is likely to induce violent behaviour in children, especially among those predisposed to act aggressively and to bully others.

There are some media presentations that seem more likely to induce bullying than others. Among these are television wrestling shows. In a recently reported case in the USA a 13-year-old boy was convicted of brutally assaulting and killing his 6-year-old sister in the course of imitating his television wrestling heroes. The boy (75kg) was reported as having hit his sister (21kg) about 40 times while tossing her around the room in a series of wrestling moves, resulting in the girl suffering horrific injuries, including a fractured skull, lacerated liver, a broken rib, internal haemorrhaging, cuts and bruises, from which she subsequently died. It is hard to believe that observing heroic figures ramming their opponents' heads into metal chairs (however faked) could fail to stimulate bullying behaviour on the part of children who are predisposed to hurt and enjoy hurting others.

Action with the bully

What should one do to, with, or for the bully? The prepositions 'to', 'with' and 'for' are significant. For some people the question is simply what should we do 'to' the bully – what does he or she deserve to have happen and what might act as a deterrent to others. 'Making the punishment fit the crime' is a well respected principle in jurisprudence, widely supported. But is bullying a crime? Does it call for a response that is applicable to offences we call criminal? The case described above, leading to a conviction by a Florida court – though the question of the penalty was not immediately resolved – suggests that it can be so regarded. In some writings about bullying the word 'crime' is used loosely, to express the writer's feelings of repugnance. I think we should be clear that where bullying has been involved, legal action has been applied in relation to the nature of the assault and the damage it caused, rather than because it constituted 'bullying' as such. From a legal standpoint, it appears that bullying per se is not a crime, but actions that accompany bullying may be criminal, and incur legally justified punishment.

Most of what we call bullying does not invoke the law, nor is it likely to do so. Yet quasi-legal structures are being mooted and in some cases introduced to cater for the relatively extreme forms of bullying, for instance, in the form of tribunals in industry which may examine cases of sexual and racial bullying and even personal bullying. In schools, procedures are sometimes introduced leading to decisions about the kinds of sanctions that should be applied, and these may include suspensions. Some writers have advocated the setting up of bully courts in which students may play a leading role in 'trying' suspected bullies and recommending to the principal of a school that one or more of their peers be punished for 'bullying' (see Elliott 1991). The notion of retributive justice as applicable to bullying, especially extreme forms, is also not without its supporters.

The buzz word until recently has been 'consequences'. This sounds better than 'punishment', in part perhaps because the latter has, for some, a sense of being arbitrary and vengeful, though of course it need not have. The appeal of 'consequences' also lies in its apparent independence of volition on the part of authorities who do hurtful things to rule-breakers. If rules can be formulated that are entirely reasonable then whoever breaks them brings the consequences on themselves. The rules relating to behaviour are seen as having an unquestionable validity. They are 'natural laws' akin to the law of gravity. Defy that and you are almost literally riding for a fall. The snag lies in the difficulty of formulating entirely reasonable rules for everything. Rules are always there to be questioned and defended or changed. Nevertheless, there is some evidence that in those US schools where students are more knowledgeable of the school rules for behavioural infractions and also know the consequences for infractions of those rules, the level of school disorder is significantly lower (Mayer and Leone 1999).

Responses to bullying sometimes invoke the concept of zero tolerance. Tolerate nothing. The theory of James Q. Wilson, the academic who introduced the notion, was that allowing small crimes to pass unpunished will encourage contempt for the law in larger matters. For instance, a school in which children tease and call each other names will also be one in which children physically assault each other. In practice, if we stamp on teasing we will simultaneously be reducing physical violence. The plausibility of this theory appeared to be supported by the introduction of zero-tolerance policing in New York and a corresponding observed reduction in crime in that city. Unfortunately for the theory, its introduction coincided with a period during which there was a dramatic reduction in the numbers of young men in New York between the ages of 15 and

24 years, the demographic category most associated with crime statistics (see 'Defeating the bad guys', *The Economist* 1998).

The Columbine killings in 1998 gave considerable impetus to the employment of zero-tolerance policies for schools in each of the 50 US states (Cloud 1999). The slogan has gained credence in other parts of the world, for example in Britain and Australia.

What disturbs people about the zero-tolerance policy is that in its execution, if not in its conception and intention, it appears to be undiscriminating. Cases of minor infringement have been treated as major crimes meriting suspension. In their examination of legal issues in the prevention of school violence, Yell and Rozalsky (2000) describe zero tolerance as relating to 'policies in which any violation of a specified type (e.g. violence, drug use) results in severe consequences (e.g. expulsion, arrest)' (p.190). This suggests that the theory of zero tolerance applies to really serious anti-social activities. But this goes against the line of thinking that says don't let people get away with small things or they will go on to do the big things. No wonder people are confused. What is missing is a reasonable view on adjusting the reaction of school authorities to correspond to the seriousness of the student's misbehaviour.

We need a reasonable typology of seriousness as applied to bullying. I have proposed the basis for such a typology in Chapter 2. What can be added to this is an examination of the variety of motives or reasons for bullying. These may include an exaggerated sense of 'getting one's own back'; just having (misplaced and harmful) 'fun' as a member of a group; coldly practising extortion by threatening vulnerable individuals; not knowing how to resolve a dispute with a less powerful person in any other way; and pure unadulterated sadism. Delwyn Tattum, the Welsh authority on bullying, has advised teachers to gather all the relevant evidence, then 'exercise the wisdom of Solomon'. Certainly an answer cannot be given in a nutshell. Unfortunately, that is what teachers and authorities in general want, and the notion of an irrefutable correspondence between offence, rule and consequence is what is yearned for. Some authorities have sought to provide guidelines to help teachers to gauge the seriousness of offences and the severity of the options open to them (Rigby 2001a).

But when the focus is on the bully, the question is not just or simply what shall be done to him or her, because that would be just and that would deter others. There is also the question of what can be done with and for such a person. Tattum, for instance, has argued that it is not enough simply to apply an appropriate sanction to the school bully. We have to think about the miscreant's future. Should the label 'bully' remain like an albatross around his or her neck in perpetuity? Clearly not, if one wants to motivate that person to make a fresh start and, in time, wipe the slate clean.

Some would argue that (whether the individual wants it or not) bullies must be 'helped'. The means by which a bully can be helped to abandon bullying and act more pro-socially may, of course, vary from person to person. For example, some bullies do have well developed social skills; others may bully because they lack such accomplishments and can in fact be helped by appropriate social training. There are bullies who simply lack self-control and these people may benefit from anger-management training, whilst others are very deliberate and calculating and cannot be helped in this way. Some can be helped by being provided with better opportunities for cooperating with others or even leading others in pro-social activities. Alternatives for helping children who bully at school are examined in the handbook *Stop the Bullying* (Rigby 2001a). It would be foolish, however, to assume that all can be helped in the same way, or that every alternative is equally practicable. One may, for instance, seek to reform a bully in the workplace by promoting him to a position of greater authority (where he is less frustrated) only to find that this gives him greater scope for bullying and that his promotion is, in any case, deeply resented by other workers.

Finally we should recognise that there is one enormously important advantage in working 'with' bullies or 'for' bullies as opposed to against them. If one is successful in changing the basic motivation of people who bully (and no-one should underrate this difficulty) the task of monitoring what goes on in the school or workplace is made much easier. In fact, as far as the less overt forms of bullying are concerned, as in indirect aggression, rumour spreading, etc. – forms that are often highly destructive of individuals – they are practically impossible to stamp out by punitive action and sustained surveillance.

Focus on the bully or bullies and the victim

They say it takes two to tango – and at least two, often more, to produce a bully/victim situation. Hence some authorities have argued that it is no good dealing with each in isolation. The bully and the victim must be brought together and their conflict resolved in a satisfactory way. Accordingly, emphasis has been placed in some schools on conflict resolution. This has sometimes involved the training of selected students in ways in which they can intervene to stop bullying from continuing. There can be no doubt that some students are apt trainees and can develop useful conflict resolution skills and apply them in situations where aggressors and victims are prepared to talk about their differences. Indeed, some students are more willing to work with a fellow student-counsellor than with a teacher whom they think would be less able to understand the situation. However, as it has been frequently observed, mediation ideally requires a situation in which there is an equality in power between the people in dispute and a readiness in both of them to find a mutually acceptable solution. By definition bullying occurs when there is an imbalance of power, sometimes a very large imbalance of power. Moreover the bully often does not want his or her dominance over the other to end. There is little therefore for the bully to gain from mediation; much, it seems, to lose. What can be done directly through the use of it to resolve conflict in bully/victim cases must therefore be limited. (I should add that it may nevertheless help greatly in creating an ethos in a school or place of employment which is conducive to constructive relations between people; an ethos in which bullying is unlikely to thrive.)

Authority is generally seen as needed to redress the imbalance of power between bully and victim. In schools this means teachers; in the workplace, management – or a suitable tribunal or even a court of law. Typically, the bully or bullies are to be denounced; the victim (or victims) roundly supported. In schools I often hear of such a thing. The gang of bullies are 'invited' to the principal's office and dressed down in no uncertain terms in the presence of the child whom they have been tormenting. They are then each invited to go up and apologise sincerely to the poor child who is wishing the ground would swallow him up. Afterwards, he – or it could be she – has a fair idea of what will happen. The subsequent bullying could be more subtle but no less intense and no less hurtful.

Anatol Pikas (1989) has proposed a way in which authorities – that is credible authorities – can work with both bullies and victims. His method of dealing with bullies and victims is known as the Method of Shared Concern. It has been applied in numerous schools in Europe and in Australia, often with considerable success. It seems likely that the approach can be adapted for use in the workplace. The method is applicable especially in cases in which there is evidence of group bullying. It is assumed that bullies are generally insensitive to the harm, or the extent of the harm, they are doing to the victim. This insensitivity is due to their involvement in a group which seems to give legitimacy to their bullying activities and prevents them from feeling personally responsible for the outcomes. What they appear to gain mostly through bullying is a sense of being part of a group which is 'having fun'. Yet as individuals, bullies commonly feel uncomfortable about what is being done. Further, a hostile blaming attitude on the part of an authority figure is likely to increase the desire to continue bullying and unite the group of bullies more strongly.

Pikas recommends that one should work with members of a known bullying group individually, and always begin by sharing with them one's own sincere concern for the victim before asking them what they know about what has been happening to the victim. The method is in a sense confrontational – it does not involve making any accusations but it does strongly invite and expect a responsible response. Typically promises are elicited from each person in the group separately on how they will improve the situation for the victim. (A possible script for

an encounter is given in Ken Rigby's website: http://www.education.unisa.
edu.au/bullying/) What transpires is then carefully monitored.

Pikas believes strongly that victims should not be interviewed first, because
then the bullies will suspect that they have informed on them and the victims will
become more endangered. Victims, he points out, are not always 'innocent', and it
is important to understand what they may be doing to provoke the bullying. One
may need to work directly on changing the victim's provocative way of behaving.
Once the victim becomes involved in the proceedings, the counsellor may sometimes need to engage in 'shuttle diplomacy', between the victim and members of
the bullying group in a mediational role. Although the aim is to re-individualise
bullies, the idea is *not* to 'break up' groups (students have a right to enjoy being in
a group) but eventually to change their attitudes and behaviour towards the
victim and other potential victims.

Finally, in employing this method, it is important to see the whole group of
'bullies' together, to congratulate them on what they have been able to achieve,
and to work through any residual problems with the victim present. An important
benefit from this approach is that it can lead to a 'change of heart' on the part of
bullies and remove the need for constant surveillance. He points out that the use
of punishment is often ineffective. It may breed resentment, increase group solidarity, jeopardise the victim further, and challenge bullies to practise ways of
bullying that are hard to detect. There is research evidence that the method is
effective in at least two cases in three and contributes significantly to reduction in
peer victimisation (see Petersen and Rigby 1999; Smith and Sharp 1994).

Include the peers

A wider perspective on dealing with bully/victim problems includes not only
bullies and victims but also peers. We can identify two contrasting ways in which
this may be done, based upon quite different philosophies and premises. Both
ways have been applied only in schools.

One way is to include peers in reaching a judgement about the culpability of
the bully or bullies and the penalty or sanction that is to be applied. This
approach was suggested by Michelle Elliott (1991) who advocated the setting up
of so-called bully courts. The process (as described in Rigby 1997b) can begin
when, and only when, a student makes a formal complaint against another
student. For this an official form is provided on which the details are written. The
bully or bullies are invited to attend the next meeting of the bully court. The complainant is also to be present, together with any witnesses of the event(s). There is
no audience. Each person attending the proceedings is asked to give evidence and
is then questioned by the panel of students and staff. The panel then discusses
each case in private and make their judgement. Penalties or sanctions may be pre-

scribed and steps are taken to see that they are administered, unless there is a successful appeal to the principal who may apply a veto. Finally, as in a system of law, a record is kept of all proceedings and verdicts and these become precedents for other case.

Another, radically different way has been suggested by Maines and Robinson (1992) and is known as the No Blame Approach. The authors have provided a detailed description of the method; a critique is to be found in Rigby (1997b). Again the use of the method has been limited to schools. They have proposed that a teacher or counsellor who learns about a child being bullied should discover as accurately as possible from the victim both how he or she has been feeling about the treatment and who the perpetrators are. With the victim's permission (and with assurances that it is safe to do so) the bullies are approached and a meeting convened which includes some peers of the bullies as well as the bullies themselves. At this meeting the convener describes in graphic detail the predicament of the victim and the distress that has been felt by him or her. As a group, they are asked to put things right, and left to do so. As with the Method of Shared Concern, the outcome is carefully monitored.

Despite involving the same persons – bullies, victim and peers – in an attempted resolution of the problem, the underlying rationales could hardly be more different. The bully courts assume there is probably somebody to blame, somebody to be tried and probably convicted. The No Blame Approach assumes that the allocation of blame is unnecessary and even counter-productive. The important thing is to change the situation for the victim. The role of the peers in bully courts is to apply principles of justice, as in the public courts. The role of the peers in the No Blame Approach is to help to exert positive social influence on the bullies so that they will be encouraged to do the right thing by the victim. The philosophy behind the bully courts is that bullies need to be punished and any would-be bullies deterred by the knowledge that they can be brought to justice. The philosophy behind the No Blame Courts is that punishment is unnecessary and, moreover, bullies and would-be bullies will behave well if their consciences can be touched and if they are influenced – but not coerced – by others who know what is the right thing to do.

There is one more distinctive feature of the No Blame Approach setting it apart. The exponents believe that it is absurd to believe that the victim is in any sense to blame. He or she, they assert, are actually doing their best. They would stop the bully if they could. It is outrageous to suggest in any way that the victim is to blame, for example, in not having the necessary social skills or in being somehow provocative. Curiously, I have found that some people feel that the victim *is* being blamed if the bully is not punished, so deeply ingrained is the notion that one cannot reasonable deal with bullying cases without punishing someone.

Include the friends and families

Perhaps the broadest perspective employed is one in which the net is spread so wide as to include virtually everyone who has a personal interest in the way bullies and victims are going to be dealt with. This most inclusive approach has been advocated by those who run community or school conferences for the resolution of particularly extreme kinds of bullying, as in cases involving serious assaults which do not have to go to court. At such a conference the victim of bullying is encouraged to describe what had happened and the distress that resulted. Friends and relatives of both parties – bully and victim – listen to what is said. The victim has the satisfaction of knowing that what has happened has indeed been heard. The bully is expected to provide compensation for the hurt that was done, and typically feels shame. When this is done with the support of family and friends this can be 'reintegrative shame' rather than an enduring stigma (see Braithwaite 1989).

This approach is controversial and clearly requires a careful selection of cases that are suitable for conferences and the employment of a trained facilitator to manage proceedings. One difficulty is that if teachers are used as facilitators, the fact that they may be well known to the persons involved in the conflict, and are, in any case, seen as representing the school, may call in question their objectivity and reduce their effectiveness. Yet there have certainly been successful resolutions of bully/victim issues using this approach, and more important, true reconciliations between bullies and victims. The view of bullying as a community problem requiring a community response rather than one that involves a counsellor, detached from the broader social context and 'fixing up' individuals, has considerable appeal.

Who should help?

It is generally assumed that action to stop bullying is to be taken by authorities. This is understandable. As we have seen, in bullying there is an imbalance of power between perpetrator(s) and victim. An authority – with greater power than the bully, who can apply sanctions, suspend, dismiss or take legal action – is seen by many as necessary.

This view that adults must be there to dispense justice has greatest appeal when we look at the more severe end of the bullying continuum. Yet a great deal of bullying, as we have repeatedly noted, does not even approach being a crime, but should definitely be discouraged. Should all the work of discouraging bullying be done by authorities? Some people think not. They recognise that intervening in severe cases of bullying is potentially dangerous and people are often understandably unwilling to do or say anything. Still, in the bulk of cases the danger is not great and being willing to express displeasure (or at least withhold admiration!) is not a great deal to ask. Hence the growing interest in bystander reactions to bullying. This view is expressed strongly in a recent letter from Mary Stephen to *The Australian* (24/2/01) which commented on a case of two boys who were found to have engaged in a particularly violent form of bullying at an Australian boys' boarding school, Trinity Grammar, in Sydney.

> Far more disturbing than the two boys found guilty of indecent assault at Trinity Grammar is that there were 35 witnesses who failed to defend the victim. More necessary than the anti-bullying initiatives the school has undertaken would be programs instructing the students to stand up and be counted – to act upon an injustice being perpetrated, to have the courage to speak out. There is obviously a pressing need for some action in this regard. Over time, this instruction would have a two-fold effect of character-building for the students resulting in the bullying and abuse being curtailed... Let their schooling prepare them...so that they go into the workforce well equipped to stand up and speak out or act should the need arise, and be able to shoulder any unsavoury consequences.

This letter illustrates several important features in contemporary public reactions towards bullying: a deep concern that severe acts of bullying should not continue; a belief that it is the responsibility of everyone present to act to stop it; and a sense that bullying is a whole-community problem, not one confined to schools, but capable of being solved through what can happen when young people are encouraged to 'stand up and be counted'.

Against this one should recognise the real dangers of intervening in situations in which one can become a victim oneself. Educating bystanders so that they can apply reasonable judgements about when and how to intervene, after counting possible costs and gains, is urgently needed.

Bullying in other places

The discussion on what can be done to counter bullying is heavily weighted towards the school situation. This is inevitable. As we have seen, this is where most bullying in fact occurs; this is where bullying has been most intensively studied; this is where interventions to stop bullying seem most practicable; and finally, if people can be educated not to bully, the school is where such education is likely to happen – with positive consequences for the quality of life in workplaces, homes and indeed wherever people interact with each other.

Nevertheless many parallels have been drawn between bullying in schools and bullying in other places and it is instructive to compare the approaches advocated to counter bullying in schools with what happens elsewhere.

Perhaps the most obvious contrast between schools and other places in the countering of bullying lies in the emphasis upon legal means open to victims when adults rather than children are involved. For example, the Dignity at Work Bill proposed in the UK in 1997 is largely concerned with facilitating access to legal means of redress for victims of bullying in the workplace via industrial tribunals. It is true that taking legal action against schools for not protecting children adequately from peer victimisation is an option that some parents have made use of (see Slee and Ford 1999). Again there have been cases in Australia of 'restraining orders' being taken out by parents to keep a legally enforceable distance between their child and another child who has bullied their son or daughter. But these are exceptional actions, seen as more applicable to relations between adults in the workplace or couples involved in domestic disputes in which one member is being seriously threatened.

Rather than treat bullying as a quasi-legal matter, it has sometimes been considered as basically a health issue. Anti-bullying policy is thereby seen as a means of protecting the mental and physical health of individuals. Evidence reviewed in Chapter 5 clearly supports the view that bullying is a highly significant health hazard experienced in both schools and the workplace. Not surprisingly, organisations concerned with occupational health and safety have added their perspective on bullying. For example, in New Zealand in 1995 the Occupational Health and Safety Service provided a guide for employers and employees on dealing with violence at work, especially from external sources, such as from clients who might physically bully them. More recently in Victoria, Australia, the state Work Cover Organisation has produced an issues paper suggesting a code of practice for the prevention of workplace bullying (Victorian Work Cover Authority 2001). This is of particular interest because it explores the possibility of preventing bullying in the workplace by applying principles that have been used in addressing occupational health problems.

The rationale underlying the Work Cover proposal is that just as there can be hazards in the workplace that are likely to lead to injury or illness – for example handling hazardous substances or working with unsafe machinery – so there can be conditions in the workplace that are likely to lead to a person or group being bullied by others. Such conditions, it is argued, need to be identified and rectified.

The precise analogy between these conditions of potential danger is rarely explored in detail. Sometimes the parallel appears crude. Toxic fumes and guys who bully, it is suggested, are equivalent, and require similar action. Remove them! Fill in a form, stating the source of the hazard and Occupational Health

Officers will, in due course, arrive and arrange for the offending substances or persons to disappear. Presto. It may indeed be the case that the forcible removal of some pathological bullies is desirable. But as a routine way of dealing with bullying, few would support it.

A more sophisticated view is that there may be organisational or social conditions in a given workplace that give rise to bullying and thereby constitute a threat to the health of workers just as there may be physical conditions in the work environment that may undermine a person's health. Such organisational or social conditions might include the following: the exercising of power by managers and bosses beyond what is required to ensure efficient direction of operations; role ambiguity leading to unnecessary disputes between workers; uncertainty about rights and responsibilities at work that could in fact be clarified; and confusing or misleading induction and training procedures. As in schools, there may be measurable aspects of 'workplace climate' analogous to 'classroom climate' (see Chapter 3) that are likely to give rise to bullying and indeed are amenable to change. If boredom is – as some have suggested – a precursor to bullying among schoolchildren, one may question whether this could not give rise to some bullying in some workplaces.

We are thus confronted with two solutions to workplace bullying, depending on how the relevant health hazards are identified. The first is identify those noxious people (labelled 'bullies') who need to be removed. The second is to remove those conditions that give rise to people doing noxious things – what we call bullying. At best, these appear to be partial and often less than adequate solutions. Much bullying is done by people who cannot reasonably be regarded as incorrigible. Much bullying is done by people in conditions or circumstances that appear to be conducive to the most impeccable conduct. Faith in the potential of well designed environments to overcome the tendency of people to abuse power has a utopian ring, which would be touching if it were not so unrealistic.

This is not to say that nobody should be removed from where they are doing great harm; nor that conditions that give rise to bullying should not be identified (if possible) and rectified. The objection is that these 'solutions' appear to block or invalidate a third way – that of working with individuals who bully and doing so in ways that invite responsible behaviour rather than seeking to coerce it.

Chapter 12

Beyond blame

The man who gets angry at the right things, and with the right people and in the right way and at the right time and for the right length of time, is to be commended.

– Aristotle, *Nicomachean Ethics*, Book 4

To get as far as allocating blame for bullying is an achievement. At least there is a recognition that bullying is wrong and that somebody or something is responsible for it. It is, one might say, better than a resigned acquiescence to things as they are; infinitely better than a toadying admiration for those who wield power regardless of how they do so. Blame looks for a cause so that its source can be condemned. It does so with righteous anger. It cries out to high heaven that bullying should not be. And it points the finger.

The prime target is the bully. But we find that this is not the only target. The victim, too, may be in the line of fire. Or for those who seek a deeper cause, the school or workplace or home. Or more pervasively 'the system'.

Blaming the bully

Let us begin with the prime villain, the bully. The bully is the one we most want to blame. Typically, he or she is seen as entirely responsible and must take all the blame. Since time immemorial this is the way most of us have responded. We have seen how thousands of years ago the Jewish people, as described in the Psalms, agonised through persecution, clamouring for justice and desperate for revenge, heaped blame upon blame on their oppressors. Those who bullied them were 'man-eating lions', 'evil men', 'wicked ones gloating over our suffering'. They deserved to die. 'May they be like snails that dissolve into slime,' cried the Psalmist. Or worse: better that they had never lived – 'May they be like a baby born dead that never saw the light.'

We find this furious condemnation of the ultimate bully, the child abuser, in the words of Jesus Christ:

> Whosoever shall offend one of these little ones which believe in me, it would be better for him that a millstone were hanged about his neck, and that he were drowned in the depth of the sea.
>
> Matthew 18:5–6

No less condemning are the words that appear on the internet today describing workplace bullies. Recall the litany of Tim Field (1999). 'They are vile, vicious, devious, glib, shallow, slippery, slimy…' They deserve no mercy. Or recall the illustration in *Bully-Proof Your School* (p.9) with its repeated depiction of the bully as the mad dog (see Chapter 6).

In these outpourings we may choose to see something wildly unbalanced, even absurd. Yet, it would be better to hear in them the sound of anguish of people driven to and beyond breaking point, of people striking out in desperation and anger for all they are worth at the sheer injustice of how they are being treated. And just as the words of the Psalms brought comfort to the oppressed in the ancient world, so too do the words we may speak today, denouncing bullying in equally wild and vindictive ways, serve to ease the pain of victims of school and workplace bullying. We are insisting that bullies are to blame, not the victims. In their misery and defeat the victims had even come to think that they were themselves at fault. Not so. Their rights had been recognised. They had not deserved to be treated that way. They could be free to be themselves. By demonising the bully, it seems, we may humanise ourselves.

I recall a meeting I attended of men and women who had been bullied out of work. It was a very emotional meeting of sad and angry people. People spoke about those who had bullied them into a state in which they could no longer continue as employees. Not only had they been bullied by others but – so they recognised – they had in fact been bullying themselves, as people who somehow deserved no consideration. But as the meeting progressed they seemed to take heart. They were all in the same boat and it was emphatically the bullies, not they, who were to blame. The burden of undeserved shame began to lift.

Once we have appreciated the psychological gain from demonising the bully we can begin to count the long-term costs. One aphorism of Bernard Shaw which I cherish is this admittedly hard saying: 'Hatred is the coward's revenge for being intimidated.' Perhaps it is a counsel of perfection. It is not easy to rise above the desire for revenge, especially against those who have mercilessly bullied you. It is easy to say 'rise above it', much harder to do so.

Yet if we do not, the hatred for the bully rankles and festers and may destroy the hater. Richard Nixon is quoted as saying: 'Those who hate you don't win unless you hate them – and then you destroy yourself' (Fitzhenry 1986, p.91). Moreover, the bully can become an infinitely enduring frozen figure. He or she cannot change. Neither the internal force of conscience (the bully doesn't have one) nor the external force of persuasion to which the bully is always impervious can make the slightest difference. The bully will always be like that – vile, vicious, devious, always a mad dog. A leopard cannot change his spots. When the hatred is obsessive, no other factors can be seen as having any relevance. What has been happening is to be understood entirely as the outcome of the evil will of the bully. The bully must be destroyed, so it is said, at all costs.

Blaming the victim

Full-blown contempt for all victims is unusual enough to be pathological. One suspects it of Hitler and other homicidal maniacs. But it is not unusual to find people who express contempt for some victims, and it is not unusual, as we have seen, for people to feel ambivalent towards those who are habitually victimised. What function does the blaming of victims serve?

It helps to steer us away from those who are victimised so that we will not share their fate. This is such an ignoble thought that we may wish to deny that it happens. And yet when children tell us that they wouldn't be friends with kids who don't stand up for themselves, we have to believe them. When we learn from children, as we do, that being bullied has led to them being isolated and without companions, we are further convinced. The 18th-century poet John Clare (1793–1864), said to be 'much addicted to the pernicious habit of rhyming verses' and confined to an asylum for his eccentricities, wrote movingly of the loss he suffered (Martin 1865):

My friends forsake me like a memory lost
I am the self-consumer of my woes.

For those who blame such a victim there is a gain. They are no longer to be associated with the loser.

There is a weird comfort in blaming the victim. It enables one to identify more clearly the kind of person we do not want to be. We will strive to avoid his or her mistakes. Moreover, we can maintain undisturbed the fiction that this is a just world. Bad things do not happen to good, innocent people, people like us.

By their behaviour some victims appear to provide some justification for others disliking and blaming them. Here I have in mind the provocative victim.

Olweus (2001) points out that these children often have the characteristics of both the passive victim – in being depressive, socially anxious and of low self-esteem – and of the bully – in having 'elevated levels of dominant, aggressive and anti-social behaviour and problems with concentration, hyperactivity and impulsivity' (p.13). Not surprisingly, their behaviour can appear irritating and create tension. According to Olweus 'some teachers and students alike seem to think that these victims actually deserve the rough treatment they get' (p.12). We should be careful not to exaggerate the prevalence of such children among victims. Most victims are passive victims with perhaps one or two in ten 'provocative'. Yet their existence does help us to understand why victims sometimes elicit blame rather than support.

But the blaming of victims extends far beyond understandable reactions to 'provocative' types of the kind described by Olweus. Vulnerability itself may appear blameworthy. Being unable or unwilling to protect oneself may be construed as 'asking for it'. At times the behaviour of victims must appear extraordinary. The observer may readily see what the victim could do to avoid or even overcome the situation. But from the victim's point of view there are no ways out and there will be no ways out. The vulnerability and the impotence of the victim appears fixed for ever. To the observer such self-perception is both irrational and contemptible.

Sometimes shyness or congenital introversion may be seen as signs of 'superiority'. Those who do not join in may be branded as uncooperative, outsiders, not 'one of us', even disloyal. Their non-joining is a serious criticism of what we are doing. Who do they think they are?

Blaming the victim thus has its rewards. It may increase your sense of security by ensuring that you stay with the strong and are not undermined by associating with the weak. It may provide a sense of comfort in the thought that only bad or stupid people – who deserve to be bullied – are victimised. Surely, never me. It can build group cohesion by defining who are the unworthy. One may begin to wonder where victims can ever get support.

And yet some do. The Canadian researcher Debra Pepler claims that in bully/victim encounters witnessed by bystanders, on about one in four occasions somebody does express support for the victim. Sometimes, one may assume, this is despite the risk that must be taken that one will be identified with the victim and incur the wrath of the bully or bullies.

Blaming the family

For some people the aberrant behaviour of children is the product of inadequate parenting. Hence children who bully and children who are victimised are not to be blamed. The fault lies with their parents.

This is a particularly attractive idea for schools and many developmental psychologists. Take schools first. If it can be accepted that behavioural problems of children at school are the responsibility of parents and that the difficulties teachers experience with their delinquent charges are in essence 'imported', then the schools cannot be blamed for any bullying that occurs on their premises. I have more than once been interrupted by an outraged principal to be told that it all stems from the home. They learn to be violent in the home from their mums and dads. They learn to be helpless victims from the maters and paters who molly-coddle them. Result: bullying.

As we have seen there are many developmental psychologists who appear to support such an explanation of bullying and do so on almost entirely correlational evidence. Certain kinds of behaviour – including bullying others and being victimised by others – go with certain kinds of parenting and family dynamics. This is indisputable. There has been much elaborate theorising to explain the connection. Victims of peer abuse, we are told, tend to have a history of insecure attachment to parents or carers in infancy, especially anxious/resistant attachment. Subsequently at school they are often anxious, cry easily and behave timidly. And, in addition, they think poorly of themselves. All this invites bullying. Thus parents fail to provide children who are subsequently victimised at school with the right kind of love and security they need. They, not their children, are to blame.

A somewhat different tack is taken by those who lay the blame on inadequate child-rearing practices extending throughout childhood. Years of parental over-protection – so it is argued – take their inevitable toll, reducing the unfortunate children to impotent wrecks unable to defend themselves at school. If only the parents had given their children more space, had encouraged independence more, had simply got out of the way, all would have been well. As for the bully, another kind of parenting produces him or her. By their insensitive, uncaring, aggressive behaviour, parents of bullies provided a model that their children took on board and found more than handy when it came to intimidating others at school. Or was it that the parents made them so angry and frustrated that they had to take it out on other poor kids? Maybe both. Parents are further to blame, one might add, for not teaching their children right from wrong, not monitoring their behaviour, not stepping in when their children struck someone, and so on. As for the provocative victim, he or she can be seen as having the worst of both worlds: sometimes being over-protected, horribly spoiled; sometimes neglected, sometimes harshly controlled – in short, treated with disturbing inconsistency.

The assumption that 'parents are to blame' can become psychiatric dogma. Here is an extract from a biographical account of childhood written by a Canadian college student, as reported by Ambert (1994):

Up to the age of 11 years I had been quite happy at school but then something happened to me. I stopped growing and I became in no time the shortest and the skinniest and soon the pimpliest little runt at my grade level. The other boys used to pick on me, hide my coat, steal my lunches, and would never include me in their games. They'd laugh at me openly and the girls started avoiding me too because it wasn't cool being seen with the most unpopular boy… You can't imagine how many times my mother had to keep me at home because I'd start throwing up. I became scared shitless…and to this day I feel insecure around other guys… The funny thing is that my parents had to send me to a psychiatrist and he turned around and he blamed them for not being supportive and for whatever else. That's kind of sad when you think that my kind of problem had nothing to do with my parents. My parents were sort of being made miserable because of the little runt I was and now by this psychiatrist, and to this day they have never blamed me and have always been supportive. (p.114)

Although numerous research papers have been published showing that bullying behaviour and being victimised are correlated with certain parenting practices and family dysfunctionality, it has yet to be confirmed that there is a direct causal link between the two. As we have seen, Harris (1998) has argued strongly that genetic factors and forces operating within the school environment, emanating largely from peers, are more potent determinants of children's behaviour at school than parenting practices, which have their effects largely in the home itself and possibly also in the very early years of kindergarten or primary school.

Blaming of parents for bullying is certainly popular. I encounter it regularly in the schools I visit. What can you expect of bullying in this school, they tell me, given the sorts of parents in this area. It absolves the school of responsibility; it takes away the blame from children themselves (their parents made them); and (happily) it is in line with what many developmental psychologists seem to think. Unfortunately, it dumps the blame unfairly on some if not all the parents of bullies and victims. Emboldened by reading about 'family determinants of bullying', one principal I know arranged for copies of his favourite article on how parents produce bullies and victims to be sent home to the parents of every one of his students. I guess he felt better afterwards.

Blaming the school

Parents commonly blame the school. They do so especially when their own child is being bullied and the school appears unable or unwilling to help matters. The school becomes the enemy. Whatever the school does – or fails to do – it is culpable.

Some years ago a parent, maddened by the way she believed the school had reacted – or failed to react – to her daughter being bullied, documented from memory, as best she could, what had transpired between herself and the principal in phone calls between the two of them. She gave me permission to use it as an example of how things can go wrong. (The names are invented.)

Earlier in the day the parent's child, a girl aged 13 years, had sustained an injury during a lacrosse game at school. She had received a blow to her back and a black eye from a lacrosse stick. The girl (Jennifer) had subsequently gone home. At about 4 pm the school Principal (Mr B) phoned the parent (Mrs P) about the incident.

The reconstruction begins after Mrs P had phoned the Principal to complain about her daughter's injury.

Mr B: Tell me what happened, Mrs P? (*said in a patronising manner*)

Mrs P: What! It happened in your own school and you don't know what happened, you should be telling *me* what happened!

Mr B: I was in a meeting.

Mrs P: Which one is more important, your meeting or Jennifier's condition?

Mr B: When I came out of the meeting I didn't have a chance to see Jennifer, because *you* had already taken her.

Mrs P: Obviously you didn't bother to check anything. You assumed I took her. A social worker took Jennifer because I was not at home. Secondly, she had waited 40 minutes, and I repeat to you she had to wait 40 minutes in the sick room, crying and in pain. The only one who comforted her was the nurse teacher. According to the nurse teacher, it was serious, and Jennifer needed to get out of the school environment because she was stressed out and needed medical attention. Are you aware of the letter I gave to the Deputy Principal?

Mr B: Yes, I am aware of it.

Mrs P: Finally, Jacob Turner, the boy I had previously complained about to the Deputy Principal, had carried out his threat and hit her in the back and eye – and now she has a black eye.

Mr B: No, this was an accident.

Mrs P: Every time he hits her you call it an accident. How can this be an accident when the boy said: 'This is just the beginning'?

Mr B: I need to investigate the matter.

Mrs P: Does this mean you have not talked to the boy yet?

Mr B: No.

Mrs P: Why not?

Mr B: Because I was in a meeting.

Mrs P: But, it is now 4 pm and still you don't know! (*Pause*) And how did you come to the conclusion that this was an accident?

Mr B: (*No answer*)

Mrs P: I hold you and the Deputy Principal responsible for failing to carry out your duty and neglecting to take any action now and before.

Mr B: Why did you go to the media? I have a name to look after (*said in a sharp tone of voice*).

Mrs P: Yes, and I have a daughter to look after. Which one is more important: my daughter's safety, or the name of the school?

Mr B: (*No answer*)

Mrs P: I suppose you are angry I went to the police?

Mr B: No, I would have advised you to go to the police.

Mrs P: Why?

Mr B: Because she has been physically assaulted.

Mrs P: But just now you said it was an accident.

Mr B: (*Pause*) I am *not* happy you went to the media because I have a name to look after (*said in a sharp tone of voice*).

Mrs P: So you only rang me because the media is involved, not because you care about Jennifer.

Mr B: Remember I have a name to look after (*said in an angry voice. Hangs up*).

The following day, at 11 am approximately.

Mrs P: I need to know what have you done about the boy who assaulted my daughter. Has he been suspended?

Mr B: No! (*in a sharp tone of voice*).

Mrs P: Why not?

Mr B: Because I need to investigate the matter.

Mrs P: What! Since yesterday and today you have not done anything?

Mr B: (*No answer*)

Mrs P: Who are you covering for Mr B?

Mr B: I am not covering for anybody.

Mrs P: I am holding you and the Deputy Principal responsible for failing to carry out your duty, and neglecting to take any action now and before. I will make sure that justice is done.

Mr B: I need to see Jennifer to take details from her.

Mrs P:	In no way will I let her come to school until you can provide her with safety. How do you expect me to send her to school when the boy said: 'This is just the beginning'?
Mr B:	(*No answer*)
Mrs P:	I take this as a 'no', that you will not provide her with safety. (*Pause*) Thank you very much for your caring.
Mr B:	Huh, thank you (*in a taunting manner*).
Mrs P:	(*Hangs up*)

It must be emphasised that this was the parent's version of events. We do not, unfortunately, have the Principal's side of the story.

The incident was never satisfactorily resolved. In fact, not surprisingly, it escalated. It reached the press. Parent and child were distraught. Letters were written to people in high places: to the Education Department; even to the Prime Minister of Australia (who did not reply). Eventually a meeting was convened with numerous school and department representatives and witnesses. To no avail. The child left the school and, I am glad to say, settled down well in her new school. But one positive thing did come out of this sorry tale of blame and counter blame. The mother fighting for her child and the daughter for whom the battle was fought grew closer.

This saga illustrates the strong feelings of outrage that parents can sometimes have towards the school where their child has been bullied. From the parent's point of view the blame is clearly merited. The school is *in loco parentis* and failed to discharge a sacred duty of care. From the school's point of view it is impossible to prevent everything. There are other things a teacher or principal must do. One can't do everything at once. And there is the reputation of the school to defend. The latter, once expressed, is a red rag to a raging parent.

Blaming the nation

It is common to characterise nations at times as "bullies." Generally the term has been used to condemn military action or the threat of military action by more powerful nations against weaker ones: for example, the US against Iraq in the Gulf War; Russia against the Chechen rebels; China against Formosa; Indonesia against East Timor; Jews against Arabs in Israel; and so on. The list could be extended almost endlessly.

What the appellation of "bully" does is to focus on a self- evident mismatch, a David and Goliath contest in which one's sympathies are with the diminutive David. It captures and encourages a sense of indignation at the prospects of the stronger party trampling on the weaker party. We see Arab children throwing stones and Israeli soldiers firing bullets. The emotional impact of such an image, seen nightly on television newsreels, is redoubled when we pronounce the word "bullies." We are predisposed to think and feel that might is not right; so much so that we forget that it is equally the case that might may sometimes be right. In short, a conception of a nation as a bully simply because it is stronger than its adversary can be very misleading.

We also need to remind ourselves that nations are not people. When we read in the history of the Second World War that "Germany marched into Poland" we must pause, translate and say: " German soldiers under instruction from military leaders entered Poland." We are dealing in personification, handy for propaganda, not so useful for analysis.

So is the term "bully" useless as a concept for analysing conflicts between countries ? Not I think if we are ready to admit other considerations into the definition, especially the notion that bullying involves not only an imbalance of power and a desire to hurt, but also actions that are unjustifiable. It is tempting at this point to dismiss such talk as idealistic, unreal, much as did Nicolo Machiavelli (1469-1527) in his famous analysis of political actions. And there is indeed considerable scope for cynicism when one considers the actions (or non-actions) of the United Nations in the twentieth century in its response to conflicts between nations.

We must not forget either the assumption we are making in attributing bullying behaviour to nations. We are assuming that the citizens of a country do have some responsibility for bullying acts perpetrated by their nation. The more democratic the institutions of a country, the more representative the government, the more justified is this assumption.

Blaming the system

We are all caught up in it. All of us: fathers, mothers, sons, daughters, brothers, sisters, teachers, policemen, politicians, sportsmen and sportswomen, the bus driver, the telephone operator… the list is endless. We must change the whole system.

What constitutes 'the system' can encompass relatively small units such as the family; larger units such as the school or workplace; larger still, as in the Education Department or company; or it might encompass the whole caboodle – our politico-economic apparatus. With increasing levels of generality, it becomes more difficult to see in practical terms what things can be changed for the better, but the potential pay-off becomes ever bigger.

As bullying as a phenomenon is increasingly examined we see how bullying operates in more and more areas of life: not just in the school; not just at work; not just in the family; seemingly everywhere. More and more we see the interconnections. We become more aware of its scope and complexity.

We may conclude that what happens at the level of individuals cannot be understood except by reference to the collectivity. We may seek to deny Margaret Thatcher's oft quoted statement that there is no community, only a collection of individuals. We see that what can be achieved by the implementation of a good system is far greater than what can be achieved through skilled individuals working alone. The prevalence of bullying is an indictment of the system within which bullying occurs. Bullying is to be overcome by replacing old bad systems by new good ones.

When education departments encourage a 'systemic approach' they have in mind the need for schools to involve everybody at a school in working together according to a sensible well-coordinated plan. Few object, but many are prone to ask: what sensible plan do you have in mind? A system may have good or bad effects. The Inquisition was a bad system. When parents are asked whether they believe there should be a policy in a school specifically directed against bullying, they mostly agree that there should be, but some worry about its possible misdirection or its inflexibility. Applied to their child they want flexibility. To them their child is an individual, not a unit in an organisation. A 'system' often suggests rigidity.

A current buzz phrase is 'whole school approach', which implies a well-coordinated plan for preventing bullying, which everyone participates in implementing. If bullying continues, then either the plan was flawed or people were not implementing it properly. In either case individuals for whom the system was intended were not to blame. The logical conclusion is that it is inappropriate to identify anybody as a bully. There are, according to this well-meaning view, no bullies, only bullying. It follows there are no drunkards, only excessive drinking; no smokers, only smoking; no pickpockets, only pockets being picked. Laying the blame on the system exculpates the individual. One may vainly protest that much of the bullying can be traced to a small number of individuals. It is not to be seen that way.

Few educators in practice deny that children who persistently bully others have responsibility in the matter. However, 'systems' perspective on bullying emphasises that it is how the total system in a school operates that largely determines the level of bullying, if not who actually engages in bullying people. The level of bullying is normally what concerns the educational administrator. The micro level of who does what to whom and why is somebody else's concern.

Concern with how a system works – say in a school or workplace or family – may of course lead to useful changes. It may lead at times to a realisation that radical changes will be necessary if a real impact is to be made. Yet it may also be apparent that the actions of individuals, including potential actions to change or improve the system for the benefit of others, are severely limited by the demands of the organisation. If a middle manager, for instance, is to keep his or her job, and the economic viability of the organisation is at stake, some people must be forced to leave their place of employment. He or she may be constrained to act the part of the bully. If a political party is to stay in power, it must do what it takes, and support its 'head kickers' in the dirty work that is necessary, no matter who is victimised in the process. If teachers want promotion they must gain their principal's approval – even if that involves severely controlling their students and limiting the freedom they should enjoy. They must act like tyrants.

Viewed as a system, the media is sometimes singled out for special blame. Although it may be objected that the media do not speak with one voice, generalisations about the sort of impact 'it' has are common. Commercial stations live or die according to their ratings. Sensationalising news stories and issues is a way of surviving. We may see this in the treatment of bullying – an issue that lends itself to the sensational. Hence the almost exclusive focus in the media on the extremely violent end of the bullying continuum. A recent example was a programme on bullying that appeared on an Australian *Sixty Minutes*. The studio was packed mainly with schoolchildren, with a few teachers and assorted 'experts'. Children were encouraged to speak up about the awful things that happened to them at the hands of school bullies. Predictably, there were stories of violent assaults; heads down toilet bowls; children terrified of going to school. We heard about the intense fear of ever reporting such incidents; bystanders who stood dumbly by or moved away, fearful of getting involved; teachers who couldn't care less. Situation hopeless – and calculated to evoke strong feelings, violent judgements. The media can be – and often is – blamed for preventing reasoned discourse and thoughtful discussion of practical steps that can be taken to reduce bullying.

As the level of generality rises, the practicality of changing the system diminishes. The macro-system has been variously labelled. Once it was seen as capitalism: the force that impels people to seek to survive through ruthless competition with one's neighbour. The salvation was seen by many as communism, a practical alternative to an economic system based upon the science of Marxism and the yearning for the brotherhood of man. The inhuman excesses of communist states and the disintegration of the Russian empire has, for the time being at least, put paid to the old analysis. In its place we have the bogeys of 'globalisation' and 'economic rationalism'. The rise of feminism has led to the identification of patriarchy as the crucial system that must be endured or overthrown.

Targeting of the whole system can have different outcomes, depending on the level at which change is aimed. Many would argue that at the lowest level, sensitively directed or encouraged, pressure to change an old, authoritarian system can lead to increases in efficiency: in practical terms, significant reductions in bullying. However, blaming the system in some cases may be no more than scapegoating and denying any responsibility to individuals. We may personally feel better saying it's the system that's at fault, not people. One may come to see everyone in an organisation as being in the body of the whale, going whither it goes. It can induce fatalism. Or by dwelling on the vices of the *ancien régime* it can lead to revolution!

Towards the end of his life, the noted essayist and social critic Aldous Huxley reflected on what changes might be brought about by individual effort. He concluded that it might just be possible with the utmost exertion to change one small part of the order of things to a minute degree; that part being one's self.

Blame and responsibility

Look up 'blame' in the dictionary and you will be told it is to hold somebody responsible. And yet it is not quite that. 'Blame' has acquired connotations that 'holding responsible' does not have. Blame is hot-blooded. It rushes in angrily to judgement. It denounces. It is blinkered. It sees nothing else but what is in the immediate line of fire. It seeks justice, revenge, punishment, a revolution, Armageddon.

- The bully has hurt me. I shall have justice.
- The victim provoked her. He deserved to suffer.
- The family drove him mad. They should be punished.
- The school failed to protect my child. It shall be made to pay.
- Everyone is doing it. Society must change.
- We are 'fallen' people. God help us!

To 'hold responsible' is like blame in that it does not take excuses. It assumes that there is at the core of each individual a will that is free, that can be used for good or ill, and that it were better if it were used for good. But unlike blame it may resist the urge to compel. It is mindful that under external compulsion the will can stop being free and a sense of individual responsibility lost.

Beyond blame

To those who seek to resolve bully/victim problems, blaming someone is generally a practical hindrance. This does not mean that it is wrong to make a careful assessment of the factors that may have led to a person or group of persons bullying someone, or of the factors that may have led to a person being selected as a victim. This can be useful. Nor does it mean that we must stop making moral judgements. We should always bear in mind that bullying is an abuse of power and to abuse power is wrong. Going beyond blame is about how one treats people for their own good and the good of others.

It emphatically does not mean that people are to be treated as if they were automata pulled here and there by past and present environmental forces. This is not behavioural determinism along the lines of B. F. Skinner. I do not think we will ever satisfactorily solve the philosophical problem of free will and determinism. All we can say, along with Dr Johnson, is that all the evidence is for determinism and all our experience is against it. If we are working with people, let us listen to our experience.

Our experience is that if someone tries to compel us to do something or desist from doing something, we are prone to mount opposition. The psychologist Brehm called it 'reactance' – a negative reaction to efforts by others to reduce our freedom by getting us to do what they want us to do (Brehm 1966). Of course if the compulsion is sufficiently strong – if, for example, by not acquiescing we will go to prison – we may go along with the compeller, thereby preserving one kind of freedom – freedom from being in prison – at the expense of another. But we are talking about bullying and that is usually a different matter.

Once again we must recall that acts of bullying are rarely crimes. Because 'bullying' typically evokes thoughts of rampant violence – encouraged by the media, doing their job responding to sensational events – we tend to focus exclusively on the violent end of the continuum. This is not helped by those who like to get attention by declaring that bullying is a crime. It usually isn't. School, workplace and domestic bullies know that. Not only do they know that they cannot be legally compelled to desist, they also know that whatever promises that are forced out of them to desist, they can, with a little imagination, easily be got round. As we have seen, quite unspectacular indirect, social or relational bullying are extraordinarily difficult to monitor and probably produce more harm to individuals than any other kind.

The basic problem of dealing with bullying is how to induce a person to freely acknowledge that he or she is treating someone who is less powerful than themselves unfairly, and then to act constructively with that person. By and large we think the way to do it is to demand an apology, to say one is sorry. Under duress such a response is rarely sincere. Yet interrogation, harangue followed by punishment, a demand for apology and threats as to what will follow if you do it again, is the usual way. But are there alternatives?

There are several. One of the most well known is the so-called No Blame Approach of Maines and Robinson (1992). This was described earlier in Chapter 11. Here we may consider why this innovative approach deserves our serious attention. By confronting people with the consequences of their actions in a non-blaming manner we are giving them the opportunity to reflect on what they have done. There is, of course, the implication that what was done was wrong. What is absent is the finger-pointing, fist-waving denunciation that is character-istic of most encounters between those who would change things and those prepared to resist. Change, real change, in human relations can only come from inside.

It is not uncommon to ridicule this approach on the grounds that it is unreal-istic. Real bullies, it is said, have no empathy. And one can point to the research lit-erature – for instance Slee and Rigby (1993) and Farley (1999) – as support for the contention that bullies are relatively low in empathy. Note: less empathic than average. This easily becomes 'lacking in empathy' – I have seen this happen. Again the bully has become the psychotic killer, devoid of human feeling. Whether a 'no-blame approach' is realistic depends on results. In the hands of people who know what they are doing it often works.

A no-blame approach also depends upon the influence of peers. Is it realistic to believe that children on the whole do want to see bullying stopped? Again writers with a thirst for the sensational and a taste for hyperbole would like to persuade us that: (i) children, especially adolescent macho boys pumped full of testosterone, are hell-bent on world domination; (ii) bullying is drama to be observed and enjoyed; and (iii) bullying is far too dangerous a thing for anybody to become voluntarily mixed up with. We need to remind ourselves that at least half the children surveyed believe that bullying is something to be ashamed of; that most children want to work with others (including teachers) to stop it; and that despite the risks involved when bystanders are present, on one occasion in four somebody actually speaks out against it. Maines and Robinson found that children are generally prepared to influence their peers to desist from bullying and to put things right – if only they are encouraged to do so.

The Method of Shared Concern likewise avoids blame. But at the same time it assumes the need for the individual to take responsibility for the harm he or she is doing. It works from a basis of acknowledgment of harm to an acceptance of a responsibility for overcoming that harm. It invites responsibility rather than demanding it. But it cannot be done without the building of a real relationship between the bully that we see before us and ourselves.

That to many is the snag. We had hoped that there was a neat, nicely defined method, a set of rules, scientifically and precisely applied. A clinical, non-messy way of dealing with people: rule – consequence – deterrent; in principle, fully automated. Ideally we need not be there. To be told that we have to actually encounter these nasty bullies, treat them as we would be treated – this is a shock to the system. But, we say desperately, they are not like us. They are mad dogs, vile, vicious, bereft of empathy and decency, fit only for blame.

Then are we never to punish? I answer sorrowfully that sometimes we must. I would first like to repeat the lines of Moberley (1968), with apologies to those who read them in my earlier book, *Bullying in Schools – And What to Do about It*. I can think of no better way of expressing how I feel about the act of punishing others.

> Though it is often right to punish, this is only because no better alternative is available at the moment to those in authority. For punishment always entails some loss as well as gain; it includes some element of pretension on the one side and of surrender to coercion on the other; it rests on presumptions that are never wholly true. Like some physic, it includes an element of poison and is not chiefly good for food. *To be obliged to punish offenders, not only implies that we blame them; in some degree it implies our own moral incapacity...* (p.381, my italics)

I would have these words inscribed above every school principal's desk and prominently displayed in workplaces, homes, everywhere in fact where the illusory short cut to reforming the bully beckons.

I would like to believe that the removal of privileges, the suspension of children from school, the dismissal of employees, the instituting of legal proceedings, the holding of community or school conferences leading to compulsory acts of restorative justice, all these and more of the same did not constitute punishment. Just consequences. But to the child who is suspended (and more so for his or her parents), to the dismissed worker, to those about to be 'tried' – each of these inevitably sees it as punishment. And although once in a while it comes home to a bully that this is no more than was deserved and a new start can be made, we know that this is nearly always wishful thinking on our part.

The debate about blaming versus non-blaming as an approach to bullying is widely misunderstood. Both sides try to paint the opposition in ways they do not recognise. The no-blame people are apt to see their opposition as 'brutalitarians' who enjoy inflicting pain; the blamers (if one may coin the term) see their opposition as 'sentimentalists' who can see no real harm in anybody. But in fact the debate has more to do with means than ends. The blamers and the non-blamers are generally equally committed to the view that people who bully others are responsible for what they do and should learn to act more responsibly. They both want to see people behave responsibly. The blamers think they can do it by force; the non-blamers by persuasion.

To some extent the debate may be settled by empirical means. There have been few good studies comparing alternative means of changing the behaviour of bullies. By contrast, there have been a number of pronouncements from high places castigating 'no-blame approaches', for example from the former British Minister of Education, Mr Blunkett, who has been quoted as saying that 'it was time to end the no-blame culture of the 90s' (Smithers 2000). What is rarely acknowledged is that different approaches may be more (or less) appropriate for different levels or degrees of bullying.

It is surely good that the question of what is to be done about bullying is now being asked and asked with more vigour than ever before. Inroads are being made, slowly. Properly conceived as the systematic abuse of power it is a gigantic question that has always been with us. In documenting and reflecting on the perspectives on bullying, as they have been and are being expressed, I hope to have illuminated some of the paths that are being taken, dead ends maybe as well as promising trails which others can follow, to help rid us of this enduring social evil.

Appendices

Appendix I

Reported frequencies of different forms of bullying					
		Aged 8–12 yrs		Aged 13–18 yrs	
		Boys	Girls	Boys	Girls
Being teased in an unpleasant way	Sometimes	38.6	38.9	35.3	34.4
	Often	12.9	9.7	10.6	8.8
Being called hurtful names	Sometimes	37.9	39.5	33.6	34.3
	Often	14.9	12.5	11.3	10.7
Being left out deliberately	Sometimes	27.1	32.4	19.5	24.3
	Often	7.8	9.6	5.9	6.8
Being threatened with harm	Sometimes	24.7	13.0	20.3	10.3
	Often	6.3	3.2	6.4	2.8
Being hit or kicked	Sometimes	31.2	20.0	22.0	9.3
	Often	9.3	4.4	6.9	2.4

Note: The sample sizes upon which these results were based were as follows:

Boys Aged 8–12 yrs: 4777; 13–18 yrs: 15,168

Girls Aged 8–12 yrs: 3790; 13–18 yrs: 10,699

Source: Rigby (1997c)

Appendix 2

Percentages of school students reporting being bullied during the school year by groups and/or individuals, according to frequency, age group and gender					
Bullied by		Young (8–11years)		Older (12–18 years)	
Individual	Group	Boys *(n = 1,850)*	Girls *(n = 1,618)*	Boys *(n = 17,654)*	Girls *(n = 12,382)*
Often	Often	3.6	2.5	3.3	2.1
Often	Sometimes	4.8	3.8	3.2	2.1
Often	Never	2.9	2.5	1.5	1.4
Sometimes	Often	5.2	4.1	2.5	2.2
Sometimes	Sometimes	15.7	18.7	15.9	14.5
Sometimes	Never	24.9	22.2	21.3	19.8
Never	Often	1.6	1.7	0.7	0.5
Never	Sometimes	7.2	6.8	6.2	5.1
Never	Never	34.1	37.6	45.4	52.2

Source: Rigby (1997c)

Appendix 3

Percentages of school students reporting bullying others at school, according to whether as an individual or as a group member, according to age group and gender				
	Students (8–11 years)		Students (12–18 years)	
	Boys	Girls	Boys	Girls
As individuals only	11.6 (26.7)	7.5 (21.9)	9.6 (18.2)	6.8 (16.9)
As members of a group	10.2 (23.5)	14.1 (41.1)	14.4 (27.2)	15.6 (38.7)
As individuals and as group members	21.6 (49.7)	12.6 (36.7)	28.8 (54.5)	18.0 (44.6)
Did not bully	56.6	65.7	47.1	59.7

Note: In parentheses are the percentages for each subgroup, excluding those who did not bully. Source: Rigby (1997c)

Appendix 4

Reported gender of the bully or bullies, coeducational schools only				
	Boys		Girls	
Bully is:	8–12 yrs	13–18 yrs	8–12 yrs	13–18 yrs
always a boy	71.4	72.5	21.9	26.6
always a girl	1.9	4.0	22.9	24.3
sometimes boy, sometimes girl	26.7	23.5	55.2	49.1

Note: Based on a sample of 15,024 Australian schoolchildren (7b1998). Source: Rigby (1997c)

Appendix 5

Percentages of students reporting that they had been abused in the current year in designated ways by boys and by girls						
	Gender of the person(s) abusing					
	A boy or boys			A girl or girls		
Gender of victim and kind of treatment received	Some	Often	Total	Some	Often	Total
Boy verbally abused	60.0	15.8	75.8	36.9	10.0	46.9
Girl verbally abused	54.2	19.8	74.0	57.6	10.6	68.2
Boy physically abused	51.6	11.1	62.7	19.6	7.6	27.2
Girl physically abused	13.2	3.8	17.0	21.9	2.8	24.7
Boys indirectly abused	19.5	6.3	25.8	22.4	8.7	31.1
Girls indirectly abused	28.8	4.2	33.0	43.8	7.8	51.6

Source: Rigby and Bagshaw (2001)

Appendix 6

Reported hurtfulness of treatments by peers for male and female schoolchildren: Percentages reporting							
Item (abbreviated)	**Boys**			**Girls**			**p <**
	not	a bit	a lot	not	a bit	a lot	
Breaking friendship (R)	22.7	33.3	43.9 (66)	7.3	37.6	55.1 (178)	.01
Ganged up on (R)	28.6	38.1	33.3 (42)	10.3	43.1	46.6 (58)	ns
Got excluded (R)	25.8	43.5	30.6 (62)	10.4	42.7	46.9 (96)	.05
Sexual touching (P)	34.6	30.8	34.6 (26)	20.6	38.2	41.2 (34)	ns
Secrets told (R)	27.4	46.8	25.8 (62)	11.4	44.0	44.6 (166)	.01
Lies spread (R)	30.4	51.1	18.5 (92)	15.5	43.2	41.2 (148)	.001
Threat with harm (V)	47.1	35.6	17.2 (87)	31.3	29.7	39.1 (64)	.01
Being 'labelled' (V)	27.7	51.8	20.5 (83)	15.0	31.1	33.8 (133)	.05
Avoided (R)	34.1	43.2	22.7 (88)	16.9	54.8	28.3 (166)	.01
Phone harassment (R)	43.8	31.3	25.0 (32)	32.9	42.1	25.0 (76)	ns
Weapon threat (P)	53.7	29.3	17.1 (41)	50.0	21.4	28.6 (14)	ns
Spat at (P)	37.5	33.9	28.6 (56)	39.1	45.7	15.2 (46)	ns
Called names (V)	40.4	44.0	15.7 (166)	14.2	61.8	24.0 (204)	.001
Rumours about me (R)	69.3	22.0	8.7 (218)	43.5	33.6	22.9 (253)	.001
Remarks on appearance (V)	56.9	32.9	10.2 (225)	35.6	35.6	28.8 (264)	.01

Being deliberately hit (P)	53.6	33.3	13.1 (153)	33.3	41.3	25.3 (75)	.01
Kicked (P)	44.7	37.2	18.1 (94)	38.6	45.6	15.8 (57)	ns
Face slapped (P)	62.9	28.6	8.6 (35)	26.0	50.0	24.0 (50)	.01
Stopped talking (R)	70.2	22.5	7.3 (218)	32.5	44.9	22.6 (265)	.001
Jokes about me (V)	43.8	44.9	11.2 (178)	26.3	55.6	18.2 (198)	.001
Pressured to fight (P)	68.2	24.7	7.1 (85)	21.9	59.4	18.8 (32)	.001
Tripped (P)	55.7	33.0	11.3 (106)	47.8	37.8	14.4 (90)	ns
Possessions moved (P)	48.6	38.3	13.1 (107)	34.2	53.5	12.3 (114)	ns
Continually stared at (R)	62.9	25.8	11.3 (62)	41.2	45.9	12.8 (148)	.05
Thrown at (P)	51.9	38.5	9.6 (135)	47.2	38.6	14.2 (127)	ns
Being 'put down' (V)	59.2	32.0	8.7 (103)	37.7	49.1	13.2 (114)	.01
Been 'paid out' (V)	46.9	45.1	8.0 (175)	29.2	58.4	12.4 (226)	.01
Picked argument (V)	73.3	23.9	2.8 (176)	34.9	51.8	13.3 (195)	.001
Being sworn at (V)	80.2	15.0	4.8 (227)	64.1	28.9	7.0 (270)	.001
Teased (V)	93.6	6.4	0.0 (235)	87.5	12.5	0.0 (287)	.05

Note: In parentheses are the numbers reporting having had that experience during the school year. Source: Rigby and Bagshaw (2001)

Appendix 7

Percentages of boys and girls approving of husband's response to wife's action				
Wife's action:		**Husband's response:**		
		Spoke sharply to her	Yelled or shouted at her	Hit her
1. Swore at husband without reason	Boys	33.1	7.3	4.9*
	Girls	23.5	4.9	0.9
2. Continually flirted with other men after being asked not to do so	Boys	54.9	37.7	6.6
	Girls	55.3	29.2	3.5
3. Deliberately destroyed something valuable of his	Boys	62.0	43.8	11.6**
	Girls	63.1	42.2	3.5
4. Always refused to help in the home	Boys	43.0	27.3	5.8
	Girls	53.2	30.6	3.6
5. Continually ridiculed or belittled husband	Boys	48.3	33.3	11.7***
	Girls	54.1	33.9	2.8
6. Abused one of the children	Boys	72.7	66.1	24.0
	Girls	79.6	77.3*	21.8
7. Lied about husband to his friends	Boys	59.5	41.7	11.7*
	Girls	62.3	42.5	4.5
8. Had been sexually unfaithful to husband	Boys	68.1	60.2	21.8***
	Girls	75.7	68.3	7.8
9. Seriously neglected their children	Boys	65.5	52.5	18.5
	Girls	76.6*	70.6***	14.2
10. Spent all of the house-keeping money on herself	Boys	65.5	48.7	14.3**
	Girls	69.7	53.2	5.0

Note: Significance by chi square: * = .05; ** = .01; *** = .001

Source: Rigby, Whish and Black (1994)

Appendix 8

	Tendency to bully		Tendency to be victimised	
	Boys	Girls	Boys	Girls
Parental care				
From mother	-0.04	-0.19***	-0.22***	-0.19***
From father	-0.16***	-0.23***	-0.19***	-0.21***
Parental control				
By mother	0.07	0.26***	0.16***	0.15***
By father	0.20***	0.31***	0.09	0.27***

Correlations between scores on the Parental Bonding Instrument (PBI) and tendencies to bully others or be victimised by others at school

Note: *** indicates the correlation was significant at the 0.001 level. Source: Rigby, Slee and Martin (1999)

Appendix 9

		Close friends	Mother	Father	Teacher
Bullying behaviour:					
Teasing in a group	Boys	14.6	5.0	6.8	5.1
	Girls	4.5	1.6	2.2	1.1
Pushing weaker kids around	Boys	15.9	4.7	5.5	4.6
	Girls	4.0	1.2	1.9	1.2
Making other kids scared	Boys	21.2	7.0	9.6	6.0
	Girls	6.8	2.6	3.2	2.4
Getting into fights with kids easy to beat	Boys	20.2	5.7	7.6	5.2
	Girls	7.6	2.2	2.9	1.9

Percentages of students indicating support from others for bullying in specified ways

Source: Rigby (1997d)

Appendix 10

Percentages of students agreeing with selected scale items						
	Boys			Girls		
Items	Agree	Unsure	Disagree	Agree	Unsure	Disagree
I like it when someone stands up for kids who are being bullied	80.9	13.7	5.4	84.1	11.9	4.0
It makes me angry when a kid is picked on without reason	78.0	15.9	2.5	85.8	11.6	2.5
It's a good thing to help children who can't defend themselves	65.6	22.3	12.1	60.1	30.9	9.1
Nobody likes a wimp	30.3	26.8	43.0	25.8	27.2	47.0
I wouldn't be friends with kids who let themselves be pushed around	22.0	26.1	51.9	19.0	37.4	43.6
Soft kids make me sick	19.1	29.0	51.9	12.7	23.8	63.5
Kids should not complain about being bullied	17.5	20.4	62.1	12.2	27.8	60.1
Kids who are weak are just asking for trouble	11.8	13.1	75.2	8.2	12.5	79.3
It's OK to call some kids nasty names	22.3	22.6	55.1	15.6	19.8	64.6
Kids who get picked on a lot usually deserve it	19.4	30.9	49.7	10.2	39.7	50.1
It is funny to see kids upset when they get teased	11.8	11.1	77.1	4.0	9.3	86.7

Source: Rigby and Slee (1991)

Appendix II

Attitudes to victims: Parent responses to selected scale items	
A small amount of bullying can be a good thing because it helps to toughen people up	6%
Some kids get teased because they ask for it	12%
It can be funny to see people being teased	14%
Kids shouldn't run to the teacher every time somebody teases them	41%
Everybody should be able to stand up for themselves	54%

Source: Adapted from Eslea and Smith (2000)

References

Adams, A. (1992) *Bullying in the Workplace and How to Confront It.* London: Virago Press.

Adorno, T. W., Frenkel-Brunswik, E., Levinson, D. and Sanford, R. N. *et al.* (1950) *The Authoritarian Personality.* New York: Harper.

Agnew, S. (1989) 'Aggressive behaviour in boys: to what extent is it institutionalised?' In D. P. Tattum and D. A. Lane (eds) *Bullying in schools.* Stoke on Trent: Trentham Books.

Ahmad, Y. and Smith, P. K. (1994) 'Bullying in schools and the issue of sex difference.' In J. Archer (ed) *Male Violence.* London: Routledge.

Ajzen, I. and Fishbein, M. (1980) *Understanding Attitudes and Predicting Social Behaviour.* Eaglewood Cliffs, NJ: Prentice-Hall.

Almeida, A. (1999) 'Portugal.' In P. K. Smith, Y. Morita, J. Junger-Tas, D. Olweus, R. Catalano and P. T. Slee *The Nature of School Bullying: a cross-national perspective.* London: Routledge.

Alsaker, F. D. and Valkanover, S. (2001) 'Early diagnosis and prevention of victimization in kindergarten.' In J. Juvonen and S. Graham (eds) *Peer Harassment in School.* New York: Guilford.

Ambert, A. M. (1994) 'A qualitative study of peer abuse and its effects: theoretical and practical implications.' *Journal of Marriage and the Family 56,* 119–130.

American Bible Society (1984) *The Bible in Today's English Version.* Nashville: Thomas Nelson Publishers.

Anderson, I. and Swainson, V. (2001) 'Perceived motivation for rape: Gender differences in beliefs about female and male rape.' *Current Research in Psychology 6,* 8, April (http://www.uiowa.edu/-grpprod/crisp/crisp.8.htm).

Andrews, F. M. and Withey, S. B. (1976) *Social Indicators of Well-Being.* New York: Plenum.

Archer, J. (2000) 'Sex differences in aggression between heterosexual partners: a meta-analytic review.' *Psychological Bulletin 126,* 651–680.

Arora, C. M. G. (1996) 'Defining bullying.' *School Psychology International 17,* 317–329.

Askew, S. (1989) 'Aggressive behavior in boys: to what extent is it institutionalised?' In D. P. Tattum and D.A. Lane (eds) *Bullying in Schools*. Stoke on Trent: Trentham Books.

Austin, A. B. and Lindauer, S. K. (1990) 'Parent–child conversation of more-liked and less-liked children.' *Journal of Genetic Psychology 151*, 5–23.

Australian Bureau of Statistics (1996) *Women's Safety, Australia, 1996*. Canberra: Australian Bureau of Statistics.

The Australian Early Intervention Network for Mental Health in Young People (2000) *National Stocktake of Early Intervention Programs, July 1998*. Adelaide, SA: Glenelg Press.

Baldry, A. C. (2001) *What about bullying? An experimental field study to understand students' attitudes towards bullying and victimization in Italian middle schools*. Unpublished paper.

Baldry, A. C. and Farrington, D. P. (1998) 'Parenting influences on bullying and victimisation.' *Criminal and Legal Psychology 3*, 237–254.

Baron-Cohen, S., Jolliffe, T., Mortimore, C. and Robertson, M. (1999) 'Another advanced test of theory of mind: Evidence from very high functioning adults with autism or Asperger Syndrome.' *Journal of Child Psychology and Psychiatry and Allied Disciplines 38*, 813–822.

Berdondini, L. and Smith, P. K. (1996) 'Cohesion and power in the families of children involved in bully/victim problems at school: an Italian replication.' *Journal of Family Therapy 18*, 99–102.

Berkowitz, L. (1986) *A Survey of Social Psychology*. New York: CBS College Publishing.

Berne, S. (1996) *Bully-Proof Your Child*. Port Melbourne: Lothian.

Besag, V. E. (1989) *Bullies and Victims in Schools*. Buckingham: Open University Press.

Betjeman, J. (1960) *Summoned by Bells*. London: John Murray.

Biddulph, S. (1997) *Raising Boys: Why Boys Are Different, and How to Help Them Become Happy and Well-Balanced Men*. Sydney: Finch Publishing.

Billingham, R. E., Bland, R. and Leary, A. (1999) 'Dating violence at three time periods: 1976, 1992 and 1996.' *Psychological Reports 85*, 2, 574–578.

Bjorqvist, K. (1994) 'Sex differences in physical, verbal and indirect aggression: a review of recent research.' *Sex Roles 30*, 177–188.

Bjorqvist, K. and Osterman, K. (1998) *Scales for research on interpersonal relations*. Abo Akademi University: Faculty of Social and Caring Sciences.

Bjorqvist, K., Ekman, K. and Lagerspetz, K. (1982) 'Bullies and victims: Their ego picture, ideal ego picture and normative ego picture.' *Scandinavian Journal of Psychiatry 23*, 307–313.

Bjorqvist, K., Lagerspetz, K., Salmivalli, C. and Kukainen, A. (1992) 'Do girls manipulate and boys fight? developmental trends in regard to direct and indirect aggression.' *Aggressive Behavior 18*, 117–127.

Borg, M. G. (1998) 'The emotional reaction of school bullies and their victims.' *Educational Psychology 18*, 4, 433–444.

Boulton, M. J. (1993) 'Aggressive fighting in British middle school children.' *Educational Studies 19*, 19–39.

Boulton, M. J. (1995) 'Patterns of bully/victim problems in mixed race groups of children.' *Social Development 4*, 277–293.

Boulton, M.J. (1997) 'Teachers' views on bullying: Definitions, attitudes and ability to cope.' *British Journal of Educational Psychology 67*, 223–234.

Boulton, M. J. and Underwood, K. (1992) 'Bully/victim problems among middle school children.' *British Journal of Educational Psychology 62*, 73–87.

Boulton, M. J. and Smith, P. K. (1994) 'Bully/victim problems in middle school children: stability, self-perceived competence, peer perception and peer acceptance.' *British Journal of Developmental Psychology 12*, 315–329.

Bowers, L. Smith, P. K. and Binney, V. (1992) 'Cohesion and power in the families of children involved in bully/victim problems at school.' *Journal of Family Therapy 14*, 371–387.

Bowie, V. (2001) 'The reluctant executioners.' In P. McCarthy, J. Rylance, R. Bennett and H. Zimmermann (eds) *Bullying: From Backyard to Boardroom.* Second Edition. Sydney: Federation Press.

Bowlby, J. (1969) *Attachment and Loss,* Vols 1 and 2. New York: Basic Books.

Boycott, G. (1991) *Boycott on Cricket.* London: Corgi Books.

Braithwaite, J. (1989) *Crime, Shame and Reintegration.* Cambridge: Cambridge University Press.

Brehm, J. W. (1966) *A Theory of Psychological Reactance.* New York: Academic Press.

Brookes, M. (1993) *Reducing Bullying at HMP Ranby.* East Midlands, UK: Psychological Research Report, no. 8.

Broome, A. and Llewelyn, S. (1995) *Health Psychology: Process and Application.* Second Edition. London: Chapman and Hall.

Brown, R. (1986) *Social Psychology.* New York: New Press.

Bulbeck, T. (2001) 'Bullying the elderly.' In P. McCarthy, J. Rylance, R. Bennett and H. Zimmermann (eds) *Bullying: From Backyard to Boardroom.* Second Edition. Leichhardt, NSW: Federation Press.

Bullock, A. (1964) *Hitler, A Study in Tyranny.* London: Odhams.

Burt, M. (1980) 'Cultural myths and support for rape.' *Journal of Personality and Social Psychology 38*, 217–230.

Butler, S. (1936) *The Way of All Flesh*. London: Oxford University Press.

Cairns, B. C. and Cairns, B. D. (1994) *Lifelines and Risks*. Hemel Hempstead: Simon and Schuster.

Callaghan, S. and Joseph, S. (1995) 'Self-concept and peer victimisation among school children.' *Personality and Individual Development 18*, 161–163.

Casdagli, P., Goki, F. and Griffin, C. (1990) *Only Playing, Miss!* London: Trentham Books.

Chagnon, N. A. (1977) *Yanomamo: The Fierce People*. New York: Holt, Rinehart.

Chesterton, G. K. (1912) *Miscellany of Man*. London: Methuen.

Cloud, J. (1999) 'The Columbine Effect.' *Time 154*, 23, 51–53.

Collins, C., Batten, B., Ainley, J and Getty, C. (1996) *Gender and School Education*. Melbourne: ACER.

Connolly, P. and Keenan, M. (2000) *Racial Attitudes and Prejudice in Northern Ireland*. Belfast: NISRA (http://www.nisra.gov.uk/featpub/opps.html)

Cowie, H., Smith, P., Boulton, M. and Laver, R. (1994) *Cooperation in the Multi-Ethnic Classroom*. London: David Fulton.

Cox, T. (1995) 'Stress, coping and physical health.' In A. Broome and S. Llewelyn (eds) *Health Psychology: Process and Applications*. Second Edition. London: Singular Publication Group.

Craig, W. M., Henderson, K. and Murphy, J. G. (2000) 'Prospective teachers' attitudes toward bullying and victimization.' *School Psychology International 211*, 5–21.

Crick, N. R. and Dodge, K. A. (1994) 'A review and reformulation of social information-processing mechanisms in children's social adjustment.' *Psychological Bulletin 115*, 1, January, 74–101.

Crick, N. R. and Dodge, K. A. (1999) '"Superiority" is in the eye of the beholder: A comment on Sutton, Smith and Swettenham.' *Social Development 8*, 128–131.

Crick, N. R. and Grotpeter, J. K. (1995) 'Relational aggression: Gender and social-psychological adjustment.' *Child Development 66*, 710–722.

Crick, N. R., Casas, J. F. and Mosher, M. (1997) 'Relational and overt aggression in preschool.' *Developmental Psychology 33*, 579–588.

Crozier, W. R. and Dimmock, P. S. (1999) 'Name-calling and nicknames in a sample of primary school children.' *British Journal of Educational Psychology 69*, 4, December, 505–516.

Dahl, R. (1984) *Boy: Tales of Childhood*. New York: Penguin.

Darwin, C. (1859, 1871) *The Descent of Man*. London: John Murray.

Davis, M. H. (1980) 'Measuring individual difference in empathy: evidence for a multidimensional approach.' *Journal of Personality and Social Psychology 23*, 113–126.

Dawkins, J. L. (1996) 'Bullying, physical disability and the paediatric patient.' *Developmental Medicine and Child Neurology 38*, 603–612.

Dawkins, R. (1989) *The Selfish Gene*. Second Edition. Oxford: Oxford University Press.

'Defeating the Bad Guys' (1998) *The Economist 340*, 35–38.

Dentan, R. K. (1968) *The Semai*. New York: Holt, Rinehart.

Department of Health and Children (1999) *Children First: National guidelines for the protection and welfare of children*. Dublin: Stationery Office.

Dietz, B. (1994) 'Effects on subsequent heterosexual shyness and depression on peer victimization at school.' *Children's Peer Relations Conference*. Adelaide: University of South Australia.

Dodge, K., Pettit, G. S. and Bates, G. E. (1994) 'Socialisation Mediators of the relation between socio-economic status and child conduct problems.' *Child Development 65*, 649–666.

Dollard, J., Dood, L., Miller, N., Mowrero, H. and Sears, R. R. (1939) *Frustration and Aggression*. New Haven, Conn.: Yale University Press.

Duncan, N. (1999) *Sexual Bullying: Gender Conflict and Pupil Culture in Secondary Schools*. London: Routledge.

Duncan, R. D. (1999) 'Maltreatment by parents and peers: The relationship between child abuse, bully victimization and psychological distress.' *Journal of the American Professional Society on the Abuse of Children 4*, 1, 45–55.

Duyme, M. D. (1990) 'Antisocial behaviour and postnatal environment: A French adoption study.' *Journal of Child Psychology & Psychiatry & Allied Disciplines 31*, 5, July, 699–710.

Egan, S. K. and Perry, D. G. (1998) 'Does low self-regard invite victimization?' *Developmental Psychology 34*, 299–309.

Ehrenreich, B. (1997) *Blood Rites*. New York: Holt.

Einarsen, S. (1999) 'The nature and causes of bullying at work.' *International Journal of Manpower 20*, 1/2, 16–27.

Elliot, M. (1991) *Bullying: A Practical Guide to Coping in Schools*. London: Longman.

Elms, A.C. (1972) *Social Psychology*, 2nd edition. New York: Free Press.

Emery, C., Hayes, R. T. and Parlett, M. K. (1999) 'Bullying of, and retaliation by, Aboriginal students in an Australian Urban High School.' *South Pacific Journal of Psychology 10*, 2, 43–59.

Eron, L. D., Walder, L. O., Toigo, R. and Lefkowitz, M. M. (1963) 'Social class, parental punishment for aggression and child aggression.' *Child Development 34*, 849–867.

Eslea, M. and Smith, P. K. (2000) 'Pupil and parent attitudes towards bullying in primary schools.' *European Journal of Psychology in Education 25*, 207–219.

Espelage, D., Bosworth, K. and Simon, T. (2000) 'Examining the social context of bullying behaviours in early adolescence.' *Journal of Counselling and Development 78*, 326–344.

Eysenck, S. (1965) 'A new scale for personality measurement in children.' *British Journal of Educational Psychology 35*, 3, 362–367.

Fabre-Cornali, D., Emin, J. C. and Pain, J. (1999) 'France.' In P. K. Smith, Y. Morita, J. Junger-Tas, D. Olweus, R. Catalano and P. T. Slee *The Nature of School Bullying: a Cross-National Perspective.* London: Routledge.

Farley, R. L. (1999) *Does a Relationship Exist Between Social Perception, Social Intelligence and Empathy for Students With a Tendency To Be a Bully, Victim or Bully/Victim?* Honours Thesis. Adelaide: Psychology Department, University of Adelaide.

Farrington, D. P. (1993) 'Understanding and preventing bullying.' In M. Tonny and N. Morris (eds) *Crime and Justice 17.* Chicago: University of Chicago Press.

Fears, J. R. (ed) (1985) *Selected Writings of Lord Acton*, Vol. 2. Indianapolis: Liberty Fund.

Field, E. M. (1999) *Bully Busting.* Lane Cove, NSW: Finch Publishing Pty.

Field, T. (1999) http://www.successunlimited.co.uk/defns.htm

Finkelhor, D., Hotaling, G., Lewis, I. A. and Smith, C. (1990) 'Sexual abuse in a national survey of adult men and women: prevalence, characteristics and risk factors.' *Child Abuse and Neglect 14*, 1, 19–28.

Fitzhenry, R. I. (ed) (1986) *The David and Charles Book of Quotations.* Newton Abbot, London: David and Charles.

Forero, R., McLellan, L., Rissel, C. and Bauman, A. (1999) 'Bullying behaviour and psychosocial health among school students in NSW, Australia.' *British Medical Journal 319*, 344–348.

Francis, L. J. and Jones, S. H. (1994) 'The relationship between Eysenck's personality factors and fear of bullying among 13–15 year olds in England and Wales.' *Evaluation and Research in Education 8*, 111–118.

Frankl, V. E. (1964) *Man's Search for Meaning.* London: Hodder and Stoughton.

French, J. R. and Raven, B. (1959) 'The basics of social power.' In D. Cartwright (ed) *Studies in Social Power.* Ann Arbor: University of Michigan Press.

Fremouw, N. J., Westrup, D. and Pennypacker, J. (1997) 'Stalking on campus: The prevalence and strategies for coping with stalking.' *Journal of Forensic Science 42*, 4, 666–669.

Frey, C.and Hoppe-Graff, S. (1994) 'Serious and playful aggression in Brazilian girls and boys.' *Sex Roles 30*, 249–269.

Fuller, A. (2000) *Raising Resilient Young People, a Parents' Guide.* Sydney: Australian Scout Publication.

Galen, B. R. and Underwood, M. K. (1997) 'A developmental investigation of social aggression among children.' *Developmental Psychology 33*, 4, 589–600.

Garrity, C., Jens, K., Porter, W., Sager, N. and Short-Camilli, C. (1997) *Bully-Proofing Your School: A Comprehensive Approach for Elementary Schools.* Longmont, Colorado: Sopris West.

Gehring, T. M. and Wyler, I. L. (1986) 'Family–System–Test (FAST): A three dimensional approach to investigate family relationships.' *Child Psychiatry & Human Development 16*, 235–248.

Gilbert, R. and Gilbert, P. (1998) *Masculinity Goes To School.* St Leonards, NSW: Allen and Unwin.

Gilmartin, B. G. (1987) 'Peer group antecedents of severe love-shyness in males.' *Journal of Personality 55*, 467–489.

Goldberg, D. and Williams, P. (1991) *A Users' Guide to the General Health Questionnaire.* Windsor: NFER-Nelson.

Golding, W. (1954) *Lord of the Flies.* London: Faber and Faber.

Gordon, M. (2000) 'Definitional issues in violence against women: surveillance and research from a violence research perspective.' *Violence Against Women 6*, 747–783.

Harlow, H. F. and Harlow, M. (1962) 'Social deprivation in monkeys.' *Scientific American 207*, 136–146.

Harris, J. R. (1998) *The Nurture Assumption.* New York: Free Press.

Harrison, F. (1990) *Trivial Disputes.* London: Fontana Paperbacks.

Hart, C. H., Ladd, G. W. and Burleston, B. R. (1990) 'Children's expectations of the outcomes of social strategies: relations with sociometric status and maternal disciplinary styles.' *Child Development 61*, 127–137.

Hastings, B. M. (2000) 'Social information processing and the verbal and physical abuse of women.' *Journal of Interpersonal Violence 15*, 651–665.

Hawley, P. H. (1999) 'The ontogenesis of social dominance: a strategy-based evolutionary perspective.' *Developmental Review 19*, 97–132.

Hazler, R. J., Carney, J. V., Green, S., Powell, R. and Jolly, L. S. (1997) 'Areas of expert agreement on identification of school bullies and victims.' *School Psychology International 18*, 1, 5–14.

Heinemann Australian Dictionary (1992) Port Melbourne, Victoria: Rigby Heinemann.

Heinnemann, P. P. (1972) *Mobbning – Gruppvald Bland Barn Och Vuxna.* Stockholm: Natur Och Kultur.

Henderson, A. (1996) 'Gerontology (Elderly Abuse).' *Women's Health Weekly,* 1/8/96, 18.

Henggeler, S. W., Edwards, J. J., Cohen, R. and Somerville, M. B. (1991) 'Predicting changes in children's popularity: the role of family relations.' *Journal of Applied Developmental Psychology 12,* 205–218.

Henry, M. E. (1992) 'School Rituals as Educational Contexts: Symbolising the World, Others and Self in Waldorf and College Prep Schools.' *Qualitative Studies in Education 7,* 295–309.

Hoel, H. and Cooper, C. L. (2000) 'Workplace bullying in Britain – results from a study of 5,288 employees.' Unpublished paper.

Hoffman, M. L. (1984) 'Interaction of affect and cognition in empathy.' In C. E. Izard, J. Kagan and J. Strayer (eds) *Emotions, Cognitions and Behaviors.* Cambridge: Cambridge University Press.

Holzbauer, J. J. and Berven, N. L. (1996) 'Disability harassment: a new term for a long-standing problem.' *Journal of Counselling & Development 74,* 5, 478–486.

Hughes, T. (1968, first published 1857) *Tom Brown's School Days.* New York: Airmont Publishing Company.

Hugh-Jones, S. and Smith, K. (1999) 'Self-reports of short- and long-term effects of bullying on children who stammer.' *British Journal of Educational Psychology 69,* 141–158.

Huxley, A. (1920) 'Fifth Philosopher's Song.' In D. Watt (ed) (1971) *The collected poetry of Aldous Huxley.* London: Chatto and Windus.

Ireland, J. L. (2000) '"Bullying" among prisoners: a review of research.' *Aggression and Violent Behavior 5,* 201–215.

Ireland, J. L. and Archer, J. (1996) 'Descriptive analyses of bullying by male and female adult prisoners.' *Journal of Community and Applied Social Psychiatry 6,* 35–47.

Janoff-Bullmann, R. (1992) *Shattered Assumptions: Towards a new psychology of Trauma.* New York: The Free Press.

Johnson, D. W. and Johnson, R. T. (1991) *Teaching Students To Be Peacemakers.* Minnesota: Interaction Book Company.

Johnson, M., Munn, P. and Edwards, L. (1991) *Action Against Bullying: A Support Pack for Schools.* Edinburgh: The Scottish Council for Educational Research.

Junger, M. (1990) 'Intergroup bullying and racial harassment in the Netherlands.' *SSR 74,* 65–72.

Junger-Tas, J. (1999) 'The Netherlands.' In P. K. Smith, Y. Morita, J. Junger-Tas, D. Olweus, R. Catalano and P. T. Slee *The Nature of School Bullying: A Cross-National Perspective.* London: Routledge.

Kaltialo-Heino, R., Rimpela, M., Marttunen, M., Rimpela, A. and Ratenen, P. (1999) 'Bullying, depression and suicidal ideation in Finnish adolescents: school survey.' *British Medical Journal 319*, 348–350.

Kaukainen, A., Bjorqvist, K., Lagerspetz, K., Osterman, K., Salmivalli, C., Rothberg, S. and Ahlbom, A. (1999) 'The relationships between social intelligence, empathy, and three types of aggression.' *Aggressive Behavior 25*, 2, 81–89.

Kelly, D. (1992) 'Identifying physical abuse, sexual abuse and neglect in older people: implications for Medical and Health Care Professionals.' In *Dignity and Security: Conference Proceedings.* Brisbane: Queensland Taskforce on Elder Abuse Prevention.

Kochenderfer, B. J. and Ladd, G. W. (1996) 'Peer Victimisation: Cause or Consequence of School Maladjustment.' *Child Development 67*, 1305–1317.

Kohlberg, L. (1984) *The Psychology of Moral Development.* San Francisco: Harper and Row.

Kohn, M., Flood, H. and Chase, J. (1998) 'Prevalence and health consequences of stalking', *Morbidity & Mortality Weekly Report 49*, 29, 653–655.

Kumpulainen, K., Rasanen, E., Henttonnen, I., Almquest, F., Kresanov, K., Linna, S. I., Moilanen, I., Piha, J., Puura, K. and Tamminen, T. (1998) 'Bullying and psychiatric symptoms among elementary school-age children.' *Child Abuse and Neglect 22*, 7, 705–707.

Ladd, G. W., Kochenderfer, B. J. and Coleman, C. C. (1997) 'Classroom peer acceptance, friendship and victimization: distinct relational systems that contribute uniquely to children's social adjustment?' *Child Development 68*, 6, 1181–1197.

Lamb, M. E. and Nash, A. (1989) 'Infant–mother attachment, sociability and peer competence.' In T. J. Berndt and G. W. Ladd (eds) *Peer Relationships in Child Development.* New York: Wiley.

Lane, D. A. (1989) 'Violent histories: bullying and criminality.' In D. P. Tattum and D. A. Lane (eds) *Bullying in Schools.* Stoke on Trent: Trentham Books.

Larson, D. G. and Chastain, R. L. (1990) 'Self-concealment: conceptualization, measurement and health implications.' *Journal of Social and Clinical Psychology 9*, 4, 439–455.

Larzelere, R. E. (1986) 'Moderate spanking: model of deterrent of children's aggression in the family?' *Journal of Family Violence 1*, 27–36.

Latane, B. and Darley, J. (1970) *The Unresponsive Bystander: Why Doesn't He Help?* New York: Appleton-Crofts.

Leane, T. (1999) *Bystander Responses of Children to Bully/Victim Situations.* Honours Thesis. Adelaide: University of South Australia.

Lerner, M. J. (1980) *The Belief in a Just World: A Fundamental Delusion.* New York: Plenum.

Levine, M. (1999) 'Rethinking bystander nonintervention: Social categorization and the evidence of witnesses at the James Bulger murder trial.' *Human Relations 52*, 9, September, 1133–1155.

Levy, D. M. (1966) *Maternal Overprotection.* New York: Norton.

Lewin, K. (1951) *Field Theory in Social Science.* New York: Harper and Row.

Lewis, C. S. (1943) *Perelandra.* London: John Lane.

Lewis, C. S. (1956) *The Last Battle.* London: Bodley Head.

Lewis, D. (1999) 'Workplace bullying – interim findings of a study in further and higher education in Wales.' *International Journal of Manpower 20*, 1/2, 1106–1118.

Lewis, T.J., Calvin, G. and Sugai, G. (2000) 'The effects of pre-correction and active supervision on the recess behaviour of elementary students.' *Education and Treatment of Children 23*, 2, 109–121.

Leymann, H. (1996) 'The content and development of mobbing at work.' In D. Zapf and H. Leymann (eds) *Mobbing and Victimization at Work.* A Special Issue of the *European Journal of Work and Organizational Psychology.*

Leymann, H. and Gustafsson, A. (1996) 'Mobbing at work and the development of post traumatic stress disorders.' *European Journal of Work and Organizational Psychology 5*, 251–275.

Loach, B. and Bloor, C. (1995) 'Dropping the bully to find the racist.' *Multicultural Teaching 13*, 2, 18–20.

Lockhart, L. L., White, B. W., Causby, V. and Isaac, A. (1994) 'Letting out the secret: violence in lesbian relationships.' *Journal of Interpersonal Violence 9*, 469–492.

Loehlin, J. C. (1997) 'A test of J. R. Harris's theory of peer influences on personality.' *Journal of Personality and Social Psychology 72*, 1197–1201.

Lorenz, K. (1969) *On Aggression.* London: University Paperback, Methuen.

Losel, F. and Bliesener, T. (1999) 'Germany.' In P. K. Smith, Y. Morita, J. Junger-Tas, D. Olweus, R. Catalano and P. T. Slee *The Nature of School Bullying: A Cross-National Perspective.* London: Routledge.

Lyons, R., Tivey, H. and Ball, C. (1995) *Bullying at Work: How to Tackle It. A Guide for MSF Representatives and Members.* London: MSF.

The Macquarie Dictionary (1987) Second Edition. McMahons Point, NSW: Macquarie Library.

Madsen, K. C. (1996) 'Differing perceptions of bullying and their practical implications.' *Education and Child Psychology 13*, 14–22.

Main, N. (1999) 'Children's Perception of violence in early childhood.' Paper presented at the *Children and Crime: Victims' and Offenders' Conference.* Australian Institute of Criminology, Brisbane, 17–18 June.

Maines, B. and Robinson, G. (1992) *Michael's Story: The 'No Blame' Approach.* Bristol: Lame Duck Publishing.

Maras, P. and Brown, R. (2000) 'Effects of different forms of school contact on children's attitudes toward disabled and non-disabled peers.' *British Journal of Educational Psychology 70*, 337–351.

Marjoribanks, K. (1994) 'Families, Schools and Children's Learning Environment.' *International Journal of Educational Research 21*, 4, 439–555.

Marmot, M. G. and Bosma, H. (1997) 'Contribution of job control and other risk factors to social variations in coronary heart disease incidence.' *Lancet 350*, 235–240.

Marmot, M. G., Davey Smith, G., Stansfeld, S., Patel, C., North, F., Head, J., White, I., Brunner, E. and Feeney, A. (1991) 'Health inequalities among British civil servants: the Whitehall II study.' *Lancet 33*, 1387–1393.

Martin, F. (1865) *The Life of John Clare.* London: Macmillan.

Martlew, M. and Hodson, J. (1991) 'Children with mild learning difficulties in an integrated and in a special school: Comparisons of behaviour, teasing and teachers' attitudes.' *British Journal of Educational Psychology 61*, 355–369.

Mayer, M. J. and Leone, P. E. (1999) 'A structural analysis of school violence and disruption: implications for creating safer schools.' *Education and Treatment of Children 22*, 333– 356.

Mellor, A. (1999) 'Scotland.' In P. K. Smith, Y. Morita, J. Junger-Tas, D. Olweus, R. Catalano and P. T. Slee *The Nature of School Bullying: A Cross-National Perspective.* London: Routledge.

Menesini, E., Eslea, M., Smith, P. K., Genta, E., Gianetti, E., Fonzi, A. and Constabile, A. (1997) 'Cross-national comparisons of children's attitudes towards bully/victim problems in schools.' *Aggressive Behavior 23*, 245–257.

Mieko, Y. (1999) 'Domestic violence against women of Japanese descent in Los Angeles: two methods of estimating prevalence.' *Violence Against Women 15*, 869–898.

Milgram, S. (1965) 'Some conditions of obedience and disobedience to authority.' *Human Relations 18*, 57–76.

Miller, D. (1999) 'Time to tell 'em off! A pocket guide to overcoming ridicule.' Unpublished manuscript.

Minaker, K. L. and Frishman, R. (1995) 'Love gone wrong.' *Harvard Heath Letter*, 20, 1–4.

Moberley, W. (1968) *The Ethics of Punishment*. London: Faber.

Moir, A. and Jessel, D. (1991) *Brainsex: The Real Difference Between Men and Women*. London: Mandarin.

Morita, Y. (1996) 'Bullying as a contemporary behaviour problem in the context of increasing "Societal Privatisation" in Japan.' *Prospects: Quarterly Review of Comparative Education 26*, 311–329.

Morita, Y., Soeda, H., Soeda, K. and Taki, M. (1999) 'Japan.' In P. K. Smith, Y. Morita, J. Junger-Tas, D. Olweus, R. Catalano and P. T. Slee *The Nature of School Bullying: A Cross-National Perspective*. London: Routledge.

Morrison, B. (2001) 'From bullying to responsible citizenship: a restorative approach to building safe school communities.' Unpublished manuscript. Research School of Social Sciences, Australian National University.

Murphy, H. A., Hutchison, J. M. and Bailey, J. S. (1983) 'Behavioral school psychology goes outdoors: the effect of organised games on playground aggression.' *Journal of Applied Behavioral Analysis 16*, 29–35.

Murray, L. A. (1994) 'The culture of hell.' *The Independent Monthly*, February, 18.

Myers, D.G. (1999) *Psychology*. New York: Worth Publishers.

Mynard, H. and Joseph, S. (1997) 'Bully/victim problems and their association with Eysenck's personality dimensions in 8 to 13 year-olds.' *British Journal of Educational Psychology 66*, 447–456.

Nabuzka, O. and Smith, P. K. (1993) 'Sociometric status and social behaviour of children with and without learning difficulties.' *Journal of Child Psychology and Psychiatry 34*, 1435–1448.

Namie, G. and Namie, R. (1998) *Bullyproof Yourself at Work! Personal Strategies to Recognize and Stop the Hurt from Harassment*. Benicia, California: DoubleDoc Press.

Neary, A. and Joseph, S. (1994) 'Peer victimisation and its relationship to self-concept and depression among schoolgirls.' *Personality and Individual Differences 16*, 138–186.

Nettelbeck, T., Wilson, C., Potter, R. and Perry, C. (2000) 'The influence of interpersonal competence on personal vulnerability of persons with mental retardation.' *Journal of Interpersonal Violence 15*, 46–62.

Neuman, J. H. (2000) 'Justice, stress and bullying can be expensive.' Paper presented at the *Workplace Bullying 2000 Conference*, Oakland, California, January 28.

Nietzsche, F. (1891, 1952) *Thus Spoke Zarathustra*. Translated by A. Tille, revised by M.M. Bozman. London: Dent.

O'Connor, M., Foch, T., Todd, S. and Plomin, R. (1980) 'A twin study of specific behavioral problems of socialisation as viewed by parents.' *Journal of Abnormal Child Psychology 8*, 189–199.

Olweus, D. (1973) 'Personality and aggression.' In J. K. Cole and D. D. Jensen (eds) *Nebraska Symposium on Motivation 1972*. Lincoln: University of Nebraska Press.

Olweus, D. (1978) *Aggression in Schools. Bullies and Whipping Boys*. Washington DC: Hemisphere Press (Wiley).

Olweus, D. (1992) 'Victimisation by peers: antecedents and long term outcomes.' In K. H. Rubin and J. B. Asendorf (eds) *Social Withdrawal, Inhibition and Shyness in Children*. Hillsdale, NJ: Erlbaum.

Olweus, D. (1993) *Bullying at School*. Cambridge, MA: Blackwell Publishers.

Olweus, D. (1999) 'Sweden.' In P. K. Smith, Y. Morita, J. Junger-Tas, D. Olweus, R. Catalano and P. T. Slee *The Nature of School Bullying: A Cross-National Perspective*. London: Routledge.

Olweus, D. (2001) 'Peer harassment.' In J. Juvonen, and S. Graham (eds) *Peer Harassment in School: The Plight of the Vulnerable and Victimized*. New York: The Guilford Press.

O'Moore, A. M. and Hillery, B. (1991) 'What do teachers need to know?' In M. Elliott (ed) *Bullying: A Practical Guide to Coping in Schools*. Harlow: David Fulton.

Ortega, R. and Mora-Merchan, J. A. (1999) 'Spain. In P. K. Smith, Y. Morita, J. Junger-Tas, D. Olweus, R. Catalano and P. T. Slee *The Nature of School Bullying: A Cross-National Perspective*. London: Routledge.

Parker, G., Tupling, H. and Brown, L. B. (1979) 'A Parental Bonding Instrument.' *British Journal of Medical Psychology 52*, 1–10.

Parker, T. (1990) *Life After Life*. London: HarperCollins.

Pepler, D. J. and Craig, W. M. (1995) 'A peek behind the fence: naturalistic observations of aggressive children with remote audiovisual recording.' *Developmental Psychology 31*, 4, 548–553.

Perrez, M. and Reicherts, M. (1992) *Stress, Coping and Health: A Situation – Behavior Approach: Theory, Methods, Applications*. Seattle: Hogrefe and Huber.

Perry, G. D., Hodges, E. V. E. and Egan, S. K. (2001) 'Determinants of chronic victimization by peers.' In J. Juvonen and S. Graham (eds) *Peer Harassment in School: The Plight of the Vulnerable and Victimized*. New York: The Guilford Press.

Petersen, L. and Rigby, K. (1999) 'Countering bullying at an Australian secondary school.' *Journal of Adolescence 22*, 4, 481–492.

Pettit G. S., Dodge, K. A. and Brown, M. M. (1988) 'Early family experience, social problem solving patterns and children's social competence.' *Child Development 59*, 107–120.

Pettit, G. S., Harrist, A. W., Bates, J. E. and Dodge, K. A. (1991) 'Family interaction, social cognition, and children's subsequent relations with peers and kindergarten.' *Journal of Social and Personal Relationships 8*, 383–402.

Pfeffer, C. R. (1990) 'Manifestation of Risk factors.' In G. MacLean (ed) *Suicide in Children and Adolescents.* Toronto: Hogrefe and Huber Publishers.

Phares, E. J. (1988) *Introduction to Psychology.* Second Edition. London: Scott, Foresman and Company.

Pikas, A. (1989) 'The Common Concern Method for the treatment of mobbing.' In E. Roland and E. Munthe (eds) *Bullying: An International Perspective.* London: David Fulton in association with the Professional Development Foundation.

Pillemer, K. and Finkelhor, D. (1989) 'Causes of elder abuse: Caregiver stress versus problem relatives.' *American Journal of Orthopsychiatry 59*, 179–187.

Pirandello, L. (1922) 'Right you are (if you thinks so).' In *Three Plays by Luigi Pirandello*, translated by Arthur Livingston. New York: Dutton and Co.

Queensland Working Women's Service (1999) *Workplace Bullying.* Brisbane, Queensland: Queensland Working Women's Service.

Quine, L. (1999) 'Workplace bullying in NHS Community Trust: staff questionnaire survey.' *British Medical Journal 318*, 228–232.

Randall, P. E. (1991) *The Prevention of School Based Bullying.* Hull: University of Hull.

Randall, P. E. (1996) *A Community Approach to Bullying.* Stoke on Trent: Trentham Books.

Rayner, C. (1997) 'The incidence of workplace bullying.' *Journal of Community and Applied Social Psychology 7*, 199–208.

Rayner, C. (1998) *Bullying At Work: Survey Report – UNISON.* http://www.bullybusters.org/home/twd/bb/res/unison.html#stats

Rayner, C. and Hoel, H. (1997) 'A summary review of literature relating to workplace bullying.' *Journal of Community and Applied Social Psychology 7*, 181–191.

Rendell, R. (1998) *Road Rage.* London: Arrow Books.

Rigby, K. (1986) 'Attitudes to authority, self and others.' *The Journal of Social Psychology 126*, 493–501.

Rigby, K. (1993) 'School children's perceptions of their families and parents as a function of peer relations.' *Journal of Genetic Psychology 154*, 4, 501–514.

Rigby, K. (1994) 'Psycho-social functioning in families of Australian adolescent schoolchildren involved in bully/victim problems.' *Journal of Family Therapy 16*, 2, 173–189.

Rigby, K. (1996) 'Peer victimisation and the structure of primary and secondary schooling.' *Primary Focus 10*, 7, October, 4–5.

Rigby, K. (1997a) 'What children tell us about bullying in schools.' *Children Australia 22*, 2, 28–34.

Rigby, K. (1997b) *Bullying in Schools – And What to do About It.* British Edition. London: Jessica Kingsley Publishers.

Rigby, K. (1997c) *Manual for the Peer Relations Questionnaire (PRQ).* Point Lonsdale, Victoria, Australia: The Professional Reading Guide.

Rigby, K. (1997d) 'Attitudes and beliefs about bullying among Australian school children.' *Irish Journal of Psychology 18*, 2, 202–220.

Rigby, K. (1998a) 'Health effects of school bullying.' *The Professional Reading Guide for Educational Administrators 19*, Number 2, Feb/March.

Rigby, K. (1998b) 'Peer relations at school and the health of children.' *Youth Studies Australia 17*, 1, 13–17.

Rigby, K. (1998c) 'The relationship between reported health and involvement in bully/victim problems among male and female secondary school students.' *Journal of Health Psychology 3*, 4, 465–476.

Rigby, K. (1998d) 'Suicidal ideation and bullying among Australian secondary school children.' *Australian Educational and Developmental Psychologist 15*, 1, 45–61.

Rigby, K. (1999) 'Peer victimisation at school and the health of secondary students.' *British Journal of Educational Psychology 22*, 2, 28–34.

Rigby, K. (2000) 'Effects of peer victimisation in schools and perceived social support on adolescent well-being.' *Journal of Adolescence 23*, 1, 57–68.

Rigby, K. (2001a) *Stop the Bullying: A Handbook for Schools.* Melbourne: Australian Council for Educational Research.

Rigby, K. (2001b) *Beliefs of Australian Teachers about Bullying.* Adelaide: University of South Australia.

Rigby, K. and Bagshaw D. (2001) 'The prevalence and hurtfulness of acts of aggression from peers experienced by Australian male and female adolescents at school.' *Children Australia.*

Rigby, K. and Barnes, A. (2001) 'Outcomes of telling about being bullied at school.' Unpublished paper.

Rigby, K. and Cox, I. K. (1996) 'The contributions of bullying and low self-esteem to acts of delinquency among Australian teenagers.' *Personality and Individual Differences 21*, 4, 609–612.

Rigby, K. and Keogh, L. (1997) 'Perceptions of Australian teachers of peer-victimization in schools: a preliminary investigation.' Unpublished paper.

Rigby, K. and Slee, P. T. (1991) 'Bullying among Australian school children: reported behaviour and attitudes to victims.' *Journal of Social Psychology 131*, 615–627.

Rigby, K. and Slee, P. T. (1993a) 'Dimensions of interpersonal relating among Australian school children and their implications for psychological well-being.' *Journal of Social Psychology 133*, 1, 33–42.

Rigby, K. and Slee, P. T. (1993b) 'Children's attitudes towards victims.' In D. P. Tattum (ed) *Understanding and Managing Bullying.* Melbourne: Heinemann Books.

Rigby, K. and Slee, P. T. (1993c) *The Peer Relations Questionnaire (PRQ).* Adelaide: University of South Australia.

Rigby, K. and Slee, P. T. (1999a) 'Suicidal ideation among adolescent school children, involvement in bully/victim problems and perceived low social support.' *Suicide and Life-threatening Behavior 29*, 119–130.

Rigby, K. and Slee, P. T. (1999b) 'The self esteem of Australian adolescents reporting peer-victimisation at school.' Unpublished paper.

Rigby, K., Cox, I. K. and Black, G. (1997) 'Cooperativeness and bully/victim problems among Australian schoolchildren.' *Journal of Social Psychology 137*, 3, 357–368.

Rigby, K., Metzer, J. C. and Ray, J. J. (1986) 'Working class authoritarianism in England and Australia.' *Journal of Social Psychology 126*, 261–262.

Rigby, K., Slee, P. T. and Martin, G. (1999) 'The mental health of adolescents, perceived parenting and peer victimisation at school.' Unpublished paper.

Rigby, K., Whish, A. and Black, G. (1994) 'Implications of school children's peer relations for wife abuse in Australia.' *Criminology Australia*, August, 8–12.

Rivers, I. and Soutter, A. (1996) 'Bullying and the Steiner school ethos.' *School Psychology International 17*, 359–377.

Roelefse, R. and Middleton, M. R. (1985) 'The Family Functioning in Adolescence questionnaire: a measure of psycho-social family health.' *Journal of Adolescence 8*, 33–45.

Roland, E. (1989) 'Bullying: the Scandinavian research tradition.' In D. P. Tattum and D. A. Lane (eds) *Bullying in Schools.* Stoke on Trent: Trentham Books.

Romain, T. (1997) *Bullies are a Pain in the Brain.* Minneapolis: Free Spirit Publishing Co.

Rosenberg, M. (1986) *Conceiving the Self.* Malabar, FL: Kreiger.

Ross, D. M. (1996) *Childhood Bullying and Teasing: What School Personnel, Other Professionals and Parents Can Do.* Alexandria, VA: American Counselling Association.

Salmon, G., Jones, A. and Smith, D. M. (1998) 'Bullying in school: self-reported anxiety and self-esteem in secondary school children.' *British Medical Journal 317*, 7163, 924–925.

Sapolsky, R. M. (1997) *The Trouble With Testosterone.* New York: Simon and Schuster.

Saracci, R. (1997) 'The World Health Organization needs to reconsider its definition of health.' *British Medical Journal 314*, 7091, 1409.

Schneider, B. H. (2000) *Friends and Enemies: Peer Relations in Childhood.* New York: Oxford University Press.

Schwartz, D., Dodge, K. A., Cole, J. D., Hubbard, J. A., Antonius, H. N., Cillessen, E. A. and Bateman, H. (1998) 'Social-Cognitive and Behavioral Correlates of Aggression and Victimization in Boys' Play Groups.' *Journal of Abnormal Child Psychology 26*, 431–440.

Schwartz, D., Dodge, K. A., Pettit, G. S. and Bates, J. (1997) 'The early socialization of aggressive victims of bullying.' *Child Development 68*, 665–675.

Sears R. R. (1961) 'Relation of early socialisation experiences to aggression in middle childhood.' *Journal of Abnormal and Social Psychology 63*, 466–492.

Sears, R. R., Maccoby, E. E. and Levin, H. (1957) *Patterns of Child Rearing.* Evanston, IL: Row-Petereon.

Sears, R. R., Whiting, J. W. M., Nowlis, V. and Sears, P. S. (1953) 'Some child rearing antecedents of aggression and dependency.' *Genetic Psychology Monographs 47*, 135–234.

Seligman, M.E.P. (1995) *The Optimistic Child.* London: Houghton Mifflin.

Sereny, G. (1998) *Cries Unheard: The Story of Mary Bell.* London: Macmillan.

Shapiro, J. P. (1992) 'The elderly are not children.' *US News and World Report 112*, 1, 26–27.

Sharp, S. (1995) 'How much does bullying hurt? The effects of bullying on the personal well-being and educational progress of secondary aged students.' *Educational and Child Psychology 12*, 81–88.

Shaw, B. (1932) *Misalliance, The Dark Lady of the Sonnets, & Fanny's First Play.* London: Constable.

Sherif, M., Harvey, O. J., Hood, W. R. and Sherif, C. W. (1961) *Intergroup Cooperation and Competition. The Robber's Cave Experiment.* Norman, OK: University Book Exchange.

Slee, P. T. (1995) 'Peer victimization and its relationship to depression among Australian primary school students.' *Personality and Individual Differences 18*, 1, 57–62.

Slee, P. T. and Ford, D. C. (1999) 'Bullying is a serious issue – it is a crime.' *Australia and New Zealand Journal of Law and Education 4*, 1, 23–29.

Slee, P. T. and Rigby, K. (1993) 'The relationship of Eysenck's personality factors and self-esteem to bully/victim behaviour in Australian school boys.' *Personality and Individual Differences 14*, 371–373.

Smith, P. K. and Levan, S. (1995) 'Perceptions and experiences of bullying in younger pupils.' *British Journal of Educational Psychology 65*, 489–500.

Smith, P. K. and Myron-Wilson, R. (1997) 'Parenting and school bullying.' *Clinical Child Psychology & Psychiatry 3*, 405–417.

Smith, P. K. and Sharp, S. (eds) (1994) *School Bullying: Insights and Perspectives.* London: Routledge.

Smith, P. K. and Thompson, D. (1991) *Practical Approaches to B. London: David Fulton.*

Smithers, R. (2000) 'Blunkett launches anti-bullying guidelines.' *The Guardian*, 11 December.

Soutter, A. and McKenzie, A. (2000) 'The use and effects of anti-bullying and anti-harassment policies in Australian schools.' *School Psychology International 21*, 1, 96–105.

Spring, N. M. and Stern, M. B. (1998) 'Nurse Abuse? Couldn't Be! Intra-professional abuse and violence in the nursing workplace.' *Nurse Advocate*, January.

Stanley, L. and Arora, T. (1998) 'Social exclusion amongst adolescent girls: Their self-esteem and coping strategies.' *Educational Psychology in Practice 14*, 2, 94–100.

Stephen, M. (2001) Letter. *The Australian*, 24 February.

Stephenson, P. and Smith, D. (1991) 'Bullying in the junior school.' In D. Tattum and D. Lane (eds) *Bullying in Schools.* Stoke on Trent: Trentham Books.

Stones, R. (1993) *Don't Pick On Me.* Markham, ON: Pembroke.

Strassberg, Z., Dodge, K. A., Bates, J. E. and Pettit, S. (1992) 'The longitudinal relation between parental conflict strategies and children's sociometric standing in kindergarten.' *Merrill-Palmer Quarterly 38*, 477–493.

Straus, M. A. and Gelles, R. J. (1986) 'Societal change and change in family violence from 1975 to 1985 as revealed by two national surveys.' *Journal of Marriage and the Family 48*, 3, 465–479.

Sullivan, K. (1998) 'Racist bullying; creating understanding and strategies for teachers.' In M. Leicester, S. Modgil and C. Modgil (eds) *Values, Education and Cultural Diversity,* Vol 2. London: Cassell.

Sutton, J. (1998) *Bullying: Social Inadequacy or Skilled Manipulation?* Unpublished PhD thesis. Goldsmith College, University of London.

Sutton, J., Smith, P. K. and Swettenham, J. (1999a) 'Social cognition and bullying: Social inadequacy or skilled manipulation?' *British Journal of Developmental Psychology 17,* 435–450.

Sutton, J., Smith, P. K. and Swettenham, J. (1999b) 'Socially undesirable need not be incompetent: A response to Crick and Dodge.' *Social Development 8,* 132–134.

Tattum, D. P. (1993) 'What is bullying?' In D. Tattum (ed) *Understanding and Managing Bullying.* London: Heinemann.

Tattum, D. P. and Tattum, E. (1992) 'Bullying: a whole-school response.' In N. Jones and E. Baglin Jones (eds) *Learning to Behave.* London: Kogan Page.

Terry, A. A. (1998) 'Teacher as targets of bullying by their pupils: a study to investigate incidence.' *British Journal of Educational Psychology 68,* 255–268.

Tisak, M. S. and Tisak, J. (1996) 'My sibling's but not my friend's keeper: reasoning about responses to aggressive acts.' *Journal of Early Adolescence 16,* August, 324–339.

Tjaden, P. (1997) 'The crime of stalking: how big is the problem?' Presentation at the *National Institute of Justice Research in Progress Seminar,* Denver, Colorado.

Tritt, C. and Duncan, R. D. (1997) 'The relationship between childhood bullying and young adult self-esteem and loneliness.' *Journal of Humanistic Education and Development 36,* 35–44.

Troy, M. and Sroufe, L. A. (1987) 'Victimization among preschoolers: Role of attachment relationship history.' *Journal of the American Academy of Child & Adolescent Psychiatry 26,* 166–172.

Turner, A. (1994) 'Genetic and hormonal influences on male violence.' In J. Archer (ed) *Male Violence.* London: Routledge.

United Nations (1989) *Convention on the Rights of the Child.* Geneva: United Nations.

Vaernes, R. J., Myhre, G. A., Henrik, H. and Homnes, T. (1991) 'Work and Stress. Relationships between stress, psychological factors and immune levels among military aviators.' *Work and Stress 5,* 5–16.

Vash, C. L. (1981) *The Psychology of Disability.* New York: Springer Publishing Company.

Victorian Work Cover Authority (2001) *Issues Paper: Code of Practice for Prevention of Workplace Bullying.* State Government Victoria.

Voss, L. D. and Mulligan, J. (2000) 'Bullying in school: are short pupils at risk? Questionnaire study in a cohort.' *British Medical Journal 4*, 612–613.

Watson, L. (1995) *Dark Nature.* London: Hodder and Stoughton.

Watt, A., Nemec, M. and Dawe, B. (2000) *Jump into PDHPE, Book 2.* South Yarra, Melbourne: Macmillan.

Wells, S., Graham, K. and West, P. (1998) 'The good, the bad and the ugly: responses by security staff to aggressive incidents in drinking settings.' *Journal of Drug Issues 28*, 817–837.

Whannel, G. (1992) *Fields of Vision: Television Sport and Cultural Transformation.* London: Routledge.

Whitney, I. and Smith, P. K. (1993) 'A survey of the nature and extent of bully/victim problems in junior/middle and secondary schools.' *Educational Research 35*, 3–25.

Whitney, I., Smith, P. K. and Thompson, D. (1994) 'Bullying and children with special educational needs.' In P. K. Smith and S. Sharp (eds) *School Bullying: Insights and Perspectives.* London: Routledge.

Williams, K., Chambers, M., Logan, S. and Robinson, D. (1996) 'Association of common health symptoms with bullying in primary school children.' *British Medical Journal 313*, 17–19.

Wilson, C. (1984) *A Criminal History of Mankind.* New York: Carroll and Graf Publishers.

Wolfensberger, W. (1972) *The Principle of Normalisation in the Human Services.* Toronto: National Institute on Mental Retardation.

Working Women's Centre of S. A. Inc. (1998) *Workplace Bullying Project: Finding Some Answers.* Adelaide: The Working Women's Centre of S. A.

World Health Organisation (1986) *Ottawa Charter of Health Promotion.* Ottawa: Health and Welfare Canada.

Wright, B. A. (1983) *Physical Disability – A Psychosocial Approach.* Second Edition. New York: Harper and Row.

Wright, J. A., Burgess, A. G., Allen, G., Burgess, A. W. and Laszlo, A. T. (1996) 'A typology of interpersonal stalking.' *Journal of Interpersonal Violence 11*, 487–503.

Yell, M. L. and Rozalsky, M. E. (2000) 'Searching for safe schools: Legal issues in the prevention of school violence.' *Journal of Emotional and Behavioural Disorders 8*, 187–197.

Yude, C., Goodman, R. and McConachie, H. (1998) 'Peer problems of children with hemiplegia in mainstream primary schools.' *Journal of Child Psychology & Psychiatry & Allied Disciplines 39*, 533–541.

Zapf, D. (1999) 'Organisational, work related and personal causes of mobbing at work.' *International Journal of Manpower 20*, 70–85.

Zarzour, K. (1999) *The Schoolyard Bully*. Toronto: HarperCollins.

Zimbardo, P. (1972) 'Pathology of Imprisonment.' *Transaction/Society*, April, 4–8.

Zona, M. A., Sharma, K. K. and Lane, J. (1993) 'A comparative study of erotomanic and obsessional subjects in a forensic sample.' *Journal of Forensic Sciences 38*, 4, 894–902.

Zubrick, S. R., Silburn, S. R., Gurrin, L., Teoh, H., Shepherd, C., Carlton, J. and Lawrence, D. (1997) *Western Australian Child Health Survey: Education, Health and Competence*. Perth, Western Australia: Australian Bureau of Statistics and Institute for Child Health Research.

Subject index

Author index

Adams, A. 87
Adorno, T.W. 134
Agnew, S. 179
Ahmad, E. 181
Ajzen,A. 220
Almeida, A. 190
Alsaker, F.D. 55
Ambert, A.M. 267
Anderson, I. 93
Andrews, F.M. 105
Archer, J. 90, 91, 173
Arora, C.M.G. 32,37,107
Askew, S. 41
Austin, A.B. 155

Bagshaw, D. 61,64,190, 247, 284, 286
Bailey, J.S. 198
Baldry, A. 60,160
Ball,C. 76
Barnes, A. 69
Baron-Cohen, S. 132,133
Bates, G.E. 190
Berdondini, L. 161
Berkowitz, L. 30,33
Berne, S. 240,242
Berven, N.L. 39,185
Besag, V.E. 28,31,32, 145
Biddulph, S. 173

Billingham, R. E. 25
Binney, V. 161
Bjorquist, K. 37,71,83,112,174
Black, G. 231,287
Bland, R. 25
Bliesener, T. 31,32,182
Bloor, C. 194
Borg M.G. 112
Bosworth, K. 164
Boulton, M.J. 106,107,182,198, 226, 228
Bowers, L. 161
Bowie, V. 204
Bowlby, J. 125,157
Braithwaite, J. 259
Brehm, J.W. 276
Brookes, M. 94
Broome, A. 185
Brown, L.B. 114
Brown, M.M. 154
Brown, R. 187
Brown, Roger 203
Bulbeck, T. 193
Burleston, B.R. 155
Burt, M. 231

Cairns, B.C. 137
Cairns, B.D. 137
Callaghan, S. 107,112
Calvin, G. 198
Casas, J.F. 56
Casdagli. P. 45
Chagnon, N. A. 23
Chase, J. 99
Chastain,R. L. 107
Chesterton, G.K. 177
Cloud,J 254.
Coleman, C.C. 110
Collins, C. 61, 175

Connolly, P. 39
Cooper, C.L.75, 77,81,84,85,86,87
Cox, I. 107,137
Cox,T 123.
Craig, W.M. 207,208, 227
Crick, N.R. 38,56,131,132
Crozier, W.R. 62,178

Darley, J. 209
Davis, M.H. 136
Dawe, B. 135
Dawkins, J.L. 187
Dentan, R.K. 151
Dentan, R.K. 23
Dietz, B. 110
Dimmock, P. S. 62,178
Dodge, K. 131,132,154,190
Dollard, J. 195
Duncan, N. 39,178
Duncan, R.D. 89, 110,212
DuymeM.D. 190

Edwards, L. 28
Egan, S.K. 108,141
Ehrenreich, B. 179
Einarsen, S. 124
Elliot, M. 253,257
Ellis, A. 230
Elms, A.C. 213
Emery, C. 182,183
Emin, J.C. 29
Eron, L.D. 154
Eslea, M. 223, 290
Espelage, D. 164,167
Eysenck, S. 135